HEDGING INSTRUMENTS AND RISK MANAGEMENT

PATRICK CUSATIS, Ph.D.
MARTIN THOMAS, Ph.D.

McGraw-Hill

New York Chicago San Francisco Lisbon London Madrid
Mexico City Milan New Delhi San Juan Seoul
Singapore Sydney Toronto

1 2 3 4 5 6 7 8 9 0   DOC/DOC   0 9 8 7 6 5

ISBN 0-07-144312-6

This publication is designed to provide accurate and authoritative information in regard to the subject matter covered. It is sold with the understanding that the publisher is not engaged in rendering legal, accounting or other professional service. If legal advice or other expert assistance is required, the services of a competent professional person should be sought.
> —*From a Declaration of Principles Jointly Adopted by a Committee of the American Bar Association and a Committed of Publishers and Associations.*

This book is printed on recycled, acid-free paper containing a minimum of 50% recycled de-inked paper.

McGraw-Hill books are available at special discounts to use as premiums and sales promotions, or for use in corporate training programs. For more information, please write to the Director of Special Sales, McGraw-Hill Professional, Two Penn Plaza, New York, NY 10011-2298. Or contact your local bookstore.

Library of Congress Cataloging-in-Publication Data

Cusatis, Patrick.
   Hedging instruments and risk management / by Patrick J. Cusatis,
Martin R. Thomas.
      p.   cm.
   ISBN 0-07-144312-6 (hardcover : alk. paper)
   1. Derivative securities.   2. Risk management.   I. Thomas, Martin R.
II. Title.
HG6024.C874   2005
332.64'5—dc22

                                                        2004018228

To my wife, Deborah
PJC

To my wife, Janice
MRT

CONTENTS

Chapter 4

Fixed-Income Mathematics   43

Chapter 5

Term Structure of Interest Rates   75

Chapter 6

Futures Contracts 97

Chapter 7

Swaps   133

Chapter 8

Options   167

Chapter 9

Commodities   207

Chapter 14

Mortgages   335

SUMMARY OF NOTATION   351

INDEX

LIST OF EXHIBITS

PREFACE

Revolutionary changes have taken place in the field of risk management. The growth in the markets for derivative instruments has provided managers with more effective tools to manage the risks faced by companies. As new and innovative derivative products are developed, more alternatives are available to reduce or eliminate specific risks. Based on our experience, many managers at corporations or banks and in state and local governments would benefit from a more complete understanding and awareness of alternative hedging methods.

This book is intended to provide the reader with the tools to understand and evaluate hedging strategies. While there may be differences between markets, our approach recognizes that there is a core set of skills required for hedging in any market. Informed decision-making begins with an understanding of the underlying mathematical and statistical concepts and with the valuation and risks of derivative products.

This book is organized into three sections. In the first section, we introduce the basic mathematical concepts of time value of money, a statistical review, fixed-income mathematics, and the term structure of interest rates. These concepts are an important foundation for the sections that follow. In the second section, we discuss the hedging instruments: futures, swaps, and options. Finally, we discuss hedging techniques as they apply to the commodity, currency, equity, municipal, and corporate bond and mortgage markets.

We have included the important aspects of the derivatives market and hedging strategies in various markets. Since these are broad topics, we do not attempt to cover every detail of every market. We have used our judgment, based on our practical experiences and academic backgrounds, to determine the important concepts for a risk manager. The practical chapters at the end of the book provide guidance to most risk management situations.

If you have any questions or comments, please contact us at Applied Finance Partners, LLC at (814) 632–7638 or e-mail us at solutions@appfin.com.

ACKNOWLEDGMENTS

Many people assisted in the preparation of this book. Colleagues who provided insights include Charlie Barkman, Melvin Blumberg, Bill Bracken, Galen Burkhardt, Jim Cantrell, Mike Cardamone, Patricia Chambers, Mike Coco, Bill Cusatis, Chris Cusatis, Joe Cusatis, Kevin Dunphy, David Eckhart, Jacqueline Garner, Gary Gray, Mike Gombola, Vicky Hamilton, Amy Kratchman, Mukund Kulkarni, Diane Lazzaris, Ed Nelling, Constantin Nelson, Mark Saussure, Nat Singer, Oranee Tawatnuntachai, George Tsetsekos, Premal Vora, Ron Watson, and John Wilson. We would also like to thank Cortney Fanning, our graduate assistant from Penn State–Harrisburg.

We are grateful for data supplied by the following people: Brian Bellucci, Thomson Financial; Peter DeGroot, Lehman Brothers; and Martin McConnell, Wachovia Capital Markets.

Many thanks to McGraw-Hill, in particular: Stephen Isaacs, executive editor, and Laura Libretti, production supervisor.

CHAPTER 1

Introduction

Hedging is an approach to risk management that uses financial instruments to neutralize the systematic risk of price changes or cash flows. Hedging is an important risk management tool for portfolio managers, bank managers, pension fund managers, and corporate treasurers. These market participants have a number of different motivations for hedging. The nature of some businesses exposes participants to price risk that they may not be willing to accept. By reducing risk exposure, hedging allows companies to focus on their core business. Multinational corporations, for example, are exposed to the fluctuations of currency markets, which may significantly increase the volatility of their cash flows. Lenders are exposed to interest rate fluctuations because changes in interest rates affect the demand for and value of loans. Other participants such as portfolio managers may hedge to eliminate risks they are not willing to bear, such as price risk or default risk, or because of a belief in the direction of the market. Regardless of motivation, all hedgers face the challenge of selecting a hedge that provides the most protection while incurring the least amount of expense.

Each market has a unique set of characteristics that make risk management a challenge. In some markets, hedging is a simple task that requires little effort and monitoring; in others, hedging is a daily activity that requires constant monitoring. The tools required to establish and manage effective hedges may appear complex and specific to each market. In fact, most markets share a fundamental structure that can be managed with a common set of mechanics. Our objective in writing this book is to provide the reader with a self-contained, accessible guide to the mechanics and risks of hedging in various markets.

Our motivation for writing this book is the need for a comprehensive guide to hedging. The books that are available often present hedging as a secondary topic in the context of fixed-income securities or derivatives. Those that provide in-depth discussions of hedging are often highly specialized, focusing on a specific market or instrument. Example topics in the existing literature include hedge funds, hedge strategies for options, and fixed-income hedges. In our experience, most applications of hedging are far simpler than these and require a different set of skills. We have attempted to compile all of the information necessary for the portfolio manager to make informed and accurate hedging decisions.

A SYSTEMATIC APPROACH TO HEDGING

There is a great deal to be gained by taking a more comprehensive and systematic approach to hedging. A broad understanding of the mechanics of the derivatives market can lead to the construction of an effective hedging strategy. Our hedging philosophy consists of a complete understanding of (1) the mathematical and statistical concepts that apply to finance, (2) the hedging instruments or tools available in the markets, and (3) the practical application of those instruments. A complete understanding of each step is important for the effective development of a hedging strategy.

This approach has several advantages over more specialized approaches. First, because it has an analytic foundation applicable to all instruments and markets, the book flows more smoothly. This avoids the appearance that these topics are a series of disparate, unrelated concepts (as in many monographs) and highlights the common threads running through different markets. Another advantage of this approach is that it provides the reader with a set of skills that can be used to analyze new instruments and markets. Simply providing an explanation of existing instruments and markets leaves the reader at a disadvantage. Most of the instruments used to hedge today have been developed in the past 30 years, and we have every expectation that this trend will continue.

MATHEMATICAL AND STATISTICAL CONCEPTS

In the next four chapters of the book, we develop a common set of mathematical and statistical concepts that serve as the foundation for hedging in various markets. In Chapter 2, we discuss the time value of money—an important concept in all financial markets. The concepts of present value and future value are used throughout the book. We provide this chapter as a tutorial and reference. In Chapter 3, we explain basic statistical concepts, including the normal distribution, hypothesis testing, and regression analysis. These procedures are important for a full understanding of the valuation of derivative securities and the analyses used to test hedge performance.

In Chapters 4 and 5 we develop some important concepts for the fixed-income markets: fixed-income mathematics and the term structure of interest rates. The tools developed in these chapters are crucial for understanding fixed-income derivatives and for developing and applying an effective hedging strategy. Chapter 4 focuses on bond valuation and risk characteristics. Chapter 5 provides a detailed explanation of the yield curve and the calculation of forward rates. These concepts are important for market participants in the U.S. Treasury, municipal and corporate bond and mortgage markets. For some readers, these chapters will serve as a reference guide to the important concepts necessary for analyzing historic data, pricing derivatives, and calculating hedge ratios.

HEDGING TOOLS

By its nature, the hedging process is closely related to the financial derivatives market. Forwards, futures, swaps, and options are important to a risk manager. We attempt to provide a detailed understanding of and reference guide to these concepts. While we cannot fully cover all of the aspects of these complex markets, we attempt to provide the most important information for the hedging process.

In Chapter 6 we describe the futures market. We outline the characteristics of the most popular products and provide examples of hedging strategies. We also explain valuation models and risk characteristics of many of the contracts.

In Chapter 7 we explain the swap market. The swap market is perhaps the most important and well-established over-the-counter market. We provide hedging examples and discuss several valuation techniques. We discuss many types of swaps, including interest rate swaps, equity swaps, municipal swaps, and currency swaps.

In Chapter 8 we discuss the options market. This chapter includes equity options, currency options, interest rate caps and floors, options on swaps or "swaptions," and index options. We discuss option strategies and valuation. The valuation and mechanics of options are complex, and many books are dedicated to this topic alone. We attempt to isolate the important option concepts for a risk manager. We provide an overview of the most important option valuation models and indicate when each model is appropriate.

HEDGING STRATEGIES

Constructing a hedging strategy begins with identifying risk tolerance. Hedging is not appropriate for all market participants. Market participants faced with the same risks may choose to hedge risks to different degrees. As with individuals, organizations must determine their degree of risk tolerance. Once a level of risk tolerance has been determined, an analysis of hedging efficiency within that market must be performed. "Hedging efficiency" refers to the amount of risk that can be removed with a particular hedge. Although it may be the goal of a hedger to eliminate a particular risk, this may not be possible or may be too expensive. In the following sections we elaborate on these points.

IDENTIFYING RISK TOLERANCE

The starting point for investors, corporations, and portfolio managers is determining the degree of risk they are willing to accept. The risk-return trade-off is a fundamental concept in finance. With higher risk comes higher volatility and higher expected returns. The probability of loss also increases with higher risk. Hedgers pay for a reduction in risk by accepting a lower *expected* return on their portfolio.

The risk profiles of two corporations may be very different because of differences in willingness to take risk. The trade-off between risk and return must be evaluated by a corporation to determine if hedging is worthwhile. For example, if an equity fund manager is successful at removing most of the price risk from a portfolio through the use of equity futures, the expected return on the hedged equity portfolio is that of a portfolio of Treasury bills. Certainly, it is not the long-term goal of an equity fund manager to mimic the returns of the U.S. Treasury market. The portfolio manager must decide on the goals of hedging and the price at which these goals are obtained. The decision to manage risk is based on the best assessment of the available information, and there is no guarantee that the hedged position will produce a return that is in the hedger's best interest.

HEDGING EFFICIENCY

An often misunderstood concept is the degree to which risk can be reduced through hedging. In practice, price uncertainty usually cannot be completely eliminated. The effectiveness of hedging activity is often specific to the situation and depends on the strength of the relationship between the position to be hedged and the hedging instrument, which can vary greatly by market. Moreover, the goals of the hedger are typically unique to each situation. Hedgers may decide to hedge only a portion of the risk they face, either because they have a point of view on the direction of the market or because the partial hedge reduces the risk to an acceptable level.

Hedging efficiency refers to the effectiveness of a particular hedge in accomplishing the goals of a risk manager. In practice, most hedges are not riskless, and the degree of risk faced by the hedger varies greatly by instrument and market. We use real-world data and examples to help the reader develop a realistic set of expectations regarding what risks can and cannot be eliminated.

The cost of a particular hedge also affects its efficiency. Hedges incur several types of costs, including transaction costs and carrying costs. "Transaction costs" refers to the fees and commissions associated with establishing a hedge. These costs are typically small for well-functioning, liquid markets. Carrying costs are also important to a hedger. "Carrying costs" refers to the cost of carrying a hedge regardless of changes in the underlying market and can change significantly over time. We discuss the carrying costs associated with different instruments and how they can be estimated.

Exhibit 1.1 outlines the systematic approach to hedging. The goal of this book is to provide the reference material and background necessary for a market participant to complete the flow chart. Following this procedure, an efficient hedging strategy can be formulated for a given level of risk tolerance.

HEDGING APPLICATIONS

In the last six chapters of the book, we apply the techniques of the previous sections to the currency, commodity, equity, corporate, municipal

EXHIBIT 1.1

Systematic Approach to Hedging

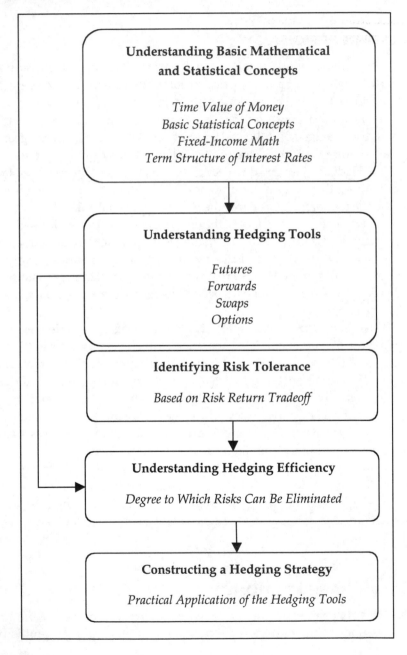

bond, and mortgage markets. These chapters of the book provide some guidance for creating a hedging strategy in these markets. We explain several hedging strategies and examine the historic performance of each of these strategies in the markets.

Chapter 9 examines the commodities market. In particular, we measure the efficiency of hedges in the crude oil, gold, aluminum, and copper markets. We examine direct and cross-market hedges in various markets and strategies for commodity swaps and commodity options.

Chapter 10 examines the currency market. In this chapter, we measure historic hedge efficiency with the use of data on the U.S. dollar, British pound, Canadian dollar, Japanese yen, and euro. We examine techniques using currency futures, forwards, swaps, and options.

Chapter 11 examines the risks of the equities market and provides examples of how to hedge portfolios and stocks by using index futures. We also discuss index option and equity swap strategies.

Chapter 12 examines the municipal bond market. Municipal bond market risk is difficult to hedge because it generally requires a cross-market hedge. We examine historic volatility in this market relative to several hedge alternatives. We examine hedge efficiency based on municipal indices and for a particular municipal bond. We also describe hedging strategies for municipal issuers.

Chapter 13 examines the corporate bond market. Like the municipal market, the corporate bond market is subject to cross-market hedging. We discuss the risk associated with hedging in the corporate bond market and examine the historic performance of corporate bonds relative to various hedges. We form a portfolio of corporate bonds and calculate hedge ratios for the portfolio. We also discuss hedging strategies for the corporation for managing its interest costs.

In Chapter 14 we examine hedging in the mortgage market. We discuss the unique risk characteristics that must be managed by mortgage lenders and investors. Mortgages exhibit negative convexity associated with the prepayment option granted to borrowers. We develop an example of hedging a portfolio of mortgages held by an investor and of hedging mortgage pipeline risk.

SUMMARY

Our goal in this book is to present the necessary information to help make informed, efficient hedging decisions. We believe that there is a basic approach that applies to all markets. The foundations of efficient hedging begin with an understanding of basic mathematical and statistical procedures. With these in place, the hedger has a better understanding of alternative hedging instruments in the derivatives market. We have attempted to provide this information in the chapters that follow.

Hedging requires constant evaluation. It is an ongoing process that requires constant monitoring and adjusting. Although historical hedge performance gives us an estimate of future performance within statistical guidelines, the markets are constantly changing and new information is always being incorporated. A hedger must stay informed and be able to adapt to changing information and markets.

CHAPTER 2

The Time Value of Money

INTRODUCTION

The value of a security is equal to the value of its expected future cash flows. To understand the value and risk of a security, it is critical to understand the time value of money. The concept of the time value of money permits the investor to compare the values of cash flows received at different times. The values of cash flows received at different points in time depend on the rate of interest per period, the number of periods until the cash flows are received, and the method of compounding.

A dollar received today is worth more than a dollar received tomorrow because the dollar could be invested and earn interest, and the investor would have more than one dollar in the future. The value of a cash flow measured in today's dollars is known as its present value (PV), and the value measured at some future time period is known as its future value (FV). We use the following notation to illustrate the time value of money concepts in this chapter:

PV = present value of a future cash flow
FV_t = future value of a cash flow measure at some future time, t
r = rate of interest earned per period
n = number of years

FUTURE VALUE

The process of going from present values to future values is known as compounding. Compounding allows an investor to determine how much a current-period cash flow will be worth at some future date. To illustrate, consider an investor who invests $100 and earns a 10.00% rate of return for one year. At the end of one year, the investor would have

$$FV_1 = PV(1 + r) = \$100(1.10) = \$110$$

In the above equation, $100 is the present value and $110 is the future value of $100 in year 1. If the funds were to be invested for an additional year at 10.00%, the value in year 2 would be

$$FV_2 = PV(1 + r)^2 = \$100(1.10)^2 = \$121$$

A more general expression for the future value of a lump sum invested for n years at a rate of interest r is given as

$$FV_n = PV(1 + r)^n$$

In the above equation, PV is the initial amount invested today, r is the rate of interest earned per year, and FV_n is the future value at time t.

Example: Suppose you invest $1,000 for five years at a 5.00% rate of interest per year. The value of the initial amount invested at the end of five years would be equal to

$$FV_5 = \$1,000(1.05)^5 = \$1,276.28$$

PRESENT VALUE

The process of going from future values to present values is known as discounting. Suppose we wish to find the present value of $1,000 received two years from now when our invested funds earn 10.00% per year. The future value in year 2, FV_2, is equal to $1,000, and the present value is unknown. According to our future value formula,

$$FV_2 = PV(1 + r)^2$$

If we solve the above equation for present value, the present value is calculated as

$$PV = \frac{\$1,000}{(1.10)^2} = \$826.45$$

Present value can be thought of as the amount that, if invested today, would compound to some future value, FV_n, at a rate of interest r. A more general expression for the present value of a future lump sum received n years from today is

$$PV = \frac{FV_n}{(1 + r)^n}$$

Note that the formula for present value is a rearranged version of the formula for calculating future value.

Most securities generate a stream of future cash flows. If we wish to calculate the value of multiple future cash flows, we simply sum the present values all of the individual cash flows. Hence, the value of a security can be thought of as the present value of the future cash flows that an investor receives from the security.

Example: Suppose an investor expects to receive two payments of $1,000. The first payment will be received two years from today, and the second payment will be received five years from today. The interest rate is 10.00% per year. The present value of these cash flows is

$$PV = \frac{\$1,000}{(1.10)^2} + \frac{\$1,000}{(1.10)^5} = 826.45 + 620.92 = \$1,447.37$$

ANNUITIES

An annuity is a series of equal payments received at fixed intervals for a specified number of periods. If the payments are received at the end of each year (i.e., the first payment is received one period from today), the annuity is known as a deferred annuity. Fixed-rate loans, such as mortgages and car loans, can be thought of as deferred annuities.[1]

---

1. If the payments are made at the beginning of each period, the annuity is known as an annuity due. Unless otherwise specified, the examples given are deferred annuities.

EXHIBIT 2.1

Payments on a Deferred Annuity

Payment		C	C		C
Year	0	1	2	...	n

Consider a deferred annuity that makes n equal payments of $\$C$ per year. Exhibit 2.1 shows the payments made on this annuity.

The present value of an annuity can be calculated as the present value of each annuity payment. Since the payments are received at the end of each year beginning one year from today, the present value is calculated as

$$PV = \frac{C}{(1+r)} + \frac{C}{(1+r)^2} + \cdots + \frac{C}{(1+r)^n}$$

If we factor out the annuity payment, C, the above equation can be expressed as

$$PV = C\left[\frac{1}{(1+r)} + \frac{1}{(1+r)^2} + \cdots + \frac{1}{(1+r)^n}\right]$$

or, equivalently,

$$PV = C\left[\frac{1}{r}\left(1 - \frac{1}{(1+r)^n}\right)\right] = C(\text{PVIFA}_{n,r})$$

In the above equation, the term in brackets is known as the present value interest factor for an annuity with n years at an interest rate of r per year ($\text{PVIFA}_{n,r}$). Using the above formula is equivalent to summing the present values of all annuity payments.

Example: Consider an annuity that pays $\$100$ per year for 10 years. The discount rate is equal to 10.00% per year. The present value of this annuity is calculated as

$$PV = 100\left[\frac{1}{0.10}\left(1 - \frac{1}{(1.10)^{10}}\right)\right] = 100(6.1446) = \$614.46$$

For the example above, the annuity factor is calculated to be 6.1446. The present value of $614.46 is identical to the sum of the present values of all of the 10 payments.

Suppose we invested each of the payments from an annuity. If we assume that we earn the same return per period on these reinvested funds, the future value of the annuity in year n can be calculated as

$$FV_n = C\left[\frac{1}{r}\left((1 + r)^n - 1\right)\right]$$

In the above equation, the term in brackets is known as the future value interest factor for an n-year annuity at an interest rate of r per year (FVIFA$_{n,r}$). If we consider the previous example, the future value of a deferred annuity that pays $100 per year for 10 years with an interest rate of 10.00% is calculated as

$$FV_{10} = 100\left[\frac{1}{0.10}\left((1.10)^{10} - 1\right)\right] = 100(15.9374) = \$1,593.74$$

COMPOUNDING PERIODS

In the above examples, we have assumed that interest is compounded once a year. However, there are many situations where interest is compounded more frequently. Many coupon bonds pay interest semiannually, and loans are often compounded monthly.

Suppose you invest $100 in an account that pays 10.00% compounded semiannually. The interest rate is stated on an annual basis. To determine the future value, we must first convert the interest to a periodic rate of 5.00% per six-month period and convert the number of periods per year to two. If we invest for one year, the future value at the end of the year is

$$FV_2 = PV(1 + r/2)^2 = \$100(1.05)^2 = \$110.25$$

In the above equation, FV_2 is the future value of the amount invested two periods from today at an interest rate of $r/2$ (5.00%) per six-month period. Once the interest rate and periods are converted, all other calculations are the same for the time value of money formulas.

Example: Suppose we wish to find the present value of a $1,000 lump sum received two years from today. The annual rate of interest is 10.00% and interest is compounded semiannually. If we convert the interest rate to 5.00% per six-month period and the number of periods to four six-month periods, the present value is calculated as

$$PV = \frac{\$1,000}{(1.05)^4} = \$822.70$$

EFFECTIVE ANNUAL RATES OF INTEREST

To compare investments with different compounding periods, we need to distinguish between quoted and effective annual rates of interest (EAR). The EAR refers to the interest rate that would produce the same end-of-period value if it were to be compounded once a year. A quoted rate of interest r may be converted to an effective rate of interest with the formula

$$EAR = (1 + r/m)^m - 1$$

where m is the number of times interest is compounded per year. For an investment earning 10.00% per year compounded semiannually, the EAR is

$$EAR = (1 + 0.10/2)^2 - 1 = 0.1025$$

The EAR of invested funds in the above example is 10.25% per year. Hence, funds invested at 10.00% semiannually grow at the same rate as funds invested at 10.25% annually.

CONTINUOUS COMPOUNDING

In the above examples, the effective annual interest rate is higher than the quoted rate when interest is compounded semiannually. Exhibit 2.2 shows the relationship between the effective annual return and the number of compounding periods for an investment with a quoted rate of 10.00%. Initially, the EAR increases as the frequency of compounding increases. However, when interest is compounded a large number of times, there is relatively little change in the EAR as the frequency of compounding increases.

EXHIBIT 2.2

Effective Annual Return (EAR) and
Compounding Periods per Year (*m*)
for a Quoted Interest Rate of 10.00%

m	EAR	*m*	EAR
1	10.00%	20	10.49%
2	10.25%	30	10.50%
3	10.34%	40	10.50%
4	10.38%	50	10.51%
5	10.41%	100	10.51%
6	10.43%	500	10.52%
7	10.44%	1,000	10.52%
8	10.45%	10,000	10.52%
9	10.46%	100,000	10.52%
10	10.46%	∞	10.52%

When interest is compounded an infinite number of times per year, it is said to be *continuously compounded*. Many derivative pricing models require the use of continuous compounding because they assume instantaneous price changes. The EAR for an investment when interest is continuously compounded is equal to

$$EAR = e^r - 1$$

where e is the natural base of logarithms, equal to 2.7182818.[2] Exhibit 2.3 shows how the EAR converges to $e^r - 1$ for a large number of compounding periods.

A general formula for the value of an investment of PV made for n years at a quoted rate of r is

$$FV_n = PVe^{rn}$$

where n is time measured in years, FV_n is the future value n years from now, and PV is the amount invested. The present value of a future cash flow is calculated for continuous discounting as

$$PV = FV_n e^{-rn}$$

2. As m becomes large, the formula $(1 + r/m)^m$ converges to the value of e^r.

EXHIBIT 2.3

Effective Annual Return (EAR) by Compounding Period and Continuously Compounded Rate of Interest at a Quoted Rate of 10.00%

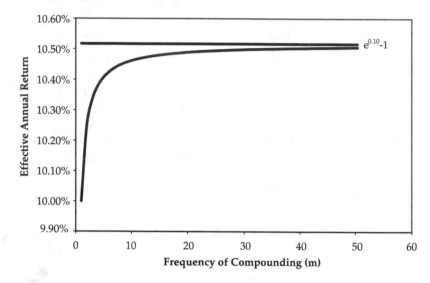

Example: Suppose you invest $1000 at a quoted interest rate of 10.00%. Interest is compounded continuously. At the end of 1.5 years, the investment would be worth

$$FV = 1,000e^{0.10(1.5)} = 1,000(1.16183) = \$1,161.83$$

In the above example, the investment earns 16.183% over the 1.5-year period.

Example: Suppose an investor expects to receive a lump-sum payment of $1,000 three years from today. The quoted rate of interest is 12.00%, and interest is compounded continuously. The present value of the future payment is calculated as

$$PV = 1,000e^{-(0.12)(3)} = \$697.68$$

AMORTIZED LOANS

Amortized loans are loans that are repaid in equal installments. Many loans made to individuals, such as mortgages and car loans, carry monthly payments. The borrower is charged interest on the unpaid balance each period. The monthly payment on the loan in excess of the interest charged is typically allocated to a reduction of the unpaid balance. Loans can be thought of as an annuity where the lender is the recipient of the payment and the amount borrowed is equal to the present value of the payments.

Consider a simple example with annual payments. Suppose an investor borrows $10,000 and agrees to repay with three equal annual payments. The interest rate charged is 6.00% per year. The present value of the payments discounted at a 6.00% rate is equal to the amount borrowed and must solve the formula

$$PV = \frac{PMT}{(1+r)} + \frac{PMT}{(1+r)^2} + \frac{PMT}{(1+r)^3}$$

where PMT is the annual payment. An alternative way to express this is the formula for an annuity,

$$PV = PMT(PVIFA_{n,r})$$

Since we know the present value and the interest rate, we can solve for PMT as follows:

$$PMT = \frac{PV}{PVIFA_{3,6.00\%}} = \frac{10,000}{2.67301} = \$3,741.10$$

Each payment consists of interest and principal. Since the investor is charged interest on the unpaid principal balance, interest is a larger component of the earlier payments. The allocation of each payment to interest and principal can be expressed in an amortization table. Exhibit 2.4 shows

EXHIBIT 2.4

Amortization Table for a Three-Year 6.00% Loan with Annual Payments

Year	Beginning Balance	Payment	Interest	Principal	Unpaid Balance
1	10,000.00	3,741.10	600.00	3,141.10	6,858.90
2	6,858.90	3,741.10	411.53	3,329.56	3,529.34
3	3,529.34	3,741.10	211.76	3,529.34	0.00

the amortization table for our three-year loan. In year 1, $600 of the payment is allocated to interest (6.00% of the $10,000 unpaid balance), and the remaining amount ($3,141.10) is allocated to principal. After the first payment is made, the borrower owes $6,858.90 (= 10,000 − 3,141.10). In year 2, the borrower is charged interest of $411.53 on the unpaid balance, and the remainder of the payment is allocated to principal. In year 3, the borrower is charged interest of $211.76. The amount allocated to principal for the final payment is equal to the unpaid balance. The remaining balance after three payments are made is equal to zero.

To calculate the payments on a loan with monthly payments, we must first convert the quoted interest rate to a monthly rate and find the number periods. The monthly interest rate is equal to the quoted rate divided by 12 payments per year, and the number of periods is equal to the number of years multiplied by 12 payments per year.

The present value interest factor of an annuity with m compounding periods per year is

$$\text{PVIFA}_{nm,r/m\%} = \left[\frac{1}{r/m} \left(1 - \frac{1}{(1 + r/m)^{nm}} \right) \right]$$

Example: Suppose a homeowner borrows $200,000 to purchase a home and agrees to repay with monthly payments for 30 years. The quoted interest rate is equal to 6.00%. The monthly interest rate on the loan is equal to 0.50% (6.00%/12), and the number of periods is equal to 360 (30 years × 12 payments/year). The $\text{PVIFA}_{360,0.50\%}$ is equal to

$$\text{PVIFA}_{360,0.50\%} = \left[\frac{1}{0.005} \left(1 - \frac{1}{(1 + 0.005)^{360}} \right) \right] = 166.7916$$

Therefore, each monthly payment is equal to

$$\text{PMT} = \frac{\text{PV}}{\text{PVIFA}_{360,0.5\%}} = \frac{200,000}{166.7916} = \$1,199.10$$

The amortization table for this loan is calculated for a payment of $1,199.10, a periodic interest rate of 0.50%, and 360 periods.

SUMMARY

The concept of time value of money is the foundation of valuation methods. In this chapter we described basic concepts of valuation. We began by discussing how cash flows received in different time periods may be compared with the methods of compounding and discounting. *Compounding* refers to the process of converting cash flows received today to future values. We have also shown how to calculate the present value of future cash flows.

Cash flows may be in the form of lump sums or annuities. We demonstrated applications of time-value concepts to these different types of investments. Loans were shown to be a special case of an annuity where the lender is the recipient of the annuity payments. We demonstrated how to calculate an amortization table for an annual-payment loan and showed how payments are calculated for loans with both monthly and annual payments.

The effective rate of interest depends on the quoted rate of interest and on the number of compounding periods per year. We explained how to calculate effective annual rates of interest from quoted rates of interest and discussed the relationship between the two. Continuous compounding was explained as a special case of the effective annual rate of interest with a large number of compounding periods.

CHAPTER 3

Statistical Review

In this chapter we review some basic statistical concepts. Assessing and managing hedging risk require a clear understanding of the relationship between price changes of the hedging instrument and target position. We spend some time in this chapter developing the fundamentals of measuring and describing the statistical relationship between variables. Price changes have characteristics that can be measured and described statistically. The statistics help us to describe individual variables as well as the relationship between variables. We begin with a discussion of random variables.

RANDOM VARIABLES

A random variable is a variable with an uncertain future value. Our discussion will focus on continuous random variables, which can take on any numerical value within some range of values. For example, consider daily percentage price changes in the spot price of Japanese yen (JPY) in U.S. dollars (USD). For a given day, there is uncertainty as to the percentage price change in JPY. The percentage price change in JPY would be considered a random variable.

The probability density function measures the relationship between probabilities and values of a continuous random variable X. A probability density function has the property that $f(x) \geq 0$ for all x, with the area under the curve equal to 1. The area under the curve between any two values of X

EXHIBIT 3.1

Probability Density Function of X

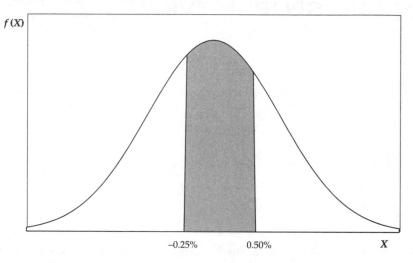

is the probability that X assumes a value within that range. Exhibit 3.1 shows the probability density function of a random variable X. The shaded area shows the probability that X assumes a value between −0.25% and 0.50%.

The cumulative density function $F(x)$ of the random variable X is useful for describing the probability that X will be less than some specific value x, that is,

$$F(x) = P(X < x) \quad \text{for all } x$$

where $P(X < x)$ is the probability that X takes on a value less than x. The cumulative density function may also be used to find the probability that X assumes a value within some interval. For example, the probability that percentage price changes in JPY are between −0.25% and 0.50% is

$$P(-0.25\% < X < 0.50\%) = P(X < 0.50\%) - P(X < -0.25\%)$$
$$= F(0.50\%) - F(-0.25\%)$$

MEAN AND VARIANCE

Statistical measures are often used to summarize characteristics of a random variable. For a random variable X, the expected value or mean $E(X)$

measures the average value that would be found if we were to choose a very large sample of X. Since the expected value is often used as a measure of central tendency for probability distributions, $E(X)$ is commonly denoted by μ_X.

The variance is a measure of variability or dispersion about the mean. The variance, σ_X^2, of a random variable X is defined as the expected squared deviation from the mean:

$$\sigma_X^2 = E\big[(X - \mu_X)^2\big]$$

Dispersion is often measured with the standard deviation of X, σ_X, which is simply the square root of the variance. The standard deviation is a more convenient and intuitive measure of dispersion because it is expressed in the same units as the original variable X.

THE NORMAL DISTRIBUTION

One of the more important examples of a continuous probability distribution is the normal or Gaussian distribution. The normal distribution is a bell-shaped curve that is symmetric around its mean, μ. If a random variable X, follows a normal distribution with mean μ_X and standard deviation σ_X, then it has the property that a fixed percentage of observations fall within a range of X values defined by the mean and standard deviation. The mean defines the center of the distribution, and the standard deviation defines the dispersion around the mean. For any normal distribution, 68.3% of the observations fall within one standard deviation from the mean, and 95.5% of the values fall within two standard deviations from the mean. This is shown in Exhibit 3.2. Stated in terms of the cumulative density function $F(x)$, this means that

$$P(\mu_X - \sigma_X < X < \mu_X + \sigma_X) = F(\mu_X + \sigma_X) - F(\mu_X - \sigma_X) = 68.3\%$$

and

$$P(\mu_X - 2\sigma_X < X < \mu_X + 2\sigma_X) = F(\mu_X + 2\sigma_X) - F(\mu_X - 2\sigma_X) = 95.5\%$$

It is often easier to work with the *standard* normal distribution, which has the properties $\mu = 0$ and $\sigma = 1$. The relationship between the normal and standard normal distributions is as follows. If a random variable X has a normal distribution, then the variable Z, defined as $Z = (X - \mu_X)/\sigma_X$, has a standard normal distribution. The probability that a normally distributed

EXHIBIT 3.2

Areas Under the Normal Distribution

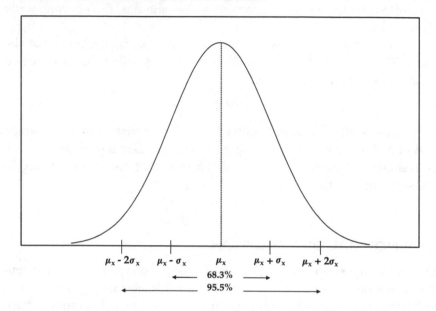

variable will fall within a range of values can be expressed as the probability that a standard normal variable falls within a related range of values. For example, the probability that a normal variable assumes a value less than 1.96 standard deviations above its mean is equal to 97.5%. This can be written in notation as

$$P(X < \mu_X + 1.96\sigma_X) = P(Z < 1.96) = N(1.96) = 97.5\%$$

The above relationship can be used to determine the probability that a normal variable falls between any two values. A table giving values of the cumulative standard normal density function, $N(Z)$, is given in Exhibit 3.3. The standard normal distribution is a useful tool for statistical inference, particularly when we wish to test hypotheses about the mean of a distribution. This is discussed further in the next section.

Example: Suppose X has a normal distribution with $\mu_X = 10$ and $\sigma_X = 50$. The probability that X assumes a value between 20 and 85 is given by

$$P(20 < X < 75) = P\left(\frac{20 - 10}{50} < Z < \frac{85 - 10}{50}\right) = N(1.5) - N(0.2)$$

E X H I B I T   3.3

Cumulative Standard Normal Distribution

z	0.00	0.01	0.02	0.03	0.04	0.05	0.06	0.07	0.08	0.09
0.0	0.0000	0.0040	0.0080	0.0120	0.0160	0.0199	0.0239	0.0279	0.0319	0.0359
0.1	0.0398	0.0438	0.0478	0.0517	0.0557	0.0596	0.0636	0.0675	0.0714	0.0753
0.2	0.0793	0.0832	0.0871	0.0910	0.0948	0.0987	0.1026	0.1064	0.1103	0.1141
0.3	0.1179	0.1217	0.1255	0.1293	0.1331	0.1368	0.1406	0.1443	0.1480	0.1517
0.4	0.1554	0.1591	0.1628	0.1664	0.1700	0.1736	0.1772	0.1808	0.1844	0.1879
0.5	0.1915	0.1950	0.1985	0.2019	0.2054	0.2088	0.2123	0.2157	0.2190	0.2224
0.6	0.2257	0.2291	0.2324	0.2357	0.2389	0.2422	0.2454	0.2486	0.2517	0.2549
0.7	0.2580	0.2611	0.2642	0.2673	0.2704	0.2734	0.2764	0.2794	0.2823	0.2852
0.8	0.2881	0.2910	0.2939	0.2967	0.2995	0.3023	0.3051	0.3078	0.3106	0.3133
0.9	0.3159	0.3186	0.3212	0.3238	0.3264	0.3289	0.3315	0.3340	0.3365	0.3389
1.0	0.3413	0.3438	0.3461	0.3485	0.3508	0.3531	0.3554	0.3577	0.3599	0.3621
1.1	0.3643	0.3665	0.3686	0.3708	0.3729	0.3749	0.3770	0.3790	0.3810	0.3830
1.2	0.3849	0.3869	0.3888	0.3907	0.3925	0.3944	0.3962	0.3980	0.3997	0.4015
1.3	0.4032	0.4049	0.4066	0.4082	0.4099	0.4115	0.4131	0.4147	0.4162	0.4177
1.4	0.4192	0.4207	0.4222	0.4236	0.4251	0.4265	0.4279	0.4292	0.4306	0.4319
1.5	0.4332	0.4345	0.4357	0.4370	0.4382	0.4394	0.4406	0.4418	0.4429	0.4441
1.6	0.4452	0.4463	0.4474	0.4484	0.4495	0.4505	0.4515	0.4525	0.4535	0.4545
1.7	0.4554	0.4564	0.4573	0.4582	0.4591	0.4599	0.4608	0.4616	0.4625	0.4633
1.8	0.4641	0.4649	0.4656	0.4664	0.4671	0.4678	0.4686	0.4693	0.4699	0.4706
1.9	0.4713	0.4719	0.4726	0.4732	0.4738	0.4744	0.4750	0.4756	0.4761	0.4767
2.0	0.4772	0.4778	0.4783	0.4788	0.4793	0.4798	0.4803	0.4808	0.4812	0.4817
2.1	0.4821	0.4826	0.4830	0.4834	0.4838	0.4842	0.4846	0.4850	0.4854	0.4857
2.2	0.4861	0.4864	0.4868	0.4871	0.4875	0.4878	0.4881	0.4884	0.4887	0.4890
2.3	0.4893	0.4896	0.4898	0.4901	0.4904	0.4906	0.4909	0.4911	0.4913	0.4916
2.4	0.4918	0.4920	0.4922	0.4925	0.4927	0.4929	0.4931	0.4932	0.4934	0.4936
2.5	0.4938	0.4940	0.4941	0.4943	0.4945	0.4946	0.4948	0.4949	0.4951	0.4952
2.6	0.4953	0.4955	0.4956	0.4957	0.4959	0.4960	0.4961	0.4962	0.4963	0.4964
2.7	0.4965	0.4966	0.4967	0.4968	0.4969	0.4970	0.4971	0.4972	0.4973	0.4974
2.8	0.4974	0.4975	0.4976	0.4977	0.4977	0.4978	0.4979	0.4979	0.4980	0.4981
2.9	0.4981	0.4982	0.4982	0.4983	0.4984	0.4984	0.4985	0.4985	0.4986	0.4986
3.0	0.4987	0.4987	0.4987	0.4988	0.4988	0.4989	0.4989	0.4989	0.4990	0.4990

Referring to Exhibit 3.3, $N(1.5) = 0.4332$ and $N(0.2) = 0.0793$; therefore the probability that X assumes values between 20 and 75 is equal to 35.39%.

SAMPLING AND STATISTICAL INFERENCE

We are often interested in drawing conclusions about the characteristics of a random variable. Determining these characteristics would be a simple matter if we could examine all possible outcomes, or the *population*, of the random variable. Population characteristics can be described by the probability density function; however, in practice, this is seldom known. Estimation is the process of estimating these population parameters with the use of a test statistic based on a sample of observations. Statistical inference refers to the process of inferring certain facts about the population from an examination of a small part of this population, which is known as a *sample*. The process of obtaining samples is known as *sampling*.

Suppose we are interested in the daily change in the spot rate of the JPY. Exhibit 3.4 contains two months of daily spot exchange rates for JPY along with daily changes in the spot rate. The rates are quoted in JPY per USD.

The mean and standard deviation of this population are unknown. We may base our inferences about these population parameters on sample statistics. The population mean can be estimated from the sample mean or the average daily change for the 42 observations in the sample. The sample mean is calculated with the formula

$$\overline{X} = \frac{\sum_{i=1}^{n} X_i}{n}$$

where $X_1, X_2, \ldots, X_n$ represent the n observations of the sample. The population standard deviation can be estimated from the *sample standard deviation*, calculated as

$$s = \sqrt{\frac{\sum (X_i - \overline{X})^2}{n - 1}}$$

In the example above, the sample mean, $\overline{X} = 2.5$, and the sample standard deviation, $s = 52.7$, are not likely to be exactly the same as the population parameters. Sample statistics calculated for a different 42-day period might be higher or lower than those calculated with these data. This difference in estimates is known as sampling variation.

The sample mean, $\overline{X}$, has a distribution known as a sampling distribution. If this sampling process were to be repeated a large number of

EXHIBIT 3.4

Spot Exchange Rates and Daily Changes
in Spot Exchange Rates for JPY per USD

Day	¥ Spot Rate	Daily Change	Day	¥ Spot Rate	Daily Change
1	9032.61	−3.26	22	9095.87	−100.38
2	9014.69	−17.91	23	9012.26	−83.61
3	9009.82	−4.87	24	9127.42	115.16
4	9096.70	86.88	25	9100.01	−27.41
5	9124.09	27.39	26	9071.12	−28.89
6	9167.58	43.50	27	9141.60	70.49
7	9203.02	35.44	28	9188.64	47.04
8	9180.21	−22.81	29	9198.79	10.14
9	9185.27	5.06	30	9186.11	−12.68
10	9129.09	−56.18	31	9249.84	63.73
11	9094.22	−34.87	32	9229.35	−20.49
12	9142.44	48.22	33	9181.05	−48.30
13	9059.61	−82.83	34	9263.55	82.50
14	9133.25	73.64	35	9147.46	−116.09
15	9175.15	41.90	36	9171.79	24.33
16	9131.59	−43.57	37	9193.71	21.92
17	9153.32	21.73	38	9144.95	−48.76
18	9214.04	60.72	39	9140.77	−4.18
19	9235.32	21.27	40	9167.58	26.82
20	9231.91	−3.41	41	9121.59	−45.99
21	9196.25	−35.66	42	9139.93	18.34

Source: Bloomberg.

times, producing a large set of sample means, the sample means them-
selves would have a mean equal to the population mean, μ, and a standard
deviation equal to

$$\sigma_{\bar{X}} = \sigma / \sqrt{n}$$

where σ is the population standard deviation. The standard deviation of
sample means, $\sigma_{\bar{X}}$, is also known as the standard error of the sampling distribution. The standard error is smaller for larger samples, which implies
that sample means become more precise estimates of the true population

mean as the sample size becomes larger. If we use the sample standard deviation as an estimate of σ, the standard error of the sampling distribution of daily changes in spot exchange rates is equal to 8.1.

CONFIDENCE INTERVALS AND HYPOTHESIS TESTING

For large samples, the sample mean will have a normal distribution, regardless of the original data from which it is calculated.[1] This is an important result because it allows us to draw conclusions about the precision of a sample mean. Since $\overline{X}$ has a normal distribution with mean μ and standard deviation $\sigma_{\overline{X}}$, it is the case that

$$P(\overline{X} - 1.96\sigma_{\overline{X}} < \mu < \overline{X} + 1.96\sigma_{\overline{X}}) = 0.95$$

In repeated sampling, the true mean will lie 1.96 standard errors above or below the estimated mean 95% of the time. This is known as a confidence interval for the mean μ. For our data on daily changes in spot exchange rates, a 95% confidence interval for the population mean μ will be 2.5 $\pm$ 1.96(8.1), or between -13.4 and 18.4.

Hypothesis testing is a related aspect of statistical inference. Hypotheses can be tested by making an assumption about the unknown population parameter and then accepting or rejecting the hypothesis on the basis of the calculated sample or test statistic. Whatever assumption is made defines what is known as the *null hypothesis*. Suppose we wish to test the hypothesis that the population mean of a distribution equals a hypothetical value μ_0. This hypothesis can be tested by initially assuming that the population mean $\mu = \mu_0$. The null hypothesis is

$$H_0 : \mu = \mu_0$$

and the alternative hypothesis is

$$H_a : \mu \neq \mu_0$$

The decision to accept or reject is made under the assumption that the null hypothesis is true. Since the sample mean, $\overline{X}$, has a normal distribution for a large sample of observations ($n > 30$), the null hypothesis is rejected

---

1. This conclusion is based on a result called the Central Limit Theorem.

EXHIBIT 3.5

Acceptance and Rejection Regions for $H_0 : \mu = \mu_0$

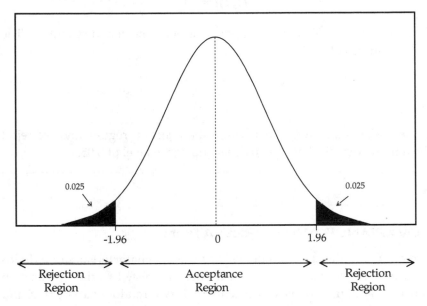

0.025

0.025

-1.96   0   1.96

Rejection   Acceptance   Rejection
Region   Region   Region

at a significance level of 0.05, commonly denoted α, if $\overline{X}$ is more than 1.96 standard errors away from μ_0. This is known as the *rejection region*. The test statistic is calculated as

$$z = \frac{\overline{X} - \mu_0}{s_{\overline{X}}}$$

where z has a standard normal distribution. The acceptance and rejection regions are shown in Exhibit 3.5. Since the rejection region lies in both tails, we have a two-tail test.

Example: Suppose we wish to test the hypothesis that the mean daily change in spot exchange rates equals 30 at a significance level of 0.05. The null hypothesis is

$$H_0 : \mu = 30$$

and the corresponding alternative hypothesis is

$$H_a : \mu \neq 30$$

Since $n > 30$, the calculated sample mean has a normal distribution. The test statistic is calculated as

$$z = \frac{\overline{X} - \mu_0}{s_{\overline{X}}} = \frac{2.5 - 30}{8.1} = -3.395$$

The calculated z statistic falls within the rejection region, and we reject the null hypothesis that $\mu = 30$ at a significance level of 0.05.

COVARIANCE AND CORRELATION

The mean and the standard deviation measure characteristics of individual variables; however, we are also often interested in the relationship between random variables. For example, if two random variables, X and Y, are positively associated with one another, they will tend to assume values larger or smaller than average at the same time. If, on the other hand, they are negatively associated, X will assume values greater (smaller) than average and Y will assume values smaller (greater) than average. One way to measure this association is to examine the product of the deviations from the mean, $(X - \mu_X)(Y - \mu_Y)$. This product will tend to be positive for variables with a positive association and negative for variables with a negative association. The expected value of this product is called the covariance between X and Y, COV(X,Y), where

$$COV(X,Y) = E[(X - \mu_X)(Y - \mu_Y)]$$

Covariance is a measure of linear association, which can assume positive or negative values, depending on the linear relationship between X and Y. It should be noted that a zero covariance does not imply that the variables are unrelated, only that they have no linear association. Covariance by itself can only be determined to be large or small if compared with the standard deviations of the variables X and Y. If COV(X,Y) is large and positive (negative), there is a strong positive (negative) relationship between the variables X and Y. An alternative measure of association that is more readily interpretable is the Pearson correlation coefficient, ρ_{XY}, where

$$\rho_{XY} = \frac{\text{COV}(X,Y)}{\sigma_X \sigma_Y}$$

The correlation coefficient, ρ_{XY}, is a measure of association that always assumes the same sign as covariance but is scaled such that the strength of the relationship does not depend on the units of measurement. The correlation coefficient has the property

$$-1.0 \leq \rho_{XY} \leq 1.0$$

If ρ_{XY} assumes values close to 1.0, this indicates that the variables X and Y have a very strong positive linear association. If, on the other hand, the correlation coefficient assumes values close to -1.0, this indicates that the variables X and Y have a very strong negative linear association. A correlation coefficient close to zero indicates a weak linear relationship.

Exhibit 3.6 illustrates the linear relationship between two variables as measured by correlation. Each figure shows a scatterplot of 100 random observations of the variables X and Y. When $\rho_{XY} = 1.0$, the relationship between X and Y is perfectly linear, that is, X and Y plot along a straight line with a positive slope, as shown in part A of Exhibit 3.6. When $\rho_{XY} = -1.0$, the relationship between X and Y is also perfectly linear, but X and Y plot along a straight line with a negative slope, as shown in part B of Exhibit 3.6. When X and Y are independent, a plot of the values of X and Y appears as random scatter and the correlation between X and Y is zero. This relationship is shown in part C of Exhibit 3.6.[2]

For a sample of n observations, the population covariance is estimated by the sample covariance

$$C_{XY} = \frac{\sum_{i=1}^{n}(X_i - \overline{X})(Y_i - \overline{Y})}{n - 1}$$

and the sample correlation coefficient is

$$r_{XY} = \frac{C_{XY}}{s_X s_Y}$$

2. A correlation coefficient equal to zero does not necessarily imply that X and Y are independent, because the relationship between them may not be linear.

EXHIBIT 3.6

Correlation and the Linear Relationship
between Two Variables

(A) $\rho_{XY} = 1.0$

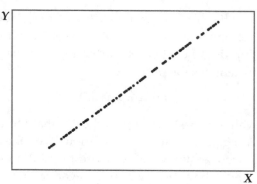

(B) $\rho_{XY} = -1.0$

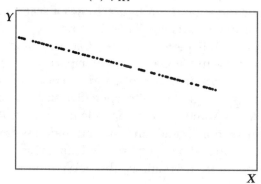

(C) $\rho_{XY} = 0$

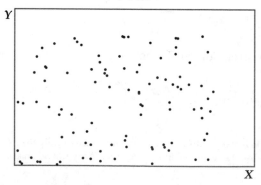

Suppose we are interested in the relationship between the daily change in the spot rate of JPY and the daily change in the futures rate of JPY. Exhibit 3.7 contains two months of daily changes in the spot and futures rate for JPY. The rates are quoted in JPY per USD.

A scatterplot of these data is shown in Exhibit 3.8. Each data point represents one daily observation of a change in spot and futures rates for JPY.

If we let Y be the daily change in the spot rate and X be the daily change in the futures rate, the sample covariance statistic is calculated as

$$C_{XY} = \frac{113,981}{41} = 2780.0$$

EXHIBIT 3.7

Daily Changes in Spot and Futures Exchange Rates
for JPY per USD

Day	Change in ¥ Spot Rate	Change in ¥ Futures Rate	Day	Change in ¥ Spot Rate	Change in ¥ Futures Rate
1	−3.26	−9.00	22	−100.38	107.00
2	−17.91	−20.00	23	−83.61	−95.00
3	−4.87	−6.00	24	115.16	130.00
4	8'.88	95.00	25	−27.41	−26.00
5	27.39	20.00	26	−28.89	−29.00
6	43.50	38.00	27	70.49	83.00
7	35.44	43.00	28	47.04	76.00
8	−22.81	0.00	29	10.14	0.00
9	5.06	−16.00	30	−12.68	−39.00
10	−56.18	−53.00	31	63.73	54.00
11	−34.87	−36.00	32	−20.49	−10.00
12	48.22	38.00	33	−48.30	−56.00
13	−82.83	−67.00	34	82.50	72.00
14	73.64	47.00	35	−116.09	−105.00
15	41.90	58.00	36	24.33	38.00
16	−43.57	−57.00	37	21.92	2.00
17	21.73	23.00	38	−48.76	−50.00
18	60.72	67.00	39	−4.18	−5.00
19	21.27	20.00	40	26.82	29.00
20	−3.41	2.00	41	−45.99	−34.00
21	−35.66	−42.00	42	18.34	0.00

Source: Bloomberg.

EXHIBIT 3.8

Daily Changes in Spot and Futures Exchange Rates for JPY per USD

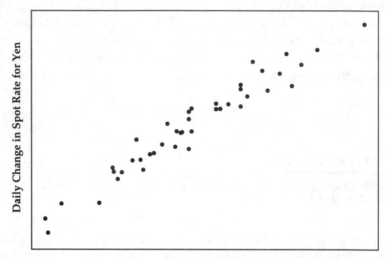

Daily Change in Futures Rate for Yen

and the sample correlation coefficient is

$$r_{XY} = \frac{C_{XY}}{s_X s_Y} = \frac{2780}{(54.3)(52.7)} = 0.972$$

These calculations show a high, positive correlation coefficient, which is consistent with the strong linear relation shown in Exhibit 3.8.

LINEAR REGRESSION

Linear regression is a method of estimating the value of one variable from another. Like correlation, regression views the association between variables as linear. Regression views this linear relationship as one in which one variable, Y, is influenced by another variable, X. The variable Y is called the *dependent variable* and the variable X is called the *independent variable*.

The linear relationship between X and Y takes the form

$$\hat{Y}_i = \beta_0 + \beta_1 X_i$$

where X_i is the ith observation of X and $\hat{Y}_i$ is the corresponding predicted or "fitted" value of Y. This relationship defines a straight line with intercept β_0 and slope β_1. Since the data points may not fall on this regression line, the exact relationship must include a stochastic term, ε, such that

$$Y_i = \beta_0 + \beta_1 X_i + \varepsilon_i$$

where Y_i is the ith observation of Y. The stochastic term ε is referred to as the error term and is assumed to be normally distributed with a zero mean and constant variance.[3]

Use of the regression model requires that the parameters β_0 and β_1 be estimated from the data to find the "best" linear relationship with the data. This estimation is usually made with the method of ordinary least squares. The ordinary least-squares method chooses estimates of β_0 and β_1 such that the sum of the squared deviations from the fitted values or sum of squared errors, SSE, is minimized:

$$SSE = \sum_{i=1}^{n} (Y_i - \hat{Y}_i)^2 = \sum_{i=1}^{n} \varepsilon_i^2$$

It can be shown that SSE is minimized by the following estimates of $\hat{\beta}_0$ and $\hat{\beta}_1$:

$$\hat{\beta}_1 = \frac{C_{XY}}{s_X^2}$$

and

$$\hat{\beta}_0 = \overline{Y} - \hat{\beta}_1 \overline{X}$$

where $\hat{\beta}_0$ and $\hat{\beta}_1$ are known as the least-squares parameter estimates.

Example: Suppose we wish to estimate daily changes in spot exchange rates in JPY from daily changes in futures exchange rates as in Exhibit 3.7. The average of the daily changes in the futures rates, $\overline{X}$, is 1.7. The least-squares estimates are calculated as

$$\hat{\beta}_1 = \frac{C_{XY}}{s_X^2} = \frac{2780.0}{2946.8} = 0.943$$

---

3. It is also assumed that the error terms have zero correlation with each other and with X.

and

$$\hat{\beta}_0 = \bar{Y} - \hat{\beta}_1 \bar{X} = 2.5 - (0.943)(1.7) = 0.897$$

and the sample regression line is

$$\hat{Y}_i = 0.897 + 0.943 X_i$$

This regression line is shown in Exhibit 3.9. The coefficient on X_i can be interpreted to mean that a one-yen increase in the futures exchange rate on JPY is associated with an increase in the spot exchange rate on JPY of 0.943 yen.

COEFFICIENT OF DETERMINATION

For a posited relationship where Y depends on X, the regression model is constructed in such a way that X is supposed to explain Y. One way to

EXHIBIT 3.9

Sample Regression Line for Daily Changes in Spot
and Futures Exchange Rates on JPY

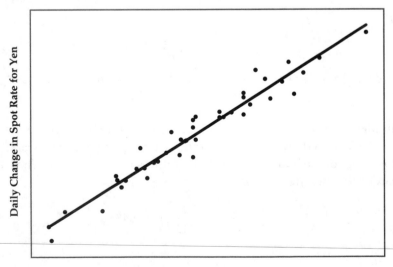

Daily Change in Futures Rate for Yen

think about this is that Y has variability because Y is related to X, which has variability. The stochastic error term, ε, represents variability in Y not due to variability in X.

A more formal way of presenting this idea is to use sum of squares decomposition:

$$SST = SSR + SSE$$

where

$$SST = \sum_{i=1}^{n}(Y_i - \overline{Y})^2$$

$$SSR = \sum_{i=1}^{n}(\hat{Y}_i - \overline{Y})^2$$

and

$$SSE = \sum_{i=1}^{n}\varepsilon_i^2$$

The total sum of squares, SST, can be thought of as the variability of Y around its sample mean. SST is the total variability we are trying to explain. SSR is the sum of squares from regression or, alternatively, the variability in predicted values around their conditional mean. SSR can be thought of as the component of variability explained by the model. SSE is the sum of squared errors or variability unexplained by the model.

In an accurate regression model, a high proportion of variability in the dependent variable is explained by the model. This is measured by the coefficient of determination R^2 calculated as

$$R^2 = \frac{SSR}{SST}$$

The coefficient of determination, the square of the sample correlation coefficient, is used to measure the strength of the relationship between X and Y. From our exchange rate data,

$$R^2 = \frac{SSR}{SST} = \frac{107,531}{113,714} = 0.946$$

The R^2 value of 0.946 can be interpreted to mean that 94.6% of the sample variability in the dependent variable is explained by the fitted regression.

INFERENCE ABOUT THE REGRESSION MODEL

The regression parameter estimates, $\hat{\beta}_0$ and $\hat{\beta}_1$, are subject to sampling variation. As we found with other sample statistics, the estimates calculated for a different 42-day period might be higher or lower than those calculated from these data. The sampling distribution of the slope term, $\hat{\beta}_1$, has a mean equal to β_1 and a standard deviation given by

$$\sigma_{\hat{\beta}_1} = \frac{\sigma_\varepsilon}{\sqrt{\sum_{i=1}^{n}(X_i - \overline{X})^2}}$$

where σ_ε is the standard deviation of the error terms from the regression. A sample estimate of this standard deviation for our exchange rate data is calculated as

$$s_{\hat{\beta}_1} = \sqrt{\frac{SSE/(n-2)}{\sum_{i=1}^{n}(X_i - \overline{X})^2}} = \sqrt{\frac{154.6}{120,818}} = 0.0358$$

The sample estimate of the slope term, $\hat{\beta}_1$, has a Student's t distribution with $n - 2$ degrees of freedom.[4]

Because the regression model is constructed such that the independent variable influences the dependent variable, it is particularly important to determine whether the slope term is different from zero. If it cannot be determined that β_1 is significantly different from zero, then we cannot conclude that X influences Y.

Example: Suppose we wish to test the hypothesis that the slope of the regression equals zero. The null hypothesis and alternative hypothesis are

$$H_0 : \beta_1 = 0$$
$$H_a : \beta_1 \neq 0$$

---

4. The Student's t distribution is a symmetrical distribution that is defined by its degrees of freedom. For small sample sizes the t distribution has more area under the tails, which means it is more likely to assume extreme values. For large sample sizes the t distribution approaches the normal distribution.

EXHIBIT 3.10

Student's *t*-distribution Table

df	α = 0.1	0.05	0.025	0.01	0.005	0.001	0.0005
∞	t_α = 1.282	1.645	1.960	2.326	2.576	3.091	3.291
1	3.078	6.314	12.706	31.821	63.656	318.289	636.578
2	1.886	2.920	4.303	6.965	9.925	22.328	31.600
3	1.638	2.353	3.182	4.541	5.841	10.214	12.924
4	1.533	2.132	2.776	3.747	4.604	7.173	8.610
5	1.476	2.015	2.571	3.365	4.032	5.894	6.869
6	1.440	1.943	2.447	3.143	3.707	5.208	5.959
7	1.415	1.895	2.365	2.998	3.499	4.785	5.408
8	1.397	1.860	2.306	2.896	3.355	4.501	5.041
9	1.383	1.833	2.262	2.821	3.250	4.297	4.781
10	1.372	1.812	2.228	2.764	3.169	4.144	4.587
11	1.363	1.796	2.201	2.718	3.106	4.025	4.437
12	1.356	1.782	2.179	2.681	3.055	3.930	4.318
13	1.350	1.771	2.160	2.650	3.012	3.852	4.221
14	1.345	1.761	2.145	2.624	2.977	3.787	4.140
15	1.341	1.753	2.131	2.602	2.947	3.733	4.073
16	1.337	1.746	2.120	2.583	2.921	3.686	4.015
17	1.333	1.740	2.110	2.567	2.898	3.646	3.965
18	1.330	1.734	2.101	2.552	2.878	3.610	3.922
19	1.328	1.729	2.093	2.539	2.861	3.579	3.883
20	1.325	1.725	2.086	2.528	2.845	3.552	3.850
21	1.323	1.721	2.080	2.518	2.831	3.527	3.819
22	1.321	1.717	2.074	2.508	2.819	3.505	3.792
23	1.319	1.714	2.069	2.500	2.807	3.485	3.768
24	1.318	1.711	2.064	2.492	2.797	3.467	3.745
25	1.316	1.708	2.060	2.485	2.787	3.450	3.725
26	1.315	1.706	2.056	2.479	2.779	3.435	3.707
27	1.314	1.703	2.052	2.473	2.771	3.421	3.689
28	1.313	1.701	2.048	2.467	2.763	3.408	3.674
29	1.311	1.699	2.045	2.462	2.756	3.396	3.660
30	1.310	1.697	2.042	2.457	2.750	3.385	3.646
60	1.296	1.671	2.000	2.390	2.660	3.232	3.460
120	1.289	1.658	1.980	2.358	2.617	3.160	3.373
∞	1.282	1.645	1.960	2.326	2.576	3.091	3.291

Since β_1 has a t distribution with $n - 2$ degrees of freedom, the corresponding test statistic at a significance level α is given by

$$t = \frac{\hat{\beta}_1 - 0}{s_{\hat{\beta}_1}}$$

The decision rule is to reject the null hypothesis whenever $|t| > t_{n-2,\alpha/2}$. The critical value for t, $t_{n-2,\alpha/2}$, is the value of a Student's t distribution with mean zero such that $P(t > t_{n-2,\alpha/2}) = \alpha/2$. The critical value for our example, $t_{40,0.025}$, is equal to 2.021. Critical values for the Student's t distribution are contained in Exhibit 3.10. For our exchange rate example, the test statistic is calculated as

$$t = \frac{\hat{\beta}_1 - 0}{s_{\hat{\beta}_1}} = \frac{0.9434}{0.0358} = 26.35$$

The calculated t statistic falls within the rejection region at a significance level of 0.05 if $t > 2.021$. Hence, we reject the null hypothesis at a level of significance of 0.05.

SUMMARY

Effective hedging requires a clear understanding of the relationship between the hedged position and the hedging instrument. In this chapter, we reviewed the statistical concepts required to construct and evaluate an effective hedge. We introduced the concepts of a random variable and discussed how to measure and describe the statistical relationship between variables.

Statistical measures, such as mean and variance, summarize the characteristics of a random variable. We discussed how to use sampling to draw conclusions about the behavior of a population, a process known as statistical inference. We show how the normal distribution is used for statistical inference about the mean of a population. Included in the description are examples of confidence intervals and hypothesis testing on the mean of a distribution.

Hedging requires an understanding of the relationship between price changes of related financial instruments. The strength and direction of the linear relationship between two variables may be measured with the use of covariance and correlation statistics. We introduced the concept of linear regression and discussed how it may be used to estimate the value of one variable from the value of another variable. Furthermore, we discussed the interpretation of regression estimates and statistical inference about the regression model.

REFERENCES

Hamburg, Morris. *Statistical Analysis for Decision Making*. San Diego: Harcourt Brace Jovanovich, 1987.

Montgomery, Douglas C., and Elizabeth A. Peck. *Introduction to Linear Regression Analysis*. New York: John Wiley & Sons, 1982.

Newbold, Paul, and Theodore Bos. *Introductory Business Forecasting*. Cincinnati: Southwestern Publishing, 1990.

CHAPTER 4

Fixed-Income Mathematics

In this chapter we explain the basics of bond pricing and measures of bond risk. The basis for bond valuation, like most asset valuation, is present value. We emphasize the assessment of bond price volatility because hedging bonds and related instruments requires an understanding of the risk of both the portfolio being hedged and the hedging instrument. In addition to bond pricing mechanics, we describe the risk and return measures of duration and convexity.

The primary risk that can be managed by hedging is known as interest rate risk.[1] Interest rate risk is the risk that changes in market levels of interest rates will adversely affect the value of an investment. For example, a bond portfolio manager may wish to hedge against the possibility of a decrease in the value of a portfolio associated with an increase in interest rates. An understanding of interest rate risk is crucial to establishing and managing an effective hedge for fixed-income investments.

---

1. There are several other types of risk associated with investment in fixed-rate debt. *Default risk* is the risk that the issuer of a bond will not make its scheduled debt service payments. *Reinvestment risk* arises from the periodic interest payment of coupon bonds. Since payments are received over the life of a coupon-bearing bond, an investor faces the risk of reinvesting coupon payments at uncertain future interest rates, which may be lower than the yield on the bond. *Prepayment risk* arises from the ability of an issuer to call bonds prior to their stated maturity. This may occur because issuers exercise their option to call bonds on or after a specified call date. Mortgage-backed securities also allow loan prepayments to be used to retire debt bonds. In either case, the prepayments tend to increase in periods of lower interest rates.

The typical method of hedging interest rate risk is to choose a hedging instrument whose price changes are closely related to those of the target portfolio. A hedged bond portfolio is one in which price changes in the hedging instrument offset price changes in the target portfolio. The more closely related the price changes, the more efficient the hedge. Hedging instruments can be long or short positions in bonds or derivative securities.

The proxy used to measure interest rate risk is called duration. Duration measures the sensitivity of bond prices to changes in interest rates. Higher duration means higher price volatility and higher expected returns.

BOND PRICING

The key to understanding the valuation of interest-bearing securities is to understand concepts of discounting and compounding. In general, bond prices are calculated as the present value of the cash flows paid by the bond. In the sections that follow, we expand on the present value techniques developed in Chapter 2 to explain the basics of bond pricing.

PRESENT VALUE OF BONDS

Consider a fixed-rate bond that pays principal and interest in one year. We will use the following notation:

F = principal or face value of the bond
c = annual coupon rate on the bond
C = interest cash flow or coupon payment in dollars equal to cF
y = market discount rate or yield on the bond

At the end of the one-year period, the investor will receive the payment of interest plus principal, $C + F$. The present value (PV) or price of the bond's cash flows is given by

$$PV = \frac{C}{(1 + y)} + \frac{F}{(1 + y)}$$

In the above equation, the present value of the bond will fluctuate as the yield fluctuates with changes in market interest rates. As yields rise, the present value or price of the bond will fall, and as yields fall the price of the bond will rise.

The coupon payment remains fixed for the life of a fixed-rate bond. When a bond is issued, if the coupon rate c is set equal to the market yield, then the bond's present value is equal to its face value. To see this, substitute c for y in the above equation:

$$PV = \frac{C}{(1+c)} + \frac{F}{(1+c)} = \frac{F(1+c)}{(1+c)} = F$$

If interest is received over more than one period, then the cash flows are summed over the time period and the discount factors are adjusted to reflect the time period in which they are received. For example, a two-period investment has the following present value:

$$PV = \frac{C}{(1+y)} + \frac{C}{(1+y)^2} + \frac{F}{(1+y)^2}$$

A more general expression for the present value of a bond with n years to maturity is given by

$$PV = \sum_{t=1}^{n} \frac{C}{(1+y)^t} + \frac{F}{(1+y)^n}$$

Interest is often compounded on a different frequency, such as semi-annually, monthly, or daily. The interest rate, coupon payment, and number of compounding periods must then be adjusted to reflect the frequency of the compounding. If m is the frequency of compounding per year, then the present value of the bond is represented as

$$PV = \sum_{t=1}^{nm} \frac{C/m}{\left(1+\frac{y}{m}\right)^t} + \frac{F}{\left(1+\frac{y}{m}\right)^{nm}}$$

As we discussed in Chapter 2, interest is said to be continuously compounded when the frequency of compounding becomes large. If the coupon payments on a bond are continuously compounded, then the present value is calculated as

$$PV = \sum_{t=1}^{n} Ce^{-yt} + Fe^{-yn}$$

where $e = 2.7182818$ is the natural base of logarithms.

FULL-COUPON BONDS

The coupon on a fixed-rate corporate or municipal bond is typically paid semiannually on a 30/360-day basis. Each year is assumed to have 360 days, called *bond days,* and each month is assumed to have exactly 30 days. The semiannual coupon is expressed in terms of an annual rate of interest or bond equivalent yield. Interest accrues beginning on the dated date; and thereafter interest is paid semiannually until maturity.

For example, consider a bond that is dated and delivered January 1, 2004 with a maturity date of January 1, 2034. The bond will make its first interest payment on July 1, 2004 for the initial period of 180 bond days and will continue to make semiannual payments each January 1 and July 1 thereafter. Exhibit 4.1 shows the cash flows for a 30-year, 6.00% full-coupon bond.

The current market price P of a bond is equal to the present value of the cash flows received over the life of the bond. The cash flow on a full-coupon bond consists of $2n$ semiannual coupons over n years paid until

EXHIBIT 4.1

Interest and Principal Payment on a 30-Year, 6.00% Full-Coupon Bond

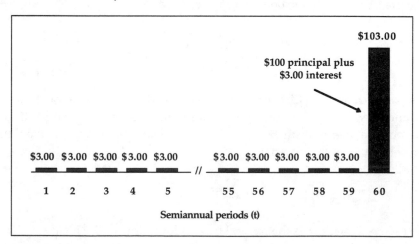

maturity and the principal or face value, F at maturity. Each semiannual coupon payment $C/2$ is discounted at the prevailing semiannual market yield $y/2$ for a bond of similar maturity and credit quality. The bond's price P is calculated as

$$P = \sum_{t=1}^{2n} \frac{C/2}{\left(1 + \frac{y}{2}\right)^t} + \frac{F}{\left(1 + \frac{y}{2}\right)^{2n}}$$

Example: At issuance, a $100 face-value, noncallable 30-year bond that pays interest at a rate of 6.00% when the market discount rate is 5.00% would be priced as

$$P = \sum_{t=1}^{60} \frac{3.00}{(1.025)^t} + \frac{100}{(1.025)^{60}} = \$115.45$$

This pricing is appropriate when all of the interest payment periods are equal and the first interest period is a full period. When bonds are sold between interest payment periods, the original owner of the bonds is entitled to the interest from the beginning of the interest payment period to the day prior to the settlement date of the sale. The interest over this time period is referred to as *accrued interest* and is calculated by multiplying the interest rate by the number of bond days in the partial interest period and dividing by 180, the total number of bond days in the semiannual period.

Example: Consider a corporate bond that makes semiannual interest payments at an annual rate of 6.00% on January 1 and July 1 of each year and matures on January 1, 2034. If the bond has a settlement date of March 15, 2004, the accrued interest (AI) is calculated for 74 bond days between January 1, 2004 and March 14, 2004, inclusive, where

$$\text{AI} = \left(\frac{74}{180}\right)(\$3.00) = \$1.233$$

The accrued interest for this time period is $1.233 per $100 of bond principal. A bond price that reflects the accrued interest that the seller is entitled to receive is known as the *full* or *dirty price* P_d. When the price of a bond is being calculated, if the first interest period is not a complete period, then the price of the bond must be adjusted to reflect the partial interest period. The compounding periods must be adjusted, and the accrued interest must be subtracted from the price. This is known as the *clean price* of the bond P_c. The clean price is calculated as

$$P_c = \sum_{t=1}^{2n} \left[\frac{C/2}{\left(1 + \frac{y}{2}\right)^{t-1+q}} \right] + \left[\frac{F}{\left(1 + \frac{y}{2}\right)^{2n-1+q}} \right] - (AI)$$

where q is equal to the portion of the 180-day period during which interest accrues. In the above example, assuming a yield of 6.00%, the clean price of the bond is calculated as

$$P_c = \sum_{t=1}^{60} \left[\frac{3.00}{(1.03)^{t-1+.589}} \right] + \left[\frac{100}{(1.03)^{59.589}} \right] - (1.233) = \$99.989$$

where

$$q = (106/180) = 0.589$$

ZERO-COUPON BONDS

Zero-coupon bonds do not make interest payments; instead, they sell at a discount from their face value and increase in value or *accrete* to the par value at maturity. There is only one cash flow associated with a zero-coupon bond, as shown in Exhibit 4.2. Therefore the value is relatively easy to calculate.

The price of a zero-coupon bond is simply the discounted value of the principal payment received at maturity:

$$P = \frac{F}{\left(1 + \dfrac{y}{m}\right)^{nm}}$$

EXHIBIT 4.2

Cash Flows on a 30-Year, Zero-Coupon Bond

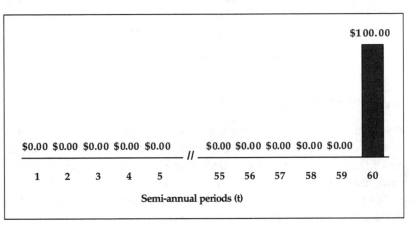

Example: With semiannual compounding, a noncallable, $100 face amount, zero-coupon bond that matures in 30 years and is priced at a yield of 6.00% would sell for

$$P = \frac{100}{(1.03)^{60}} = \$16.97$$

This pricing is appropriate when all of the interest accretion periods are equal and the first period is a full period. If the first interest period is not a complete period, we must make an adjustment to the calculation. Since zero-coupon bonds do not pay interest, there is no interest accrual between interest payments; therefore, only the compounding periods need to be adjusted. The adjustment to compounding periods is similar to the adjustment for a full-coupon bond:

$$P = \frac{F}{\left(1 + \dfrac{y}{m}\right)^{nm-1+q}}$$

Example: A zero-coupon bond has a maturity date of January 1, 2034, and interest accretes semiannually based on January 1 and July 1. The bond pays $100 principal at maturity, and the market yield is 6.00%. If the bond is purchased for settlement on March 15, 2004, the price of the bond is

$$P = \frac{100}{(1.03)^{59.589}} = 17.180$$

COMPUTATION OF YIELD

The semiannual coupon payment on a bond represents the current cash flow to an investor. Since the coupon on a long-term bond is fixed, the value of the bond fluctuates to reflect changes in market rates. The price of a bond, its maturity or redemption date, and the coupon rate jointly determine the yield on a bond. As such, yield-to-maturity is the interest rate that equates a flow of semiannual coupon payments until maturity to a given bond price. *Yield-to-maturity* is the rate of return earned on a bond at a given price from some date to maturity. *Yield-to-call* is the rate of return earned on a bond at a given price from some date to the first optional call date.

Example: A $100 face value corporate bond that pays interest semiannually at 6.00% and matures in 30 years is callable on January 1, 2014 at $102. The bond sells for $115.45 on January 1, 2004 and has a yield-to-maturity such that its price is equal to the discounted value of the cash flows:

$$115.45 = \sum_{t=1}^{60} \frac{3.00}{\left(1 + \frac{y}{2}\right)^t} + \frac{100}{\left(1 + \frac{y}{2}\right)^{60}}$$

Solving for y results in a yield-to-maturity on this bond of 5.00%. This means that an investor who buys this bond at a price of $115.45 and holds the bond until maturity will realize an annualized yield of 5.00% over the life of the bond, neglecting reinvestment risk.

The yield-to-call y_c on the same bond is calculated by solving the following equation:

$$115.45 = \sum_{t=1}^{20} \frac{3.00}{\left(1 + \frac{y_c}{2}\right)^t} + \frac{102}{\left(1 + \frac{y_c}{2}\right)^{20}}$$

In the example above, the yield to call y_c is equal to 4.25%. An investor who buys this bond at $115.45 and holds it until the first call date (at which time the bonds are redeemed for $102.00) will receive an annualized yield of 4.25% over the 10-year period.

An important concept in bond valuation is the relationship among coupon, yield, and price. If a bond is sold at its face value, or *par*, the yield on the bond will equal its coupon rate. A $100 bond that pays a 6.00% coupon is priced at par to yield 6.00%. If the bond is priced below par, the discount from par acts to increase the yield above the coupon rate. A 30-year, 6.00% bond that sells for $87.53 is priced to yield 7.00%. Conversely, if a bond is priced above par, the premium over par acts to decrease the yield below the coupon rate. A 30-year, 6.00% bond that is priced at $115.45 is priced to yield 5.00%. The price of a bond is inversely related to its yield. In Exhibit 4.3 we show the relationship among coupon, yield, and price for a 6.00% bond with 30 years to maturity.

PRICE VOLATILITY

We now address quantitative measurements of changes in the price/yield relationship of bonds. The three measurements we examine are price volatility, duration, and convexity. The price volatility of a bond is the

EXHIBIT 4.3

Prices and Corresponding Yields of a 6.00% Bond with 30 Years to Maturity

C	P	y
6.00%	$62.14	10.00%
6.00%	$69.04	9.00%
6.00%	$77.37	8.00%
6.00%	$87.53	7.00%
6.00%	$100.00	6.00%
6.00%	$115.45	5.00%
6.00%	$134.76	4.00%
6.00%	$159.07	3.00%
6.00%	$189.91	2.00%

EXHIBIT 4.4

Relationship between Maturity and Price of a Bond

		Decrease in Yield		Increase in Yield	
Maturity	Coupon	Yield	Price	Yield	Price
10 years	6.00%	5.00%	$107.79	7.00	$92.89
20 years	6.00%	5.00%	$112.55	7.00	$89.32
30 years	6.00%	5.00%	$115.45	7.00	$87.53

extent to which a bond's price changes with fluctuations in market levels of interest rates. We have shown that changes in bond prices and yields move in opposite directions, other things being equal. However, the magnitude of price movements will differ based on specific bond characteristics. For example, the price volatility of a fixed-rate bond is directly related to its maturity; a longer maturity bond will experience a sharper price adjustment for a given change in market level of interest rates than an otherwise identical shorter maturity bond.

Exhibit 4.4 demonstrates the price sensitivity of three bonds to fluctuations in market interest rates. The three bonds have an identical coupon rate of 6.00% and maturities of 10, 20, and 30 years, respectively. The chart reports price changes that correspond to a 1.00% decrease and increase in yield. For a given change in yield, the price of the 30-year bond changes the most, followed by the 20-year bond price. The 10-year bond exhibits the least price volatility. The longer maturity of the 30-year bond increases the volatility in the bond price.

THE PRICE/YIELD RELATIONSHIP

As discussed in the previous section, an important relationship exists between bond prices and yields. Recall from Exhibits 4.3 and 4.4 that bond prices increase as bond yields decrease. Conversely, as yields increase, bond prices decrease. Exhibit 4.5 shows this relationship for three 30-year, fixed-rate bonds: a zero-coupon bond, a 6.00% bond, and a 15.00% bond.

E X H I B I T   4.5

Relationship Between Price and Yield for 30-Year,
Fixed-Rate Bonds

y	Zero-Coupon Bond P	6.00% Full-Coupon Bond P	15.00% Full-Coupon Bond P
0.00%	$100.00	$280.00	$550.00
1.00	74.14	229.31	462.08
2.00	55.04	189.91	392.21
3.00	40.93	159.07	336.28
4.00	30.48	134.76	291.18
5.00	22.74	115.45	254.54
6.00	16.97	100.00	224.54
7.00	12.69	87.53	199.78
8.00	9.51	77.37	179.18
9.00	7.13	69.04	161.91
10.00	5.35	62.14	147.32
11.00	4.03	56.36	134.90
12.00	3.03	51.52	124.24
13.00	2.29	47.38	115.03
14.00	1.73	43.84	107.02
15.00	1.30	40.78	100.00
16.00	0.99	38.12	93.81
17.00	0.75	35.78	88.32
18.00	0.57	33.71	83.43
19.00	0.43	31.87	79.04
20.00	0.33	30.23	75.08

At a yield of 0.00%, the bond prices for all three bonds are equal to the sum of the expected cash flows: the zero-coupon bond has a price of $100.00, the 6.00% bond has a price of $280.00, and the 15.00% bond has a price of $550.00. As the yield on the bond increases, the price of each bond decreases because the cash flows are discounted at a higher yield.

An important aspect of this relationship is the speed at which the price decreases for an incremental increase in yield. This determines

EXHIBIT 4.6

Relationships among Prices and Yields for 30-Year Bonds

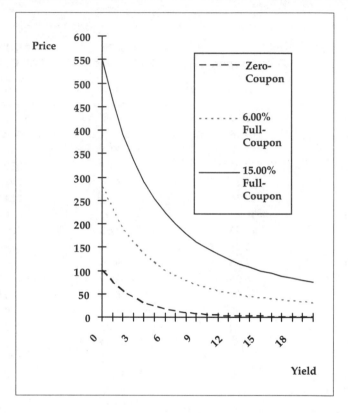

the slope of the price/yield curve or price duration. Exhibit 4.6 shows the relationships among prices and yields. The price/yield curve is convex to the origin. Initially, the price decreases significantly for a 1.00% increase in yield. When yields increase from 0.00% to 1.00%, the price drops from $100.00 to $74.14 for the zero-coupon bond, from $280.00 to $229.31 for the 6.00% bond, and from $550.00 to $462.08 for the 15.00% bond. However, this price change diminishes quickly as yield is increased. For example, when yields are increased from 10.00% to 11.00%, the price drops from $5.35 to $4.03 for the zero-coupon bond, from $62.14 to $56.36 for the 6.00% bond, and from $147.32 to $134.90 for the 15.00% bond.

DURATION

In the above example, the price of the 15.00% coupon bond is more sensitive to interest rate changes than the price of the 6.00% coupon bond or the price of the zero-coupon bond. Although the price duration of the 15.00% coupon bond is the highest among the three bonds, this should not be interpreted to mean that it is the riskiest bond. The high price duration of the 15.00% coupon bond is primarily a result of its high price.

In assessing bond risk, it is appropriate to examine percentage price changes. In the above example, as yields increase from 10.00% to 11.00%, the zero-coupon bond drops in price from $5.25 to $4.03, a decrease of $1.32. Although smaller in dollar terms, the percentage decrease in price of the zero-coupon bond is 24.7%, which is considerably higher than that of the 6.00% coupon bond (9.3%) and the 15.00% coupon bond (8.4%). The percentage change in the price of a bond is referred to as the bond's *duration*. By expressing price changes in percentage terms, we are able to compare the sensitivities of bonds with different prices.

There are two commonly used measures of bond price sensitivity. *Macaulay's Duration, D,* measures the percentage change in the price of an asset per percentage change in interest rates. As such, it is the slope of the line that is tangent to the price/yield curve for a particular security when both price changes and interest rate changes are measured in percentage terms. Macaulay's duration can be represented by the equation

$$D = -\frac{\Delta P/P}{\Delta y/(1+y)} = -\left(\frac{\Delta P}{\Delta y}\right)\left(\frac{(1+y)}{P}\right)$$

where ΔP is the change in price and Δy is the change in market yields. In the above equation, the term $\Delta P/\Delta y$ is the price duration D_p, defined as

$$D_p = -\frac{\Delta P}{\Delta y}$$

Modified duration D_m measures the percentage change in the price of an asset per change in interest rates. As such, it is the slope of the line that is tangent to the price/yield curve for a particular security when price changes are measured in percentage terms and interest rate changes are measured in absolute terms. In the above notation, modified duration is given by

$$D_m = -\frac{\Delta P/P}{\Delta y} = \frac{D}{(1+y)}$$

The duration of a bond is typically measured in years. In the simplest case, the duration of a zero-coupon bond is equal to its current maturity. That is, an investor in a zero-coupon bond holds the bond until maturity to receive the entire cash flow associated with the bond. Because interest payments are received throughout the life of the bond, a coupon-bearing investment has a duration that is somewhat less than that of a zero-coupon bond of the same maturity. Both of the duration measures above represent a bond's sensitivity for small changes in interest rates. Given the convexity of the price/yield curve, duration is only an approximate measure of sensitivity for large changes in interest rates.

MACAULAY'S DURATION

In this section we discuss how to calculate the measures of duration described above. The standard measure of duration for fixed-rate bonds is *Macaulay's duration*,[2] D. A general formula for Macaulay's duration is given by

$$D = \sum_{t=1}^{mn} \left[\left(\frac{(C/m)/(1 + \frac{y}{m})^t}{P} \right) \left(\frac{t}{m} \right) \right] + \left[\left(\frac{F/(1 + \frac{y}{m})^{mn}}{P} \right) (n) \right]$$

For a semiannual coupon bond, Macaulay's duration is calculated as

$$D = \sum_{t=1}^{2n} \left[\left(\frac{(C/2)/(1 + \frac{y}{2})^t}{P} \right) \left(\frac{t}{2} \right) \right] + \left[\left(\frac{F/(1 + \frac{y}{2})^{2n}}{P} \right) (n) \right]$$

Macaulay's Duration is often interpreted as the value-weighted average time to maturity of the cash flows received on a bond. To see this, consider the above equation, rewritten as

$$D = \sum_{t=1}^{2n} \left[w_t \left(\frac{t}{2} \right) \right]$$

---

2. See Macaulay (1938).

where

$$w_t = \frac{\left(\dfrac{C/2}{(1 + \frac{y}{2})^t}\right)}{P}, \qquad t = 1, 2, \ldots 2n - 1$$

and

$$w_{2n} = \frac{\left(\dfrac{C/2 + F}{(1 + \frac{y}{2})^{2n}}\right)}{P}$$

In the above equation, the term $t/2$ represents the maturity in years of a cash flow received in period t. For example, a cash flow received one six-month period from today has a maturity of 0.5 years. The weights w_t are value weights that measure the percentage of the bond's value that comes from each cash flow.[3]

The duration of a zero-coupon bond is equal to its maturity. Recall that the price of a zero-coupon bond is found by dividing F by the discount factor, $(1 + y/2)^{2n}$. The duration of a zero-coupon bond is calculated by substituting a coupon payment of zero into the duration formula as follows:

$$D = \sum_{t=1}^{2n}\left[\left(\frac{\dfrac{0}{(1 + \frac{y}{2})^t}}{\dfrac{F}{(1 + \frac{y}{2})^{2n}}}\right)\left(\frac{t}{2}\right)\right] + \left(\frac{\dfrac{F}{(1 + \frac{y}{2})^{2n}}}{\dfrac{F}{(1 + \frac{y}{2})^{2n}}}\right)(n) = 0 + n = n$$

---

3. The duration calculations presented here assume no partial periods. Similar to the bond valuation equations, an adjustment must be made to calculate duration when the first period is shorter than the others. The adjustments are very similar to those of the full-coupon bond equation. Accrued interest must be subtracted from the coupon cash flows, and the partial period q must be used as the first period instead of a whole first period. The adjusted equation is as follows:

$$D = \sum_{t=1}^{2n}\left[\left(\frac{(C/2)/(1 + \frac{y}{2})^{t-1+q}}{P}\right)\left(\frac{t-1+q}{2}\right)\right] + \left[\left(\frac{F/(1 + \frac{y}{2})^{2n-1+q}}{P}\right)\left(\frac{2n-1+q}{2}\right)\right]$$

For a zero-coupon bond, the weight on the final cash flow equals 1 because all of the bond's value comes from that cash flow. Hence, the duration of a zero-coupon bond equals its maturity. Because duration is a measure of the weighted average maturity of a bond's cash flows, a coupon-bearing bond that makes semiannual payments prior to maturity has a duration that is somewhat less than that of a zero-coupon bond of the same maturity.

Example: Consider a semiannual, full-coupon bond that matures in 30 years and is priced at par with a yield of 6.00%. The bond has a coupon rate of 6.00%. We calculate the duration of this bond as

$$D = \sum_{t=1}^{60} \left(\frac{\frac{3.00}{(1.03)^t}}{100} \left(\frac{t}{2}\right) \right) + \left(\frac{\frac{100}{(1.03)^{60}}}{100} \right)(30) = 14.25$$

Exhibit 4.7 shows the duration calculation for this bond. Column (1) represents the time period at which each of the cash flows is received, and Column (2) is the time in years until the cash flow is received. The cash flows for this bond are in Column (3). Column (4) shows the discount factors for each time period used to calculate the present value of each of the cash flows shown in Column (5). After we derive the present value of each cash flow, the value weight for each period is calculated by dividing the present value of each cash flow by 100. This step is accomplished in Column (6). The value weights from Column (6) are then multiplied by time in years. The final step is to sum the results in Column (7) to arrive at duration.

EFFECT OF CASH FLOWS ON DURATION

We can break down the cash flows of a bond into components to examine the contribution of specific cash flows to the duration of a bond. For example, a semiannual full-coupon bond that pays interest at an annual rate of 6.00% and matures in 30 years has cash flows as shown in Exhibit 4.1. Consider, however, the case where the bond has been broken into a series of distinct cash flows. For example, we can isolate the first 20 semiannual

EXHIBIT 4.7

Duration Calculation for a $100, 30-Year,
6.00% Full-Coupon Bond

(1) t	(2) t/2	(3) C/2	(4) 1/(1.03)^t	(5) (3)×(4)	(6) (5)/100	(7) (6)×(2)
1	0.5	3.00	0.9709	2.913	0.0291	0.015
2	1.0	3.00	0.9426	2.828	0.0283	0.028
3	1.5	3.00	0.9151	2.745	0.0275	0.041
4	2.0	3.00	0.8885	2.666	0.0267	0.053
5	2.5	3.00	0.8626	2.588	0.0259	0.065
6	3.0	3.00	0.8375	2.513	0.0251	0.075
7	3.5	3.00	0.8131	2.439	0.0244	0.085
8	4.0	3.00	0.7894	2.368	0.0237	0.095
9	4.5	3.00	0.7664	2.299	0.0230	0.103
10	5.0	3.00	0.7441	2.232	0.0223	0.112
11	5.5	3.00	0.7224	2.167	0.0217	0.119
12	6.0	3.00	0.7014	2.104	0.0210	0.126
13	6.5	3.00	0.6810	2.043	0.0204	0.133
14	7.0	3.00	0.6611	1.983	0.0198	0.139
15	7.5	3.00	0.6419	1.926	0.0193	0.144
16	8.0	3.00	0.6232	1.870	0.0187	0.150
17	8.5	3.00	0.6050	1.815	0.0182	0.154
18	9.0	3.00	0.5874	1.762	0.0176	0.159
19	9.5	3.00	0.5703	1.711	0.0171	0.163
20	10.0	3.00	0.5537	1.661	0.0166	0.166
21	10.5	3.00	0.5375	1.613	0.0161	0.169
22	11.0	3.00	0.5219	1.566	0.0157	0.172
23	11.5	3.00	0.5067	1.520	0.0152	0.175
24	12.0	3.00	0.4919	1.476	0.0148	0.177
25	12.5	3.00	0.4776	1.433	0.0143	0.179
26	13.0	3.00	0.4637	1.391	0.0139	0.181
27	13.5	3.00	0.4502	1.351	0.0135	0.182
28	14.0	3.00	0.4371	1.311	0.0131	0.184
29	14.5	3.00	0.4243	1.273	0.0127	0.185
30	15.0	3.00	0.4120	1.236	0.0124	0.185
31	15.5	3.00	0.4000	1.200	0.0120	0.186

(*continued*)

EXHIBIT 4.7

Duration Calculation for a $100, 30-Year,
6.00% Full-Coupon Bond (*Continued*)

(1) t	(2) t/2	(3) C/2	(4) $1/(1.03)^t$	(5) (3)×(4)	(6) (5)/100	(7) (6)×(2)
32	16.0	3.00	0.3883	1.165	0.0117	0.186
33	16.5	3.00	0.3770	1.131	0.0113	0.187
34	17.0	3.00	0.3660	1.098	0.0110	0.187
35	17.5	3.00	0.3554	1.066	0.0107	0.187
36	18.0	3.00	0.3450	1.035	0.0104	0.186
37	18.5	3.00	0.3350	1.005	0.0101	0.186
38	19.0	3.00	0.3252	0.976	0.0098	0.185
39	19.5	3.00	0.3158	0.947	0.0095	0.185
40	20.0	3.00	0.3066	0.920	0.0092	0.184
41	20.5	3.00	0.2976	0.893	0.0089	0.183
42	21.0	3.00	0.2890	0.867	0.0087	0.182
43	21.5	3.00	0.2805	0.842	0.0084	0.181
44	22.0	3.00	0.2724	0.817	0.0082	0.180
45	22.5	3.00	0.2644	0.793	0.0079	0.178
46	23.0	3.00	0.2567	0.770	0.0077	0.177
47	23.5	3.00	0.2493	0.748	0.0075	0.176
48	24.0	3.00	0.2420	0.726	0.0073	0.174
49	24.5	3.00	0.2350	0.705	0.0071	0.173
50	25.0	3.00	0.2281	0.684	0.0068	0.171
51	25.5	3.00	0.2215	0.665	0.0067	0.170
52	26.0	3.00	0.2150	0.645	0.0065	0.168
53	26.5	3.00	0.2088	0.626	0.0063	0.166
54	27.0	3.00	0.2027	0.608	0.0061	0.164
55	27.5	3.00	0.1968	0.590	0.0059	0.162
56	28.0	3.00	0.1910	0.573	0.0057	0.160
57	28.5	3.00	0.1855	0.557	0.0056	0.159
58	29.0	3.00	0.1801	0.540	0.0054	0.157
59	29.5	3.00	0.1748	0.524	0.0052	0.155
60	30.0	103.00	0.1697	17.479	0.1748	5.244
				Duration		14.253

EXHIBIT 4.8

Cash Flows on a 30-Year, 6.00% Bond Divided
into Three Components

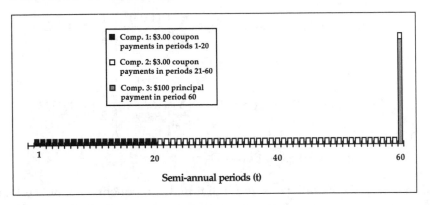

Semi-annual periods (t)

cash flows, the second 40 semiannual cash flows, and the principal. The
cash flows consist of the three components shown in Exhibit 4.8.

We calculate the duration on each of these three components by applying the duration formula developed earlier in this chapter. We begin
by calculating prices for each of the components, using a semiannual discount rate of 3.00%. The individual prices are

Component	P
1	$P_1 = 44.632 = \sum_{t=1}^{20} \dfrac{3.00}{(1.03)^t}$
2	$P_2 = 38.395 = \sum_{t=21}^{60} \dfrac{3.00}{(1.03)^t}$
3	$P_3 = 16.973 = \dfrac{100}{(1.03)^{60}}$
Total	$100.00 = \sum_{t=1}^{60} \dfrac{3.00}{(1.03)^t} + \dfrac{100}{(1.03)^{60}}$

Using the prices above, we calculate the duration for each of these cash flows as

$$\text{Component 1: Duration} = D_1 = \sum_{t=1}^{20}\left(\frac{\frac{3.00}{(1.03)^t}}{44.632}\right)\left(\frac{t}{2}\right) = 4.762$$

$$\text{Component 2: Duration} = D_2 = \sum_{t=21}^{60}\left(\frac{\frac{3.00}{(1.03)^t}}{38.395}\right)\left(\frac{t}{2}\right) = 18.325$$

$$\text{Component 3: Duration} = D_3 = 30$$

Comparing the durations of the individual components, we notice that Component 1 has a much lower duration than Components 2 and 3. Cash flows received in earlier periods act to lower duration, whereas cash flows received in later periods act to increase duration. If we weight the individual durations by the appropriate percentage prices, we can derive the duration of the total bond:

$$D = D_1\left(\frac{P_1}{100}\right) + D_2\left(\frac{P_2}{100}\right) + D_3\left(\frac{P_3}{100}\right)$$

$$D = 4.762\left(\frac{44.623}{100}\right) + 18.325\left(\frac{38.395}{100}\right) + 30.0\left(\frac{16.973}{100}\right) = 14.25$$

PORTFOLIO DURATION

The above example demonstrates that the duration of a bond is equal to a value-weighted average of the durations of bond cash flows. A similar relationship exists for portfolios. Suppose we hold a portfolio of J bonds with prices $P_1, P_2, \ldots P_J$ and durations $D_1, D_2, \ldots D_J$, respectively. The duration of the portfolio D_p is equal to a value-weighted average of the durations of individual bonds and is calculated as

$$D_p = \sum_{i=1}^{J}\left(\frac{P_i}{\sum_{i=1}^{J} P_i}\right)(D_i)$$

RELATIONSHIP BETWEEN DURATION AND MATURITY

Certain notable relationships exist among duration and maturity, current bond price, coupon, and discount rates. In general, duration increases as time to maturity increases. However, the rate at which it increases is a function of the coupon structure on the bond. The lower the coupon rate, the greater the increase in duration. For coupon-bearing bonds, duration increases at a decreasing rate as maturity increases. Current coupon payments act to decrease duration, and the effects of additional coupon payments are lessened as maturity increases. For a zero-coupon bond, the duration is always equal to its maturity. Therefore, a linear relationship exists between the two. These relationships are shown in Exhibit 4.9.

RELATIONSHIP BETWEEN DURATION AND COUPON

Because duration is a measure of the value-weighted average time of expected cash flows of a bond, increasing the coupon on a bond while keeping the required yield constant increases the price of the bond and decreases its duration. As coupon rates increase, a larger percentage of the bond's value is attributable to early cash flows; hence the value weights are higher for early cash flows. That is, if two bonds with the same maturity and yield have different coupon rates and different market values, the bond with a higher coupon and higher price P will have a shorter

EXHIBIT 4.9

Relationships between Duration and Maturity

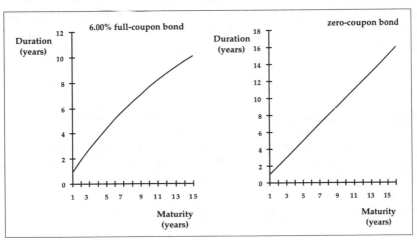

EXHIBIT 4.10

Duration and Coupon: 30-Year Maturity Full-Coupon Bond

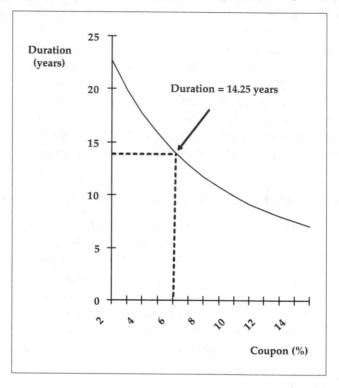

duration. Exhibit 4.10 shows the relationship between duration and coupon for a 30-year bond and a 6.00% level of market rates. Recall that this bond has a duration of 14.25. As the coupon increases (decreases) the duration decreases (increases). Assuming yield and maturity are unchanged, the duration decreases as the coupon increases.

RELATIONSHIP BETWEEN DURATION AND YIELD

A similar relationship exists between duration and yield for coupon bonds. As the yield on a bond decreases, the price increases at an increasing rate. The opposite is true for an increase in yield. As the yield on a bond increases, the price decreases at a decreasing rate. The convex nature of the price/yield relationship implies that the bond becomes less sensitive to

E X H I B I T   4.11

Duration and Yield of a 30-Year Maturity,
6.00% Full-Coupon Bond

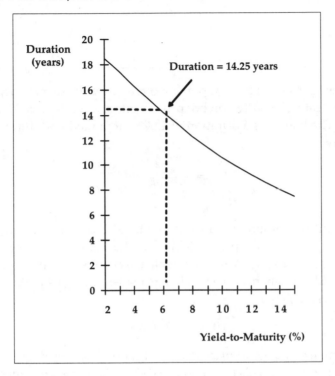

interest rate changes as yields rise. Exhibit 4.11 shows the relationship between duration and market yields for a 30-year, 6.00% full-coupon bond.
Assuming coupon and maturity are unchanged, duration decreases as
yield increases for coupon bonds. For zero-coupon bonds, duration is always equal to the maturity of the bond. Hence, as yields change, the duration of a zero-coupon bond remains constant.

MODIFIED DURATION

As we discussed, an important variation of Macaulay's duration is *modified duration* D_m, which measures the percentage change in the price of an
asset per change in interest rates. Modified duration is more easily interpreted than Macaulay's duration because interest rate changes are mea-

sured in the same units as interest rates.[4] Modified duration is a simple transformation of Macaulay's duration:

$$D_m = \frac{D}{1 + \dfrac{y}{m}}$$

Example: Consider a full-coupon bond with 30 years to maturity that has a coupon rate of 6.00%. The bond pays interest semiannually and sells for par. The bond has a duration of 14.25 and a modified duration equal to 13.83:

$$D_m = \frac{14.25}{1 + \dfrac{.06}{2}} = 13.83$$

Modified duration for a fixed-rate bond is of particular importance because of its link to the price/yield curve. Suppose the market yield on a bond rises from y to y_n. We can estimate the change in a bond price due to duration ΔP_D for an incremental change in yield Δy by using the modified duration estimate:

$$\Delta P_D = -D_m(y_n - y)P$$

The estimated change in price due to duration is a linear estimate of the actual price change. This is shown in Exhibit 4.12 by the line tangent to the price/yield curve.

Example: Consider a semiannual full-coupon bond with 30 years to maturity and a coupon rate of 6.00%. The bond has a modified duration of 13.83. If market yields rise from 6.00% to 7.00%, the estimated change in the bond price due to duration is calculated as

$$\Delta P_D = (-13.83)(0.07 - 0.06)(100) = -\$13.83$$

---

4. For example, suppose the yield on a bond rises from 8.00% to 9.00%. Modified duration measures the estimated percentage change in price associated with this 1.00% change in rates. Macaulay's duration, on the other hand, would measure the estimated percentage change in price associated with the *percentage* change $(1 + y)$, which is equal to $(0.01/1.08)$ or 0.93%.

EXHIBIT 4.12

Price/Yield Curve and Modified Duration Estimate

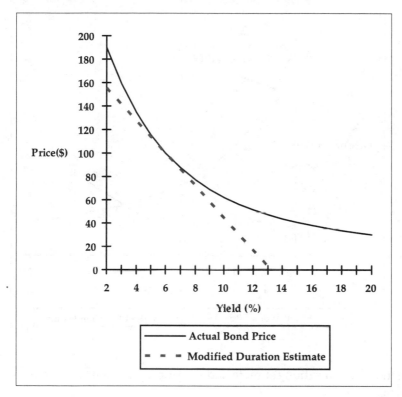

CONVEXITY

Modified duration can be used to estimate changes in bond prices. This estimate is accurate only for small changes in yields due to the convexity of the price/yield relationship. In general, modified duration will underestimate the price increase and overestimate the price decrease associated with a change in the yield. For this reason, we must adjust our estimates of price changes by using an estimate of the distance between the modified duration tangent line and the price/yield line. The distance between the two lines is commonly referred to as *convexity*.

Exhibit 4.13 depicts the convexity region for a 6.00% full-coupon bond with 30 years to maturity. The convexity region is the area between

EXHIBIT 4.13

Convexity Regions for a 6.00%, 30-Year, Noncallable Bond

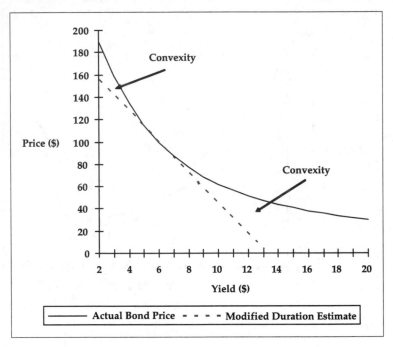

the modified duration estimate and the price/yield curve. Convexity K is calculated as

$$K = \frac{1}{2} \frac{\Delta D_p}{\Delta y} \frac{1}{P}$$

where D_p is price duration.[5] The price change can be expressed as a function of both modified duration and convexity according to the equation

$$\Delta P = \Delta P_D + \Delta P_K$$

---

5. Convexity is derived from the second-order term of a Taylor series expansion, where the percentage change in a bond price can be expressed as

$$\frac{dP}{P} = \frac{\frac{dP}{P}}{dy} dy + \frac{1}{2} \frac{d^2 P}{dy^2} \frac{1}{P} (dy)^2 = -D_m dy + K(dy)^2$$

For a further discussion of convexity, see Stoll and Whaley (1993).

where

$$\Delta P_D = (-D_m \Delta y)P$$

and

$$\Delta P_K = K(\Delta y)^2 P$$

In the above equation, ΔP_D is the modified duration estimate of the change in price associated with a change in yield Δy, and ΔP_K is the convexity adjustment to the estimate. The following is a general formula for calculating the convexity of a coupon bond with n years to maturity:

$$K = \left(\frac{1}{2m^2}\right) \frac{\left[\sum_{t-1}^{mn} \frac{C/m}{(1+\frac{y}{m})^{t+2}}(t)(t+1) + \frac{F}{(1+\frac{y}{m})^{mn+2}}(mn)(mn+1)\right]}{P}$$

where m is the number of compounding periods per year. For a coupon bond with semiannual payments, convexity is calculated as

$$K = \left(\frac{1}{8}\right) \frac{\left[\sum_{t=1}^{2n} \frac{C/2}{(1+\frac{y}{2})^{t+2}}(t)(t+1) + \frac{F}{(1+\frac{y}{2})^{2n+2}}(2n)(2n+1)\right]}{P}$$

Example: Consider a full-coupon bond that matures in 30 years that is currently trading at par with a yield of 6.00% and pays interest semi-annually at an annual rate of 6.00%. We can calculate the convexity of this bond as

$$K = \left(\frac{1}{8}\right) \frac{\left[\sum_{t=1}^{60} \frac{3.00}{(1.03)^{t+2}}(t)(t+1) + \frac{100}{(1.03)^{62}}(60)(61)\right]}{100} = 148.235$$

Since the modified duration of the above bond is equal to 13.838, the change in price resulting from a change in yield Δy is given by

$$\Delta P = \Delta P_D + \Delta P_K$$

where

$$\Delta P_D = -13.838(\Delta y)(100)$$
$$\Delta P_K = (148.235)(\Delta y)^2(100)$$

If the yield on the bond rises to 7.00% ($\Delta y = 0.01$), then

$$\Delta P_D = -13.838$$
$$\Delta P_K = 1.482$$

and

$$\Delta P = \Delta P_D + \Delta P_K = -12.355$$

Exhibit 4.14 shows the relationship between actual price changes and estimated price changes for a noncallable, 6.00%, full-coupon bond with 30 years to maturity. The estimate of price change ΔP is relatively accurate for small incremental changes in the price of a bond. When y changes by 1.00% in either direction, the estimated price change is very close to the actual price change. For yield changes greater than 1.00% in either direction, the estimated price changes become less accurate. The degree to which the estimated price diverges from the actual price is a function of the level of convexity of the underlying bond.

EXHIBIT 4.14

Convexity Measures for a 6.00%, Noncallable Bond
with 30 Years to Maturity

Δy	P	Actual Price Change	ΔP_D	ΔP_Y	ΔP
−3.00%	$159.07	+$59.07	+$41.51	+13.34	+54.85
−2.00%	134.76	+34.76	+27.68	+5.93	+33.60
−1.00%	115.45	+15.45	+13.84	+1.48	+15.32
0%	100.00	0.00	0.00	0.00	0.00
+1.00%	87.53	−12.47	−13.83	+1.48	−12.36
+2.00%	77.38	−22.62	−27.68	+5.93	−21.75
+3.00%	69.04	−30.96	−41.51	+13.34	−28.17

NEGATIVE CONVEXITY

In some cases, the price/yield line is not convex to the origin at every yield. When this occurs, there is a positive relationship between a bond's duration and interest rates and, in some circumstances, a positive relationship between bond price and yield. For example, bonds that are subject to call prior to maturity will be priced in the market to the call date and redemption price any time the yield falls below the coupon rate. Bonds backed by interest-sensitive cash flows such as mortgages may decrease in value as market yields drop, because prepayments by borrowers reduce the duration of the bond's cash flows. In general, prepayment provisions on a bond will cause this price reaction

Consider a $100, 30-year bond that is issued at 6.00% and can be called in five years at $100. This bond will be priced as a five-year bond with a redemption price of $100 when market rates fall below 6.00%. When rates are below 6.00%, it is advantageous for the issuer to call these bonds and refinance at the lower market rates. For this reason, the market views this bond as having a maturity coincident to the call date. Whenever rates are at or above 6.00%, the bond will be priced as a 30-year bond.

The tendency for duration to move in the same direction as yields gives rise to what is called *negative convexity*. Negative convexity exists when the modified duration estimate of price changes is above some or all of the price/yield line. When this occurs, modified duration overestimates the increase in price associated with a fall in yields; hence the change in price due to convexity in this area is *negative*.

As shown in Exhibit 4.15, the price yield line for a callable bond follows a pattern that is different from what is shown in Exhibit 4.13. In particular, when the yield on the callable bond falls below the coupon rate of 6.00%, the price/yield line bends back toward the price axis. This is due to the increased probability of the bond being called for refinancing at rates below the coupon. For this reason, when yields are below the bond coupon rate, the bond will be priced to the call date with a redemption price of $100 in five years. The bond exhibits negative convexity in the region where the yield is below the coupon. In this area, the price/yield line is concave to the origin. The measures of convexity are negative in this region because of the pricing aberration. When rates are above the 6.00% level, the bond is priced as a typical, 30-year, 6.00% bond, and the bond exhibits convexity in this region.

EXHIBIT 4.15

Negative Convexity for a 6.00%, 30-Year Bond
Callable in Five Years

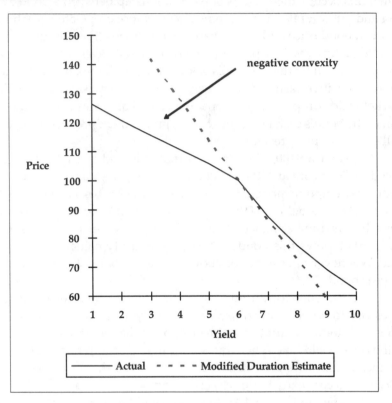

SUMMARY

Hedging the risk of fixed-income securities requires an understanding of bond risk and pricing. In this chapter, we explained the mathematics of bond pricing and risk measurement. Like most financial assets, the value of a bond is equal to the present value of the expected cash flows over the life of the security. Bond prices are determined by the bond's coupon payment, maturity, and yield-to-maturity. We began by showing how coupon bond prices and yield-to-maturity are determined. We distinguished between the dirty price of a bond, which includes accrued interest, and the clean price, which does not. The pricing of zero-coupon bonds was also discussed.

The primary risk faced by bondholders is interest rate risk. Interest rate risk refers to the risk that a bond price will fluctuate in response to changes in market interest rates. The price/yield curve shows the graphical relationship between bond prices and yields to maturity. The shape of the price/yield curve is related to some common measures of bond risk. Price volatility measures the change in bond prices as interest rates change, or the slope of the price/yield curve. Duration measures the sensitivity of bond price changes when price changes are measured in percentage terms. We discussed two measures of duration, Macaulay's duration and modified duration. In addition, we provided examples of how to calculate each measure of duration and how to estimate bond price changes from duration. Duration was shown to be related to the characteristics of a bond, such as yield-to-maturity, coupon rate, and maturity. We discussed how each of these measures affects bond risk. We showed how to calculate the duration of a portfolio by using the durations of the bonds in the portfolio.

Estimates of price changes from duration are only an approximation to true price changes due to the shape of the price/yield curve. We discussed the concept of convexity and how it may be used to develop more accurate estimates of bond price changes than estimates that are based only on duration. *Negative convexity* refers to situations where there is a positive relationship between duration and interest rates. We discussed negative convexity in the context of callable bonds and mortgage-backed securities.

REFERENCES

Gray, Gary, and Patrick Cusatis. *Municipal Derivative Securities: Uses and Valuation.* Burr Ridge: Irwin Professional Publishing, 1995.

Macaulay, Frederick. *Some Theoretical Problems Suggested by the Movements of Interest Rates, Bond Yields, and Stock Prices in the United States since 1865.* New York: National Bureau of Economic Research, 1938.

Stoll, Hans R., and Robert E. Whaley. *Futures and Options: Theory and Applications.* Cincinnati: Southwestern Publishing Company, 1993.

CHAPTER 5

Term Structure of Interest Rates

Effective hedging requires an understanding of the relationships that exist between the pricing of short-term bonds and that of long-term bonds. In this chapter, we discuss the analysis of fixed-income securities with different maturities. We explain in detail how to extract spot and implied forward rates from coupon bonds. In addition, we provide a detailed example of how to construct a swap zero-coupon yield curve from market prices.

The relationship between the yields and maturities of otherwise identical securities is generally referred to as the yield curve. The shape of the yield curve reflects the cost of credit for debt of various maturities. The yield curve has been the focus of many studies over the past 50 years. In an effort to better understand the movements of interest rates, researchers have attempted to identify processes or rational behavior by investors that will help to explain the shape of the yield curve at various points in time. We explain the pure expectations hypothesis, which is the basis for the valuation of many fixed-income securities.

U.S. TREASURY SECURITIES AND THE YIELD CURVE

A yield curve may be constructed with the use of fixed-income securities from a market segment, such as the U.S. Treasury, municipal, or corporate bond markets. The U.S. Treasury yield curve is a particularly important

EXHIBIT 5.1

U.S. Treasury Yield Curve as of January 23, 2004

Maturity	Yield	Maturity	Yield	Maturity	Yield
Feb 05n	1.12	Nov 13n	3.97	Feb 23	4.82
Feb 06n	1.63	Feb 15	4.07	Nov 24	4.85
Feb 07n	2.13	Feb 16	4.24	Feb 25	4.86
Feb 08n	2.59	May 17	4.38	Feb 26	4.91
Jan 09n	2.95	May 18	4.47	Feb 27	4.92
Feb 10n	3.23	Feb 19	4.55	Aug 28	4.95
Feb 11n	3.50	Feb 20	4.63	Feb 29	4.94
Feb 12n	3.71	Feb 21	4.70	May 30	4.93
Feb 13n	3.85	Aug 22	4.79	Feb 31	4.85

Source: *The Wall Street Journal,* January 23, 2004, page C13. U.S. Treasury note quotations are designated by the letter n.

tool because it shows the relationship between yield and maturity in the absence of default risk. A typical yield curve is plotted for maturities from one month to 30 years. Exhibit 5.1 details a series of full-coupon U.S. Treasury notes and bonds taken from the *Wall Street Journal.*

The U.S. Treasury yield curve constructed with these data is shown in Exhibit 5.2. In January 2004, longer term treasuries had higher yields than shorter term treasuries. Thus, the yield curve is upward sloping.

The shape of the yield curve is of considerable interest to market participants. Historically, yields have been higher for treasuries with longer maturities, as in the above example. According to the pure expectations hypothesis, which states that long-term yields reflect expectations of future short-term rates, yield curves are upward sloping when the consensus of market participants is that interest rates will increase in the future. One implication of an upward-sloping yield curve is that the market anticipates an economic expansion.

Exhibit 5.3 displays the yields on one-year and 10-year U.S. Treasuries from 1954 to 2004. In 1954, the yield on a 10-year bond was approximately 2.50%, and the interest rate on a one-year note was approximately 1.40%. Yields rose steadily through 1982, when both rates peaked at more than 14.00%, and have fallen steadily since that time. By January 2004, the long rate had dropped to 4.15% and the short rate had dropped to 1.24%.

EXHIBIT 5.2

The U.S. Treasury Yield Curve

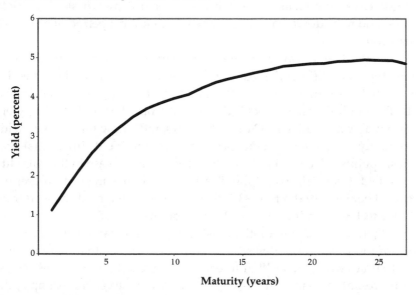

EXHIBIT 5.3

Long-term and Short-term U.S. Treasury Yields

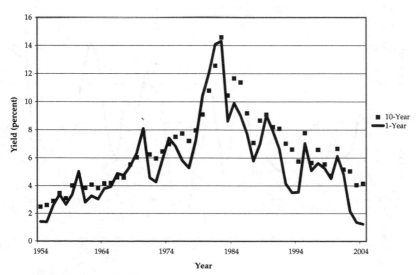

Source: Federal Reserve Bank of St. Louis.

Exhibit 5.3 also shows periods when short-term rates were higher than long-term rates, such as the mid-1960s, the late 1970s, and the early 1980s. In these cases, the yield curve is inverted or downward sloping. Yield curves tend to be downward sloping near the end of a period of economic expansion.

An alternative way to examine the shape of the yield curve is to examine the yield differential. An example of a yield differential is the difference between the yield on a 10-year bond and the yield on a one-year note. Exhibit 5.4 plots the yield differential from 1954 to 2004. The yield differential was positive in 42 of the 51 years, indicating that higher yields accompany longer term maturities. The average yield differential was 85 basis points. Also evident from the curve is an increase in the volatility of the yield differential over time. The greatest change in yield differential occurred between 1981 and 1983, when the yield differential changed from −1.51% to 1.84%, an increase of 335 basis points.

When the yield differential crosses zero, it indicates a change in the slope of the yield curve. Revisiting Exhibit 5.4, we see that there were at least 10 times when the yield differential crossed zero. Each of these crossings represents a change in the slope of the yield curve. For example, the

EXHIBIT 5.4

Yield Differential over Time

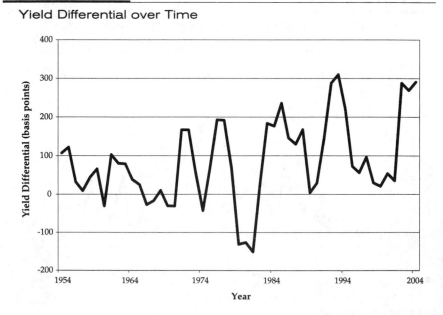

EXHIBIT 5.5

Zero-Coupon Yield Curve, 1980

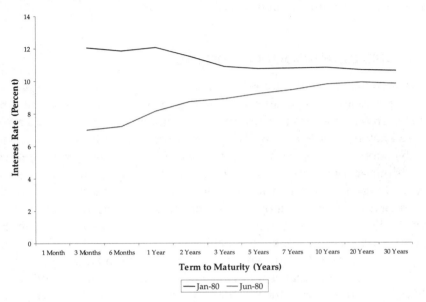

Term to Maturity (Years)

— Jan-80   — Jun-80

yield differential was nearly −1.30% in 1980. By 1981 it had changed to 0.30%. The corresponding change in the slope of the yield curve is illustrated in Exhibit 5.5. In January 1980 the yield curve was inverted. By June of 1980 the yield curve had become upward sloping. Note that the change in slope was due to the decrease in the short-term yields since the long-term yield remained essentially the same. Yields on 10-year bonds and one-year notes move together over time. In addition, U.S. Treasury yields have become more volatile, and this volatility is more pronounced for short-term yields. The fact that short-term yields are more volatile than long-term yields results in occasional inversions in the yield curve.

THE TERM STRUCTURE OF INTEREST RATES

A yield curve constructed from default-free zero-coupon bonds is known as the *term structure of interest rates*. The zero-coupon yield, or spot rate of interest, is the yield-to-maturity on a bond or investment with only one cash flow occurring on a specific date or maturity.[1] Since zero-coupon bonds make only one payment at a time, coupon bonds may be thought of as a portfolio of zero-coupon bonds.

IMPLIED ZERO-COUPON YIELDS

It is often the case that coupon bond prices are available, but zero-coupon bond prices are not available. In these circumstance, it is possible to estimate zero-coupon bond prices from full-coupon bond prices by a procedure known as *bootstrapping*. The yields associated with these estimated zero-coupon bond prices are known as *implied zero-coupon yields*. Implied zero-coupon yields are the set of discount rates implied in the par yield curve that equates the cash flows of a full-coupon bearing bond with those of a set of zero-coupon bonds. The theoretical implied zero-coupon yield adjusts the full-coupon rate for the loss or gain associated with the periodic reinvestment of interest payments.

To illustrate this concept, assume that a noncallable, full-coupon bond selling at par makes a payment of $C/2$ in each time period t, $t =$ 1,2,3,..., $2n$. At maturity, the full-coupon bond also pays a $100 face value. As shown in Chapter 4, the bond price is calculated as

$$100 = \sum_{t=1}^{2n} \frac{C/2}{(1 + \frac{y}{2})^t} + \frac{100}{(1 + \frac{y}{2})^{2n}}$$

To calculate implied zero-coupon yields with the bootstrapping procedure, we replace the yield to maturity, y, with the appropriate zero-coupon yield in each period. There is a set of zero-coupon yields r_t such that, when they are used as discount rates, will result in the current price of the bond. We begin with the zero-coupon yield for the shortest period

---

1. U.S. Treasury Bills and U.S. Treasury STRIPS are examples of default-free zero-coupon securities. U.S. Treasury STRIPS are often used to construct a representative risk-free taxable zero-coupon curve. STRIPS, which is an acronym for Separately Traded Registered Interest and Principal Securities, represent zero-coupon bonds that are created by stripping full-coupon U.S. Treasury bonds. STRIPS can be observed daily in the U.S. Treasury Bonds, Notes & Bills section of the *Wall Street Journal*. One problem with relying on actively traded zero-coupon bonds is that the they may not be traded at desired maturities and yields may have to be interpolated between maturities. For this reason, zero-coupon yields are often calculated from full coupon rates.

of time and calculate the implied zero-coupon yields for subsequent periods. The zero-coupon yield for the shortest time period can be observed in the market. The bootstrapping procedure for deriving an implied zero-coupon curve is illustrated by the following example.

Example: Exhibit 5.6 presents data for six annual coupon bonds selling at par. Bond one, which matures in one year, has a coupon rate of 2.20%. The implied one-year zero-coupon yield r_1 is equal to 2.20%, the market yield on bond one.

The implied zero-coupon yield for year 2, r_2, can be calculated as

$$100 = \frac{2.50}{(1.022)} + \frac{102.50}{(1+r_2)^2}$$

Solving for r_2, the implied two-year zero-coupon yield is equal to 2.5038%. With the use of the implied one-year and two-year zero-coupon yields, the three-year implied zero-coupon yield solves the equation

$$100 = \frac{2.80}{(1.022)} + \frac{2.80}{(1.025038)^2} + \frac{102.80}{(1+r_3)^3}$$

The zero-coupon yield that solves this equation is 2.8113%. The bootstrapping procedure requires that we solve for each subsequent zero-coupon yield and use the results to calculate the next implied zero-coupon yield. Exhibit 5.7 shows the implied zero-coupon yield curve for six years.

EXHIBIT 5.6

Yields and Maturities on Coupon Bonds

Bond	Maturity (t)	Coupon Rate
1	1.0	2.20%
2	2.0	2.50%
3	3.0	2.80%
4	4.0	3.00%
5	5.0	3.20%
6	6.0	3.50%

E X H I B I T 5.7

Implied Zero-Coupon Yields

Bond	Maturity t	Annual Full-Coupon Yield c	Implied Zero-Coupon Yield r_t
1	1.0	2.20%	2.2000%
2	2.0	2.50%	2.5038%
3	3.0	2.80%	2.8113%
4	4.0	3.00%	3.0184%
5	5.0	3.20%	3.2291%
6	6.0	3.50%	3.5548%

For an annual coupon bond of maturity n, the annualized zero-coupon yield r_n is calculated as

$$P = \sum_{t=1}^{n-1} \frac{C}{(1 + r_t)^t} + \frac{100 + C}{(1 + r_n)^n}$$

where P is the price of the bond, C is the annual coupon equal to $c(100)$, and r_t is the zero-coupon yield for a bond maturing in t years. For semiannual coupon bonds, the formula is

$$P = \sum_{t=1}^{2n-1} \frac{C/2}{(1 + r_t/2)^t} + \frac{100 + C/2}{(1 + r_n/2)^{2n}}$$

THE PURE EXPECTATIONS HYPOTHESIS

Several hypotheses have been developed to explain how the yield curve conveys information to market participants. The pure expectations hypothesis states that expected future short-term rates are equal to the forward rates implied in the yield curve. One implication of this hypothesis is that the yield curve can be decomposed into a series of expected future short-term rates that will adjust in such a way that investors receive equivalent expected holding period returns.

Under pure expectations, investors are assumed to be risk-neutral. Since risk-neutral investors apply no risk-related discount to the value of short-term bonds, the shape of the yield curve is driven only by investor expectations. If an upward-sloping yield curve prevails, investors expect higher future short-term interest rates, whereas an inverted yield curve implies expectations of lower future short-term rates. This theory implies a flat yield curve when investors expect that short-term rates will remain constant.

The pure expectations hypothesis states that the expected average annual return on a long-term bond is the geometric mean of the expected short-term rates.[2] For example, the two-period spot rate can be thought of as the one-year spot rate and the one-year rate expected to prevail one year hence. Since expected short-term rates are implied in the yield curve, an investor would be indifferent between holding a 20-year investment, a series of 20 consecutive one-year investments, or two consecutive 10-year investments.

Pure expectations is perhaps the best known and easiest of the theories of the term structure to quantify and apply. For this reason, it is widely used in the capital markets as a pricing convention for interest rate contingent securities. The set of forward rates derived under pure expectations, the implied forward yield curve, is the basis for the valuation of many fixed-income securities.

IMPLIED FORWARD RATES

Coupon bonds may be viewed as a portfolio of zero-coupon bonds with unique yields r_t for each coupon payment received at time t. As such, coupon bonds can be viewed as a series of separate bonds of different overlapping maturities. Consider bond 2 in the above example. From zero-coupon yields, the bond can be priced as

$$100 = \frac{2.50}{(1.022000)} + \frac{102.50}{(1.025038)^2}$$

---

2. Empirical evidence suggests that implied forward rates have been a poor predictor of future short-term interest rates. Fama (1975) found that a naïve forecasting method, which used current rates to predict future short-term rates, produced more accurate forecasts than one using implied forward rates.

The first cash flow is discounted at a yield of 2.2000% for one year, and the second cash flow is discounted at a yield of 2.5038% for two years. An alternative view of the second cash flow is that it is invested over two one-year periods. Since we know the yield over the first one-year period, there is an implied yield for the second period that satisfies the following relationship

$$100 = \frac{2.50}{(1.022)} + \frac{102.50}{(1.022)(1 + {}_1f_2)}$$

The implied yield for the second one-year period, ${}_1f_2$, is the forward rate on the bond from period 1 to period 2 and is equal to 2.8084%. The implied forward rate is simply the yield earned on a one-year bond from period 1 to period 2 when the investor contracts to invest in the bond today. Viewed in this way, long-term bonds can be considered a portfolio of a one-period investment at the prevailing spot rate of interest and a series of forward contracts to invest in one-period bonds at rates agreed upon today. The one-period forward interest rates are embedded in the price of long-term bonds and can be calculated from the zero-coupon yield curve with the equation

$$(1 + r_t)^t = (1 + r_1)(1 + {}_1f_2)(1 + {}_2f_3) \cdots (1 + {}_{t-1}f_t)$$

where ${}_{t-1}f_t$ is the implied forward rate for period $t - 1$ to t and r_t is the implied zero-coupon yield for time t. Solving for ${}_{t-1}f_t$, the implied forward rate for period t can be calculated as

$$_{t-1}f_t = \left[\frac{(1 + r_t)^t}{(1 + r_1)(1 + {}_1f_2)(1 + {}_2f_3)\cdots(1 + {}_{t-2}f_{t-1})} \right] - 1$$

Alternatively, this calculation can be expressed as

$$_{t-1}f_t = \frac{(1 + r_t)^t}{(1 + r_{t-1})^{t-1}} - 1$$

Exhibit 5.8 presents the implied forward rates associated with the implied zero-coupon yields from our example.

The relationship between implied zero-coupon yields and implied forward rates follows directly from the Law of One Price, which states that two assets with the same expected risk-free payoffs must have the same price. If they do not have the same price, arbitrage trading strategies permit investors to exploit the differential in price, which will eventually

EXHIBIT 5.8

Implied Forward Rates and Zero-Coupon Yields

Bond	Maturity t	Implied Zero-Coupon Yield r_t	Implied Forward Rate $_{t-1}f_t$
1	1.0	2.2000%	2.2000%
2	2.0	2.5038%	2.8084%
3	3.0	2.8113%	3.4293%
4	4.0	3.0184%	3.6421%
5	5.0	3.2291%	4.0764%
6	6.0	3.5548%	5.1986%

cause the prices to move back into equilibrium. With the implied forward rates, an investment in a two-year zero-coupon bond, which yields 2.5038%, produces the same end-of-period payoff as an investment in a one-year bond at 2.20% and a forward contract to invest in a one-year bond beginning one year from today at 2.8084%. Otherwise, an investor could exploit the price differential through arbitrage.

THE SWAP YIELD CURVE

A swap is an agreement between two parties to exchange cash flows in the future.[3] Swap cash flows are typically exchanged on several future dates. In a plain vanilla interest-rate swap, a company agrees to pay interest at a fixed rate on a notional principal in exchange for the receipt of interest at a floating rate. The floating rate used in plain vanilla interest-rate swaps is the London Interbank Offered Rate (LIBOR). LIBOR is the rate of interest offered by banks on deposits from other banks in Eurocurrency markets. LIBOR rates are quoted for loans of various maturities. Swap markets have experienced tremendous growth since their inception in the early 1980s. The swap market is largely unregulated and very liquid and has a wide range of maturities. Because of these characteristics, particularly the liquidity of long-term instruments, LIBOR swap rates are often considered a benchmark for pricing and hedging purposes.

---

3. We provide a detailed explanation of swaps in Chapter 7.

As in any interest rate market, a yield curve can be constructed from LIBOR rates. A yield curve constructed from LIBOR rates is known as a LIBOR zero-coupon curve or swap zero-coupon curve. Swap curves are constructed from the most liquid instruments for each time horizon with the bootstrapping methodology described previously in this chapter.[4] Swap curves are constructed in three-term segments: the short end of the curve is constructed from eurodollar time deposits, the middle area of the curve is constructed from eurodollar futures contracts, and the long end of the curve is constructed from LIBOR swap rates from the swap market.

THE SHORT END OF THE SWAP YIELD CURVE

The short end of the swap yield curve is based on the *LIBOR cash market,* the short-term market for eurodollar time deposits. Eurodollar time deposits are deposits traded between banks for various maturities. The rates charged on eurodollar time deposits are known as *LIBOR deposit rates.* The yields used to construct the short end of the yield curve are the most liquid LIBOR cash market transactions, with maturities of up to three months.

Cash market yields for eurodollars are quoted on a actual/360-day basis and are already zero-coupon yields. Forward rates for the time period $t - 1$ to t can be calculated from the quoted yields with the equation

$$_{t-1}f_t = \frac{r_t T_t - r_{t-1}T_{t-1}}{T_t - T_{t-1}}$$

where r_t is the quoted cash yield for t days, $_{t-1}f_t$ is the forward rate, and T_t is the number of days until the end of period t.

Example: On April 1, 2004, the quoted yield on a 30-day eurodollar time deposit was 3.00% and the quoted yield on a 90-day eurodollar time deposit was 3.30%. The 60-day forward rate for the period beginning in 30 days is calculated as

$$_{30\,days}f_{90\,days} = \frac{0.033(90) - 0.030(30)}{90 - 30}$$

---

4. For a good practical discussion of how to construct swap curves, see Ron (2000).

EXHIBIT 5.9

Eurodollar Cash Market Yields and Forward Rates

Cash Term	Quoted Yield	Forward Term			Implied Forward Rate
		t	T	# of days	
1-Day	1.0625%	0	1	1	
2-Day	1.0625%	1	2	1	1.0625%
1-Week	1.0700%	2	7	5	1.0730%
2-Week	1.0700%	7	14	7	1.0700%
3-Week	1.0700%	14	21	7	1.0700%
1-Month	1.0938%	21	29	8	1.1561%
2-Month	1.1100%	29	60	31	1.1252%
3-Month	1.1200%	60	90	30	1.1400%
4-Month	1.1363%	90	121	31	1.1834%

Source: Bloomberg 2/13/04.

or 3.45%. Using this methodology, we can calculate forward rates from quoted eurodollar cash market yields. Exhibit 5.9 presents quoted euro-dollar cash market yields and implied forward rates for maturities up to four months.

THE MIDDLE AREA OF THE SWAP CURVE

The middle area of the swap curve includes maturities from three months to two years and is typically constructed from eurodollar futures rates. Three-month eurodollar futures contracts trade on the Chicago Mercantile Exchange (CME) with maturities in March, June, September, and December for up to 10 years in the future. Exhibit 5.10 presents quotes on euro-dollar futures contracts for three years. Quotes are annualized contract prices stated as a percentage of face value and based on a face value of $1 million. If Q is the quoted price for a eurodollar futures contract, the value of one contract F is

$$F = 10,000[100 - 0.25(100 - Q)]$$

EXHIBIT 5.10

Price Quote and Contract Values
for Eurodollar Futures Contracts

Maturity	Quoted Price	Futures Rate	Contract Value
Mar-04	98.860	1.140	997,150
Jun-04	98.765	1.235	996,913
Sep-04	98.550	1.450	996,375
Dec-04	98.220	1.780	995,550
Mar-05	97.835	2.165	994,588
Jun-05	97.430	2.570	993,575
Sep-05	97.060	2.940	992,650
Dec-05	96.750	3.250	991,875
Mar-06	96.495	3.505	991,238
Jun-06	96.265	3.735	990,663
Sep-06	96.045	3.955	990,113
Dec-06	95.830	4.170	989,575
Mar-07	95.650	4.350	989,125

Source: Bloomberg 2/13/04.

Example: The June 2004 eurodollar futures price is equal to 98.765, and the corresponding contract value is calculated as

$$10{,}000[100 - 0.25(100 - 98.765)] = \$996{,}913$$

The eurodollar futures interest rate for this quote is equal to $(100 - Q)\%$ or 1.235%.

CONVEXITY ADJUSTMENT

Ideally, the middle area of the swap curve would be constructed from over-the-counter interest rate forward contracts or forward rate agreements (FRA). FRAs have a fixed time horizon and settle at maturity, which makes them directly comparable to implied forward rates. However, FRAs are considerably less liquid than eurodollar futures contracts, which makes the use of futures contracts preferable. Since FRAs are convex instruments and futures contracts have no convexity, a convexity adjustment is made when futures contracts are used. Hull and White (1994) show that a forward interest rate from times t_1 to t_2 ($t_2 > t_1$) can be estimated by subtracting the following convexity adjustment from the futures rate.[5] The convexity adjustment K is calculated as

$$K = \left(\frac{B(t_1,t_2)}{t_2 - t_1}\right)\left[B(t_1,t_2)(1 - e^{-2at_1}) + 2aB(0,t_1)^2\right]\frac{\sigma^2}{4a}$$

where

$$B(t_1,t_2) = \frac{1 - e^{-a(t_2-t_1)}}{a}$$

In the above equations, σ is the standard deviation of the annual change in short-term interest rates and a is the mean reversion rate.[6] $B(t_1,t_2)$ is the price at time t_1 of a zero-coupon bond that matures at time t_2.

Example: Suppose we wish to calculate a forward rate when the two-year eurodollar futures price is 95.00. The mean reversion rate a is 0.009, and the volatility σ is 0.020. Since $t_1 = 2.00$ and $t_2 = 2.25$, $B(t_1,t_2) = 0.2497$ and $B(0,t_1) = 1.9821$. The convexity adjustment is calculated as

$$\left(\frac{0.2497}{0.25}\right)\left[0.2497(1 - e^{(-2)(0.009)(2.0)}) + (2)(0.009)(1.9821)^2\right]\frac{0.020^2}{(4)(0.009)} = 0.0009$$

or 0.09%. Since the annual futures rate is 5.00%, the forward rate is equal to $5.00 - 0.09 = 4.91\%$.

---

5. Time periods for the convexity adjustment are measured in years. $t_i = T_i/360$, where T_i is the number of days until the end of the period.
6. Mean reversion refers to the tendency of interest rates to return to a long-run average over time. In the Hull-White model, the interest rate reverts to a time-dependent level of interest rates, $\theta(t)/a$, at rate a. For a more complete discussion of interest rate models, see Hull (2003).

EXHIBIT 5.11

Convexity Adjustments and Forward Rates
for Eurodollar Futures Contracts

Maturity	Futures Rate	Convexity Adjustment	Forward Rate
Mar-04	1.140%	0.000%	1.1400%
Jun-04	1.235%	0.000%	1.2348%
Sep-04	1.450%	0.000%	1.4495%
Dec-04	1.780%	0.001%	1.7791%
Mar-05	2.165%	0.001%	2.1635%
Jun-05	2.570%	0.002%	2.5679%
Sep-05	2.940%	0.003%	2.9371%
Dec-05	3.250%	0.004%	3.2462%
Mar-06	3.505%	0.005%	3.5001%
Jun-06	3.735%	0.006%	3.7290%
Sep-06	3.955%	0.007%	3.9477%
Dec-06	4.170%	0.009%	4.1613%
Mar-07	4.350%	0.010%	4.3398%

Exhibit 5.11 presents the convexity adjustments required for the quoted futures rates.[7] Also presented are the forward rates, which include the convexity adjustment. The calculations assume a constant mean reversion rate a equal to 0.0085 and volatility $\sigma = 0.0045$.[8]

Zero-coupon yields can be derived from the above three-month forward rates. The zero-coupon yield r_t for period t is calculated as

$$r_t = \frac{t-1 f_t (T_t - T_{t-1}) + r_{t-1} T_{t-1}}{T_t}$$

In the above equation, $t-1 f_t$ is the forward rate calculated from the Eurodollar futures contract expiring at time $t-1$ and T_t represents the number

---

7. The convexity adjustments are subtracted from the futures rates, resulting in forward rates that are lower than the futures rates. This relationship is expected if interest rates are negatively correlated.

8. The term of each contract should be based on an actual/360 basis. For our calculations, the March contract expires 32 days from the day the quotes were obtained, hence $t_1 = 0.0889$ years (32/360). For simplicity, our convexity adjustment calculations assume that each subsequent contract increases in maturity by 0.25 years, hence $t_2 = 0.3389$ years for the March contract.

EXHIBIT 5.12

Forward Rates and Zero-Coupon Yields
for Eurodollar Futures Contracts

Maturity	Days to Expiration	Forward Rate	Zero-Coupon Yield
Mar-04	32	1.1400%	1.1284%
Jun-04	123	1.2348%	1.1736%
Sep-04	214	1.4495%	1.2559%
Dec-04	305	1.7791%	1.3762%
Mar-05	396	2.1635%	1.5233%
Jun-05	487	2.5679%	1.6983%
Sep-05	585	2.9371%	1.8650%
Dec-05	676	3.2462%	2.0177%
Mar-06	760	3.5001%	2.1870%
Jun-06	858	3.7290%	2.3349%
Sep-06	949	3.9477%	2.4760%
Dec-06	1,040	4.1613%	2.6116%
Mar-07	1,131	4.3398%	2.7403%

of days until the end of time period t. The zero-coupon yields derived from the eurodollar forward rates are presented in Exhibit 5.12.

THE LONG END OF THE SWAP YIELD CURVE

The long end of the swap yield curve, typically from two years to 10 years, is derived from observed coupon rates on fixed or floating plain vanilla swaps. Quoted swap rates are LIBOR par yields and are typically compounded semiannually. Exhibit 5.13 presents quoted swap coupon rates. To use semiannual swap rates to derive zero-coupon swap yields, we must first interpolate between the maturities to estimate coupon rates at half-year intervals. Exhibit 5.13 also presents interpolated swap rates at half-year intervals.

We can apply the bootstrapping method described earlier in the chapter and use the swap rates to determine the LIBOR zero-coupon curve in this range of maturities. Because the semiannual swap contracts begin in year 2, our calculations require the zero-coupon yields for prior periods. The zero-coupon yields for periods 0.5, 1.0, and 1.5 are, respectively,

EXHIBIT 5.13

Quoted Swap Coupon Rates and Interpolated Swap Rates

Maturity	Swap Coupon Rate	Maturity	Interpolated Swap Rate
2 Year	1.9700%		
3 Year	2.5350%	2.5 Year	2.2525%
4 Year	2.9990%	3.5 Year	2.7670%
5 Year	3.3800%	4.5 Year	3.1895%
6 Year	3.6700%	5.5 Year	3.5250%
7 Year	3.9000%	6.5 Year	3.7850%
8 Year	4.1100%	7.5 Year	4.0050%
9 Year	4.2700%	8.5 Year	4.1900%
10 Year	4.4100%	9.5 Year	4.3400%

1.1750%, 1.3365%, and 1.6304% with semiannual compounding.[8] The zero-coupon yield for the two-year swap is calculated as

$$100 = \frac{\frac{1.9700}{2}}{\left(1+\frac{0.01175}{2}\right)} + \frac{\frac{1.9700}{2}}{\left(1+\frac{0.013365}{2}\right)^2} \frac{\frac{1.9700}{2}}{\left(1+\frac{0.016304}{2}\right)^3} + \frac{100+\frac{1.9700}{2}}{\left(1+\frac{r_{2.0}}{2}\right)^4}$$

Solving for $r_{2.0}$ results in $r_{2.0} = 1.9777\%$. With this two-year spot rate, we use the zero-coupon yield for the 2.5-year swap to solve the equation

$$100 = \frac{\frac{2.2525}{2}}{\left(1+\frac{0.01175}{2}\right)} + \frac{\frac{2.2525}{2}}{\left(1+\frac{0.013365}{2}\right)^2} \frac{\frac{2.2525}{2}}{\left(1+\frac{0.016304}{2}\right)^3}$$

$$+ \frac{\frac{2.2525}{2}}{\left(1+\frac{0.019777}{2}\right)^4} + \frac{100+\frac{2.2525}{2}}{\left(1+\frac{r_{2.5}}{2}\right)^5}$$

---

8. The zero-coupon yield for year 0.5 is simply the quoted six-month cash rate. The zero-coupon yields for years 1.0 and 1.5 are interpolated implied zero-coupon yields from eurodollar futures using linear interpolation.

EXHIBIT 5.14

Implied Zero-Coupon Yields and Forward
Rates for Swaps

Maturity t	Implied Zero-Coupon Yield r_t	Implied Forward Rate $_{t-1}f_t$
2.0	1.9777%	3.0231%
2.5	2.2660%	3.4236%
3.0	2.5569%	4.0178%
3.5	2.7976%	4.2475%
4.0	3.0409%	4.7522%
4.5	3.2421%	4.8592%
5.0	3.4459%	5.2894%
5.5	3.6016%	5.1646%
6.0	3.7594%	5.5037%
6.5	3.8849%	5.3967%
7.0	4.0123%	5.6757%
7.5	4.1297%	5.7812%
8.0	4.2491%	6.0480%
8.5	4.3395%	5.7917%
9.0	4.4315%	6.0022%
9.5	4.5124%	5.9730%
10.0	4.5947%	6.1655%

Solving for $r_{2.5}$ results in 2.2660%. Exhibit 5.14 presents zero-coupon yields
and implied forward rates for maturities from two years to 10 years, calculated with the bootstrapping method.

CONSTRUCTION OF THE SWAP
ZERO-COUPON CURVE

The complete swap zero-coupon curve is constructed by combination of
the zero-coupon yields from different maturities. Exhibit 5.15 presents
the calculated zero-coupon yields and forward rates calculated for each
area of the curve. As described previously, the short end of the curve is

EXHIBIT 5.15

Swap Rates by Maturity

	Short End			Middle Area	
Maturity	Zero-Coupon Yield	Forward Rate	Maturity	Zero-Coupon Yield	Forward Rate
(A) Short-End and Middle-Area Swap Rates					
1-Day	1.0625%		Jun-04	1.1284%	1.1400%
2-Day	1.0625%	1.0625%	Sep-04	1.1736%	1.2348%
1-Week	1.0700%	1.0729%	Dec-04	1.2559%	1.4495%
2-Week	1.0700%	1.0698%	Mar-05	1.3761%	1.7791%
3-Week	1.0700%	1.0696%	Jun-05	1.5233%	2.1635%
1-Month	1.0938%	1.1554%	Sep-05	1.6983%	2.5678%
2-Month	1.1100%	1.1242%	Dec-05	1.8650%	2.9370%
3-Month	1.1200%	1.1379%			
(B) Long-End Swap Rates					
Feb-06	1.9777%	3.0231%	Aug-10	3.8849%	5.3967%
Aug-06	2.2660%	3.4236%	Feb-11	4.0123%	5.6757%
Feb-07	2.5569%	4.0178%	Aug-11	4.1297%	5.7812%
Aug-07	2.7976%	4.2475%	Feb-12	4.2491%	6.0480%
Feb-08	3.0409%	4.7522%	Aug-12	4.3395%	5.7917%
Aug-08	3.2421%	4.8592%	Feb-13	4.4315%	6.0022%
Feb-09	3.4459%	5.2894%	Aug-13	4.5124%	5.9730%
Aug-09	3.6016%	5.1646%	Feb-14	4.5947%	6.1655%
Feb-10	3.7594%	5.5037%			

constructed from LIBOR cash market rates with maturities of up to three months. The middle area of the curve is constructed from eurodollar futures contract rates with maturities from three months to two years. The long end of the swap curve is constructed from LIBOR swaps with maturities greater than two years. Exhibit 5.16 shows the swap zero-coupon curve constructed from these rates.

EXHIBIT 5.16

Swap Zero-Coupon Curve

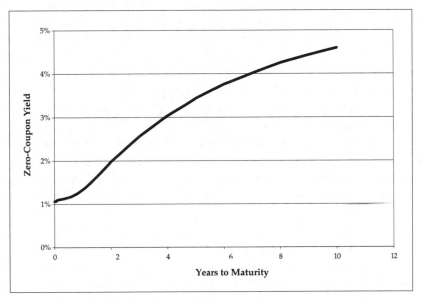

SUMMARY

The yield curve refers to the relationship between yield and maturity for debt securities that are alike in all other respects. Yield curves can be constructed from many different fixed-income securities. The U.S. Treasury yield curve is the standard that many market participants use in quantifying interest rate risks. A zero-coupon yield curve constructed from default-free U.S. Treasury securities is known as the *term structure of interest rates.*

There are several theories regarding the yield curve and what the yield/maturity relationship is supposed to explain. The methods described in this chapter are based upon the pure expectations hypothesis of the term structure of interest rates. The classical version of this theory states that expected holding period returns for a debt security over multiple periods should be the same, regardless of whether an investor rolls over a sequence of short-maturity bonds or holds a long-term zero-coupon bond. In other words, the yield curve reflects today's expectations for future short-term rates.

The yield curve that market participants observe is the par yield curve. This shows the yield to maturity on coupon-bearing bonds, where the coupon rates are the same as the yield to maturity. We showed how implied zero-coupon yields can be derived from a par yield curve. Implied zero-coupon yields are the set of discount rates that equates the cash flow of a full-coupon-bearing bond to those of set of zero-coupon bonds. The zero-coupon yield curve is constructed from yields-to-maturity on zero-coupon bonds where each has only a single cash flow.

Underlying the pure expectations model of the yield curve is a relationship between the current long-term rate and the rates on current (or spot) loans and expected future (or forward) short-term loans. The forward market is where a market participant can contract for rates on loans or investments that begin at some time in the future. Using the zero-coupon yield curve and the Law of One Price, we showed how implied forward rates can be derived.

The swap yield curve serves as a benchmark for the pricing and hedging of many securities. The swap yield curve is constructed from eurodollar cash rates, futures contracts, and swaps. We described in detail how to derive zero-coupon yields and implied forward yields for the eurodollar market and constructed a swap yield curve from these interest rates.

REFERENCES

Burghardt, G., and B. Hoskins. "A Question of Bias." *Risk* (March 1995), 63–70.

Cusatis, P., and M. Peterson. "The Term Structure of Interest Rates," Chapter 2 in *Controlling and Managing Interest Rate Risk*. Englewood Cliffs, NJ: Prentice Hall, 1997.

Fama, E. "Short-term Interest Rates as Predictors of Inflation." *American Economic Review* (June 1975), 269–82.

Hull, J. C. *Options, Futures, and Other Derivatives*. Upper Saddle River, NJ: Prentice Hall, 2003.

Hull, J., and A. White. "Pricing Interest Rate Derivative Securities." *The Review of Financial Studies* 3, no. 4 (1990), 573–92.

Kirikos, G., and D. Novak. "Convexity Conundrums." *Risk* (March 1997), pp. 60–61.

Ron, U. "A Practical Guide to Swap Curve Construction." Bank of Canada Working Paper 2000-17, August 2000.

Sundaresan, S. *Fixed Income Markets and Their Derivatives*. Cincinnati, OH: Southwestern, 2002.

CHAPTER 6

Futures Contracts

Hedgers and speculators have different needs in the market. Some market participants need to buy assets, whereas others need to sell assets. In many markets, it is costly or impossible to sell assets for settlement at a later date. Futures allow market participants to buy or sell efficiently in most markets.

A *futures contract* is an agreement to exchange cash flows based on a predetermined purchase or sale price of an asset at a specified time in the future. Positions are adjusted daily with respect to market movements and the predetermined purchase and sale price. The term of the futures contract is usually three months to one year. No money is required on the trade date; however, buyers or sellers are obligated to fulfill their contractual agreement at the end of the contract and make mark-to-market adjustments daily.

The buyer or owner of a futures contract is said to take a *long* position and can take delivery of the underlying asset at maturity for the contractual price. The seller or writer of the futures contract is said to take a *short* position and must deliver the underlying asset if held to maturity. In practice, most buyers and sellers do not hold contracts until delivery of the underlying commodity or asset is required. Instead, they close out the contract by selling or buying an offsetting amount of contracts before the delivery date. In this way, the futures market provides hedgers and speculators with an opportunity to lock in asset prices without requiring the burden of delivery.

Futures contracts are traded on a variety of commodities, financial assets, and indices. They have standard contract sizes, settlement procedures, and delivery dates. Futures contracts are exchange traded and are very liquid because of established settlement and margin procedures. The market functions efficiently because the exchange monitors the ability of participants to honor their contractual obligations. Many futures contracts trade on the Chicago Board of Trade (CBOT), the Chicago Mercantile Exchange (CME), the New York Mercantile Exchange (NYMEX), and the London International Financial Futures and Options Exchange (LIFFE). Exhibit 6.1 lists the major exchanges and the contracts that they trade.

FUTURES PAYOFF PROFILE

The payoff profile for a futures contract at maturity depends on the change in value of the underlying asset. The value of a long position in a futures contract increases as the spot or cash price on the underlying asset increases. Conversely, the value of a short futures position increases as the cash price of the underlying asset decreases. Exhibit 6.2 shows the cumulative net payoff profiles at maturity for a long and a short futures position with the same contract price.[1] The payoff profiles intersect at the initial futures contract price. Notice that the sum of the two contracts at maturity will always equal zero. Below, we formulate the payoff on long and short positions in the futures market.

With the following notation:

$$F_0 = \text{initial futures price (at settlement)}$$
$$S_n = \text{spot asset price (at maturity)}$$

Then

$$\text{Long Position Payoff} = S_n - F_0$$

and

$$\text{Short Position Payoff} = F_0 - S_n$$

and

$$\text{Long Position} + \text{Short Position} = 0$$

---

1. This does not consider the time value of money.

EXHIBIT   6.1

Sample Futures Contracts by Exchange

Chicago Board of Trade (CBOT)

Agriculture	Interest Rates	Indices	Metals
Corn	30-Year U.S. Treasury Bonds	DJIA Futures	CBOT mini-sized Gold
Soybeans	10-Year U.S. Treasury Notes	Dow Jones ($10)	
Soybean Oil	5-Year U.S. Treasury Notes	AIG Commodity Index	CBOT mini-sized Silver
Soybean Meal	2-Year U.S. Treasury Notes		
Wheat	10-Year Interest Rate Swap	Mini-sized Dow ($5)	
Oats	5-Year Interest Rate Swap		
Rough Rice	30-Day Federal Funds		
	10-Year Municipal Note Index		

Chicago Mercantile Exchange (CME)

Commodities	Equity Indices	Foreign Exchange	Interest Rates	Weather
Beef	S&P 500	Euro FX	Eurodollar	European Weather
Dairy	E-mini S&P 500	Japanese Yen	LIBOR	
E-livestock	NASDAQ-100	Swiss Franc	Swap Futures	US Weather
Hogs	E-mini NASDAQ-100	Canadian Dollar	13-week T-bills	
Lumber	E-mini NASDAQ Composite	British Pound	Euroyen	

New York Mercantile Exchange/Commodity Exchange (NYMEX/COMEX)

Metals	Indices	Energy
Gold	FTSE Eurotop 100 Index	Propane
Silver	FTSE 300 Index	Middle East crude oil
Copper		Natural gas
Aluminum		Electricity
Platinum		
Palladium		

London International Financial Futures and Options Exchange (LIFFE)

Commodities	Equity Futures	Interest Rates
Cocoa	FTSE Eurotop 300 Index	Long Gilt
Robusta Coffee	FTSE Eurotop 100 Index	Two-Year Schatz
White Sugar	FTSE 100 Index	Ten-Year Bund
Wheat	FTSE 250 Index	Japanese Government Bond (JGB)
Milling Wheat		
Corn		
Potato		

Source: www.CBOT.com, www.CME.com, www.NYMEX.com, www.Liffe.com.

EXHIBIT 6.2

Futures Contract Cumulative Net Payoff to Maturity

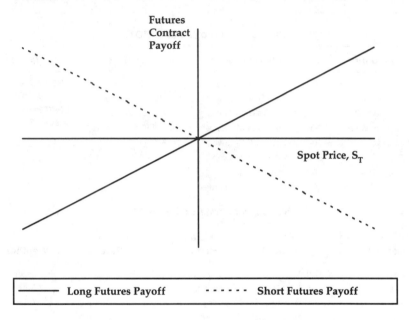

HEDGING AND SPECULATING EXAMPLES

There are two groups of participants in the futures market: *hedgers* and *speculators*. Hedgers have exposure to the price of a commodity, security, or index and use futures as a way to reduce that exposure. Speculators are risk takers who wish to capitalize on their belief about expected futures price changes. The two groups complete the market, thereby making it more efficient and allowing for the transfer of risk between parties. The examples below outline a long and a short hedge position and a speculating position in various futures markets. Assume F_t is the futures price at time t, and S_n is the spot price at the contract reversal date.

Long Hedge Example

Consider a food packaging company that wants to protect itself against an increase in the price of corn. Assume the company expects to buy 50,000

EXHIBIT 6.3

Long Hedge Example

Date	Position	F_t	Cumulative Payoff
10/13/03	Buy 10 Corn Futures	$2.17	$S_n - \$2.17$
11/13/03	Sell 10 Corn Futures	$2.40	$\$2.40 - S_n$
Cumulative Net Payoff at Maturity			$50,000(\$2.40 - \$2.17) = \$11,500$

bushels of corn one month from today. The company can purchase corn futures to hedge exposure to rising corn prices. Each CBOT traded corn contract is for the purchase of 5,000 bushels. Therefore, the initial transaction for the company would be to buy 10 corn futures contracts. Exhibit 6.3 shows actual corn futures prices and the results of this hedge over a sample one-month time period. Price quotes are in dollars per bushel, and transaction costs are not included.

In this example, the corn futures price increased from $2.17 per bushel to $2.40 per bushel in one month. The sale of 10 futures contracts on November 13, 2003 is an offsetting transaction to close the initial futures position. If the company had hedged with corn futures, it would have netted $11,500 on its futures contracts, which would have offset the higher price of corn one month later.[2]

Short Hedge Example

Consider a mining company that expects to have 1,000 troy ounces of gold for sale in one month. To ensure the sale price of the gold, the company can sell gold futures today and hedge against a decline in the price of gold. Each CBOT traded mini-sized gold contract is for 33.2 troy ounces of gold. Therefore, the initial transaction for the company would be to sell 30 gold futures contracts. Exhibit 6.4 shows actual futures gold prices and the results of this hedge over a sample one-month time period. Price quotes are in dollars per troy ounce; transaction costs are not included.

---

2. In the examples in this section, the payoff represents the cumulative effect of daily mark-to-market over the time period.

EXHIBIT 6.4

Short Hedge Example

Date	Position	F_t	Cumulative Payoff
10/13/03	Sell 30 Gold Futures	$375	$375 − S_n
11/13/03	Buy 30 Gold Futures	$394	S_n − $394
Cumulative Net Payoff at Maturity			1,000($375 − $394) = −$19,000

In this example, the gold futures price increased from $375 per troy ounce to $394 per troy ounce in one month. The purchase of 30 futures contracts on November 13, 2003 is an offsetting transaction to close the initial futures position. If the company had hedged with gold futures, it would have lost $19,000 on its futures contracts. This would have been offset by the higher sale price of gold one month later.

Speculating Example

Consider a market participant who believes that the price of crude oil is going to increase over the next month. To capitalize on this belief, the speculator can buy crude oil futures. The number of futures would be determined by the strength of the speculator's conviction. Each NYMEX traded crude oil contract is for 1,000 U.S. barrels of oil. Assume the speculator decides on an initial transaction of 10 contracts. Exhibit 6.5 shows the actual futures crude oil prices and results of this speculation over a

EXHIBIT 6.5

Speculating Example

Date	Position	F_t	Cumulative Payoff
10/13/03	Buy 10 Oil Futures	$31.60	S_n − $31.60
11/13/03	Sell 10 Oil Futures	$31.43	$31.43 − S_n
Cumulative Net Payoff at Maturity			10,000($31.43 − $31.60) = −$1,700

sample one-month time period. Price quotes are in dollars per U.S. barrel of crude oil; transaction costs are not included.

In this example, the crude oil futures price decreased from $31.60 per barrel to $31.43 per barrel in one month. The sale of 10 oil futures contracts on November 13, 2003 is an offsetting transaction to close the initial futures position. If the speculator had made these trades with crude oil futures, they would have resulted in a loss of $1,700. This would have been an incorrect market call for the speculator.

MARKING-TO-MARKET AND MARGINS

In the examples above, we focus on the cumulative net value of the trades when they are closed out and ignore intermediate cash flows. An important aspect of futures is the daily mark-to-market. The daily marking of positions, along with the posting of collateral, assures the exchange that participants will honor their obligations under the contract. This mechanism removes the risk of transacting with other parties, known as *counterparty risk*.

Investors in the futures market are required to post collateral in a margin account. At the end of each trading day, the gains or losses on outstanding futures positions are added to or subtracted from the investor's margin account. There are two primary restrictions on margin: *initial margin requirements* (IMR) and *maintenance margin requirements* (MMR). The initial margin requirement is the amount that must be deposited at the outset. The maintenance margin requirement is the minimum allowable margin or equity in the account as prices of outstanding contracts change. If the margin falls to or below the maintenance level, the investor is subject to a margin call and is required to increase the margin to the initial level. The additional margin required is known as *variation margin*. Examples of margin requirements are shown in Exhibit 6.6.

Example: A speculator buys five gold contracts on the COMEX. The current futures price is $395 per ounce, and each contract is for 100 troy ounces. The IMR is $2,025 per contract, and the MMR is $1,500 per contract. If the margin account balance decreases below $7,500, a margin call will result. Exhibit 6.7 shows the margin account balance and the variation margin for a hypothetical five-day trading period.

E X H I B I T   6.6

Example Margin Requirements

Futures Contract		Initial Margin Requirement (per contract)	
Symbol	Name	Hedger	Speculator
AL	Aluminum	$800	$1,080
HC	Copper	$1,000	$1,350
GC	Gold	$1,500	$2,025
SI	Silver	$1,000	$1,350

Source: NYMEX.com.

DELIVERY OPTIONS

Most futures contracts are canceled by an offsetting trade before expiration. In this way a hedger or speculator avoids the burden of delivering (or taking delivery of) the underlying asset. Some market participants, however, take delivery at the end of the contract. It is important as a hedger to understand the delivery options on a futures contract, since they affect trading and valuation of the contract.

The exchange determines the delivery options when it establishes the terms of the contract, and these options vary by contract. Commodity,

E X H I B I T   6.7

Margin Call Example

Day	Futures Price	Total Contract Value	Daily Change in Value	Margin Account Value	Variation Margin
1	395.00	$197,500		$10,125	
2	393.50	$196,750	−$750	$9,375	
3	390.80	$195,400	−$1,350	$8,025	
4	387.20	$193,600	−$1,800	$6,225	$3,900
5	392.20	$196,100	$2,500	$12,625	

currency, and agricultural futures require physical delivery if the contract is held to expiration. Most interest rate contracts also require delivery of the underlying security if held to maturity. Index futures, such as those written against the S&P 500, do not have a delivery requirement. The task of delivering all of the stocks in the S&P 500, for example, would be a burden. For this reason, these contracts settle in cash.

For many contracts, the delivery option is complex. Some interest rate futures are based on the value of a hypothetical bond. For example, the 10-year U.S. Treasury note contract is based on a hypothetical U.S. Treasury note with a 6.00% coupon and exactly 10 years to maturity. However, such a U.S. Treasury note does not exist. For this reason, the exchange defines acceptable grades for delivery. We discuss this concept in detail later in the chapter.

THE COST-OF-CARRY RELATIONSHIP

Cost-of-carry refers to the explicit costs associated with hedging or speculating with futures contracts. The futures market was established as a means of hedging the prices of commodities. The term *carry* or *carrying cost* was coined as a reference to the storage, insurance, and funding charges associated with delivering a commodity such as soybeans or wheat.

In general, the price of a futures contract can be expressed in terms of its carrying costs. If we refer to the carrying costs as G, then the price of a futures contract can be expressed as

$$F_0 = S_0 + G$$

If we express the carrying costs as a percentage of the spot price such that $G/S_0 = g$, then we can rewrite the pricing relationship as

$$F_0 = S_0(1 + g)$$

Therefore, in continuous time, the price of a futures contract is

$$F_0 = S_0 e^{gn}$$

where n is the time to maturity of the futures contract in years.

We assume that the pricing model above applies to futures on physical commodities. For interest rate, currency, and equity futures, the concept of cost-of-carry is less obvious, because there are no storage or insurance costs. However, there are financing charges on money borrowed to buy the underlying asset. In addition, the underlying assets may pay interest or dividends that offset the financing costs. Cost-of-carry on equity futures is based on the relationship between the financing rates and dividend yields. For interest rate futures, cost-of-carry is based on the shape of the yield curve and can be positive, negative, or zero. The shape of the yield curve contains information about expectations regarding forward interest rates. The yield curve is most often upward sloping. Under this scenario, the net cost of borrowing funds and investing in a bond in the cash market is negative. That is, the interest received on a bond exceeds the interest expense incurred from borrowing funds to buy the bond. Since a long position is replicated in the futures market by the purchase of a futures contract, the same relationship must hold. Specifically, the price of an interest rate futures contract in an upward-sloping yield curve environment must be less than the price of the underlying cash asset. The difference between spot and futures prices is a function of the difference between the short-term funding rate and the yield on the underlying asset.

The cost-of-carry relationship is important but is often overlooked by hedgers. The implication for hedgers is as follows. In a typical market, even if the spot price does not change over a period of time, there is a cost associated with hedging. In this scenario, a long portfolio that is not hedged will not change in value, whereas the hedged portfolio will typically decrease in value because of the cost-of-carry on the futures contracts. For a hedger, the cost-of-carry is an important consideration when one examines the efficiency of hedging instruments.

BASIS

Basis is the difference between the spot price and the futures price of the same commodity or asset. The relationship between these two is a concern for hedgers because the futures contract acts as a proxy for the cash market. A shift in basis occurs if changes in the futures price do not reflect movements in the cash market. This is referred to as *tracking error*. As the contract nears delivery, the cash and futures prices will converge because, as expiration approaches, the futures price becomes a spot price. Exhibit 6.8 shows the gross basis between the delivery price on the 10-year U.S. Treasury note and the cash market between August 1, 2003 and December 4, 2003. The *gross basis* is measured as the difference between the two prices at the close of each business day. Notice that the basis is decreasing over time as expiration nears. The convergence of prices eventually drives the gross basis to zero.

EXHIBIT 6.8

Gross Basis between a 10-Year U.S. Treasury Note Futures Contract and a Deliverable U.S. Treasury Note

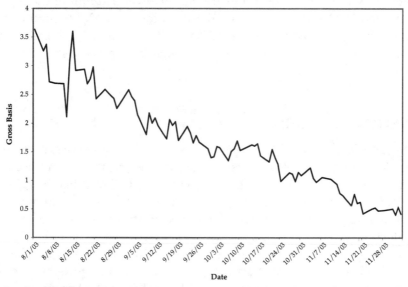

Data Source: Bloomberg, December 4, 2003.

FUTURES CONTRACTS

In this section we describe the most popular futures contracts for hedgers. We begin with metals and oil futures. Metals and oils belong to the same class of futures contracts, metallurgical commodities. We then describe agricultural futures, which are the oldest exchange traded contracts. Next we describe currency and interest rate futures. Because of their complexity and importance, interest rate futures are described in detail. Included in the interest rate futures discussion are U.S. Treasury note and bond contracts, eurodollar futures, municipal futures, and swap futures. Finally, we discuss popular equity futures contracts.

METALS FUTURES

Gold, silver, and aluminum futures contracts are used by companies in the metal industry, such as mining companies and jewelry manufacturers, to minimize their price risk. Portfolio managers also use gold and silver futures as an alternative to investing in other forms of the metals market. Including gold in an investment portfolio is a useful diversification and risk-minimizing tool because gold retains its value during periods of economic downturn. The most popular gold, silver, and aluminum contracts are traded in U.S. dollars and are listed on the COMEX Division of the New York Mercantile Exchange (NYMEX). Fewer than 1% of these contracts result in delivery. The terms of the three contracts are shown in Exhibit 6.9.

ENERGY FUTURES

Energy futures are used for the same reasons as other futures: risk minimization and price discovery. Three popular energy futures contracts are natural gas, gasoline, and crude oil. If a company believes that the price of an energy source will increase, it may want to buy an energy futures contract to guarantee future delivery at a fixed price. The price of oil affects production and transportation costs. Corporations such as airlines may protect against unexpected changes in the price of oil by using oil futures.

Crude oil futures contracts are especially volatile, since the price of oil futures is affected by conflicts in the Middle East and other areas where oil is produced. Also affecting the prices of the oil futures contracts are the activities of the Organization of Petroleum-Exporting Countries (OPEC), such as restricting oil outputs or changing production quotas. The terms of energy futures contracts traded on the NYMEX are shown in Exhibit 6.10.

AGRICULTURAL FUTURES

The futures market developed as the market for the future delivery of agricultural commodities. Corn, wheat, and other agricultural futures contracts are normally used by farmers, food industry companies, and other companies in agribusiness to alleviate price fluctuations. Crops are seasonal and weather-dependent, making their prices extremely volatile. Poor weather and growing conditions result in an increase in agricultural futures prices. Prices for corn futures are negatively affected by farm subsidies, which result in overproduction by U.S. farmers.

Corn, wheat, and oats belong to one class of agricultural futures. Other classes include oils and meals, livestock, forest products, textiles, and foodstuffs. Delivery dates follow harvest cycles. Agricultural futures

EXHIBIT 6.9

Terms of Metal Futures Contracts

	Gold 100-oz Futures	Silver Futures	Aluminum Futures
Exchange	COMEX	COMEX	COMEX
Size	100 troy oz	5,000 troy oz	44,000 lbs
Contract Grade	Troy ounces of refined gold, not less than 0.995 fineness, cast either in one bar or in three 1-kg. bars, and bearing a serial number and identifying stamp of a refiner approved and listed by the Exchange.	Troy ounces of refined silver, assaying not less than 0.999 fineness, in cast bars weighing 1,000 or 1,100 troy ounces each and bearing a serial number and identifying stamp of a refiner approved and listed by Exchange.	Primary aluminum meeting all the requirements of the P1020A designation or primary aluminum of 99.7% purity with a maximum iron content of 0.20% and a maximum silicon content of 0.10%.
Settlement Procedure	Delivery	Delivery	Delivery
Price Quotes	Cents and 1/10s of a cent	Cents and 1/2s of a cent	Cents and 1/20s of a cent
Tick Size and Value	1/10 of a cent ($10)	1/2 of a cent ($25)	1/20 of a cent ($22)
Delivery Months	February, April, June, August, October, December	January, March, May, July, September, December	January, February, March, April, May, June, July, August, September, October, November, December
Margin Limits	Speculator Hedger Initial 2025 1500 Secondary 1500 1500	Speculator Hedger Initial 1350 1000 Secondary 1000 1000	Speculator Hedger Initial 1350 1000 Secondary 1000 1000

EXHIBIT 6.10

Terms of Energy Futures Contracts

	Natural Gas	Gasoline	Crude Oil Futures
Exchange	NYMEX	NYMEX	NYMEX
Size	10,000 million British thermal units	42,000 U.S. gallons	1,000 U.S. Barrels
Contract Grade	Delivery through Sabine Pipe Line Company's Henry Hub	Phase II Complex Model Reformulated Gasoline is F.O.B. seller's facility in the New York Harbor ex-shore. Delivery may also be completed by pipeline, tanker, book transfer, or intra-facility transfer.	Specific domestic crudes with .42% sulfur by weight or less, not less than 37bp API gravity nor more than 42bp API gravity. Deliverable Grades: West Texas Intermediate, Low Sweet Mix, New Mexican Sweet, North Texas Sweet, Oklahoma Sweet, and South Texas Sweet.
Settlement Procedure	Delivery	Delivery	Delivery
Price Quotes	Cents and 1/10s of a cent	Cents	Cents
Tick Size and Value	1/10 of a cent ($10)	Cents ($4.2)	Cents ($10)
Delivery Months	January, February, March, April, May, June, July, August, September, October, November, December	January, February, March, April, May, June, July, August, September, October, November, December	January, February, March, April, May, June, July, August, September, October, November, December
Margin Limits			
	Speculator Hedger	Speculator Hedger	Speculator Hedger
Initial	5400 4400	5400 4400	3375 2750
Secondary	4000 4000	4000 4000	2500 2500

EXHIBIT 6.11

Terms of Agricultural Futures Contracts

	Corn Futures	**Wheat Futures**
Exchange	CBOT	CBOT
Size	5,000 Bushels	5,000 Bushels
Contract Grade	No. 2 Yellow at par and substitutions at differentials established by the exchange.	No. 1 Northern Spring Wheat, No. 2 Soft Red, No. 2 Hard Red Winter, and No. 2 Dark Northern Spring at par. Substitutes at differentials established by the exchange.
Settlement Procedure	Delivery	Delivery
Price Quotes	Cents and 1/4s of a cent	Cents and 1/4s of a cent
Tick Size and Value	1/4 of a cent ($12.50)	1/4 of a cent ($12.50)
Delivery Months	March, May, July, September, December	March, May, July, September, December
Margin Limits	Speculator Hedger Initial 540 400 Secondary 400 400	Speculator Hedger Initial 878 650 Secondary 650 650

contracts are traded in U.S. dollars and are listed on the CBOT, CME, LIFFE, and elsewhere. The terms of the CBOT traded corn and wheat futures contracts are shown in Exhibit 6.11.

CURRENCY FUTURES

Currency futures help companies with transactions in more than one currency to establish a fixed exchange rate. Multinational corporations borrow and lend in foreign currencies. Changes in exchange rates can significantly affect borrowing costs, investment income, and projected cash flows. Corporations use currency futures to lower the volatility in cash flows caused by exchange rate fluctuations. Like many contracts, currency futures are rarely held to the delivery date.

The futures price for a currency futures contract is a future exchange rate. Exhibit 6.12 shows the terms of two of the most popular

EXHIBIT 6.12

Terms of Currency Futures Contracts

	Japanese Yen Currency Futures	Euro Currency Futures
Exchange	CME	CME
Size	¥12,500,000	€125,000
Contract Grade	Japanese Yen	Euros
Settlement Procedure	Delivery	Delivery
Price Quotes	1/100 of a cent	1/100 of a cent
Tick Size and Value	1/100 of a cent ($12.50)	1/100 of a cent ($12.50)
Delivery Months	March, June, September, December	March, June, September, December
Margin Limits	Speculator Hedger Initial 1755 1300 Secondary 1300 1300	Speculator Hedger Initial 2498 1850 Secondary 1850 1850

currency futures contracts, the Japanese yen and the euro. Both are listed on the International Money Market division of the Chicago Mercantile Exchange (CME).

CURRENCY FUTURES VALUATION

The value of currency futures is based on the concept of interest rate parity. Under interest rate parity, it is assumed that exchange rates will adjust to equate differentials in interest rates between countries. Therefore, if foreign interest rates are higher than domestic interest rates, any gain received from investing in foreign securities will be lost when the currency is exchanged back in the future. If this relationship does not hold, other things being equal, there will be an arbitrage opportunity.

In this section, we use the following notation:

r_d = annual domestic interest rate

r_f = annual foreign interest rate

n = time-to-maturity of the futures contract in years

m = number of compounding periods per year

Interest rate parity states that the relationship between spot exchange rates and future exchange rates satisfies the following equation:

$$F_0 = S_0 \left(\frac{\left(1 + \frac{r_d}{m}\right)^{mn}}{\left(1 + \frac{r_f}{m}\right)^{mn}} \right)$$

where spot and future exchange rates are expressed as domestic currency per unit of foreign currency. In continuous time, this equation is expressed as

$$F_0 = S_0 e^{(r_d - r_f)n}$$

where r_d and r_f represent continuously compounded risk-free rates of interest.

Example: Consider a euro futures contract with 90 days to maturity. The 90-day interest rate for U.S. dollars is 2.50%, and the 90-day interest rate in euros is 3.50%. The spot exchange rate is $1.10/€. The current Euro futures exchange rate is $1.09725/€, as shown below:

$$F_0 = 1.10 e^{(0.025 - 0.035)0.25} = 1.09725$$

INTEREST RATE FUTURES

Interest rate or financial futures contracts are derived from interest rate contingent instruments or indices. They include contracts on U.S. Treasury bills, notes and bonds, eurodollar notes, interest rate swaps, and municipal bonds. They represent an important set of tools for fixed-income hedgers.

   Interest rate futures provide hedgers with protection against changes in interest rates. A long position provides protection against a decrease in interest rates and a short position provides protection against an increase in interest rates. Although these positions can be replicated in many cases in the cash market, they require an upfront outlay of cash and are less efficient than using the futures market. In the following sections, we discuss the characteristics of interest rate futures. An understanding of these contracts is important for the fixed-income hedging techniques discussed in Chapters 12, 13, and 14.

U.S. TREASURY NOTE AND BOND FUTURES

Futures on U.S. Treasury notes and bonds are structured in a similar manner. Until the U.S. Treasury stopped issuing bonds in 2001, the bond contract was the most popular long-term interest rate futures contract. The U.S. Treasury note futures contract is currently the most liquid long-term interest rate futures contract. The contract specifications for U.S. Treasury notes and bonds are listed in Exhibit 6.13.

U.S. Treasury futures are based on hypothetical note and bond values. For example, the 10-year U.S. Treasury note contract is based on a hypothetical U.S. Treasury note with a 6.00% coupon and exactly 10 years to maturity. Since an exact U.S. Treasury note does not exist, the exchange defines acceptable grades for delivery. For the 10-year note contract, deliverable grades are defined as U.S. Treasury notes with maturities from 6 1/2 years to 10 years, measured from the first day of the delivery month. Any U.S. Treasury note that fits this description can be delivered to fulfill the contract. Because many notes exist at any given time, the instrument that is most profitable to deliver against the futures contract will be delivered. This particular note is referred to as the *cheapest-to-deliver* (CTD).

The concept of cheapest-to-deliver is important for a futures market participant. Because the hypothetical grade of the U.S. Treasury note does not exist, the contract reflects changes in the value of the CTD. Exhibit 6.14 shows the relationship between the delivery price for the December 2003 U.S. Treasury note contract and the CTD between August 1, 2003 and December 4, 2003. The delivery price is the price of the futures contract adjusted for the appropriate conversion factor, as discussed in the next section.[3] The two prices move together, and the basis decreases as the futures contract approaches maturity. For a hedger, this relationship is important since the value of the futures contract tracks the value of the CTD.

CONVERSION FACTORS

Even though it is acceptable to deliver any note within the deliverable grades, the U.S. Treasury note contract is based on a hypothetical note. Therefore the contract requires a conversion from the CTD to the hypothetical 6.00% 10-year note. The contract specifications in Exhibit 6.13 refer to a conversion factor used to equate the price of a note futures contract with the various U.S. Treasury notes eligible for delivery. The

---

3. The CTD over that time period was the 5 3/4 of 8/15/2010.

EXHIBIT 6.13

Terms of U.S. Treasury Note and Bond Contracts

	2-Year U.S. Treasury Notes	5-Year U.S. Treasury Notes	10-Year U.S. Treasury Notes	Long-Term U.S. Treasury Bonds
Exchange	CBOT	CBOT	CBOT	CBOT
Size	$200,000 par value	$100,000 par value	$100,000 par value	$100,000 par value
Contract Grade	U.S. Treasury notes that have an original maturity of not more than 5 years and 3 months and a remaining maturity of not less than 1 year and 9 months from the first day of the calendar month but not more than 2 years from the last day of the calendar month.	U.S. Treasury notes that have an original maturity of not more than 5 years and 3 months and a remaining maturity of not less than 4 years and 3 months as of the first calendar day of the delivery month. The 5-year Treasury note issued after the last trading day of the contract month will not be eligible for delivery into that month's contract.	U.S. Treasury notes maturing at least 6 1/2 years but not more than 10 years from the first calendar day of the delivery month	U.S. Treasury bonds with at least 15 years remaining to maturity if not callable, or to first call if callable, as of the first calendar day of the delivery month
Settlement Procedure	Delivery	Delivery	Delivery	Delivery
Price Quotes	Points and 1/128 of a point	Points and 1/64 of a point	Points and 1/32 of a point	Points and 1/32 of a point
Tick Size and Value	1/128 of a point ($7.8125)	1/64 of a point ($15.625)	1/64 of a point ($15.625)	1/32 of a point ($31.25)
Daily Price Limit	1 point	3 points	3 points	3 points
Delivery Months	March, June, September, December	March, June, September, December	March, June, September, December	March, June, September, December
Margin Limits	Speculator Hedger Initial 1013 750 Secondary 750 750	Speculator Hedger Initial 1350 1000 Secondary 1000 1000	Speculator Hedger Initial 2025 1500 Secondary 1500 1500	Speculator Hedger Initial 3038 2250 Secondary 2250 2250

EXHIBIT 6.14

Relationship between Futures Delivery Price and
Cheapest-to-Deliver Price for a 10-Year U.S. Treasury
Note Contract

conversion factors convert the CTD into a 6.00% 10-year note and are used
to determine the amount of the CTD that must be delivered to make the
two equivalent. Exhibit 6.15 shows the conversion factors for 10 U.S. Treasury notes that qualify as deliverable grades for the December 2003 contract. Notice that the last note, which is the CTD from the previous section, qualifies as CTD only until December 2003, after which it has less
than 6 1/2 months to maturity from the first day of the delivery month.

   In general, we can calculate the conversion factor, CF, with the equation below:

$$
CF = \left(\frac{1}{1 + y/2} \right)^{x/6} \left(\frac{C}{2} + \frac{C}{y} \left[1 - \frac{1}{(1 + y/2)^{2n}} \right] + \frac{1}{(1 + y/2)^{2n}} \right)
$$
$$
- \frac{C}{2} \left(\frac{6 - x}{6} \right)
$$

where n is the number of whole years to maturity and x is the number of
months that the maturity exceeds n, rounded down to the nearest quarter.

EXHIBIT 6.15

10-Year U.S. Treasury Note Futures Contract Conversion Factors

	Coupon	Issue Date	Maturity Date	Issuance (Billions)	6% Conversion Factors					
					Dec. 2003	Mar. 2004	Jun. 2004	Sep. 2004	Dec. 2004	Mar. 2005
1.)	3 5/8	05/15/03	05/15/13	$18.0	0.8332	0.8367	0.8401	0.8437	0.8472	0.8508
2.)	3 7/8	02/18/03	02/15/13	$18.0	0.8539	0.8569	0.8601	0.8632	0.8665	0.8698
3.)	4	11/15/02	11/15/12	$18.0	0.8653	0.8683	0.8713	0.8744	0.8774	0.8806
4.)	4 1/4	08/15/03	08/15/13	$31.0	0.8747	0.8771	0.8797	0.8821	0.8848	0.8873
5.)	4 1/4	11/17/03	11/15/13	$17.0	0.8721	0.8747	0.8771	0.8797	0.8821	0.8848
6.)	4 3/8	08/15/02	08/15/12	$18.0	0.8930	0.8954	0.8979	0.9004	0.9030	0.9055
7.)	4 7/8	02/15/02	02/15/12	$24.0	0.9293	0.9310	0.9328	0.9346	0.9365	0.9382
8.)	5	02/15/01	02/15/11	$20.0	0.9435	0.9451	0.9468	—	—	—
9.)	5	08/15/01	08/15/11	$24.0	0.9403	0.9418	0.9435	0.9451	0.9468	—
10.)	5 3/4	08/15/00	08/15/10	$18.0	0.9867	—	—	—	—	—

Note: This table contains conversion factors for all long-term U.S. Treasury notes eligible for delivery as of November 13, 2003. (The next tentatively scheduled auction is December 11, 2003.)
Source: www.CBOT.com

Example: In the above example the CTD is the 5 3/4 of 8/15/2010. We can calculate the conversion factor for this CTD as of November 13, 2003. As of the valuation date, there are six whole years to maturity ($n = 6$) and approximately nine months ($x = 9$):

$$CF = \left(\frac{1}{1.03}\right)^{9/6}\left(\frac{0.0575}{2} + \frac{0.0575}{0.06}\left[1 - \frac{1}{(1.03)^{12}}\right] + \frac{1}{(1.03)^{12}}\right)$$
$$- \frac{0.0575}{2}\left(\frac{6-9}{6}\right)$$

$$CF = (0.95663)(0.02875 + 0.2862 + 0.7014) + (0.0144)$$

$$CF = 0.9867$$

CALCULATING CHEAPEST-TO-DELIVER

The conversion factors explained in the previous section are used to determine the quantity of a particular bond or note necessary to meet the delivery requirements of a contract. The reciprocal of the conversion factor determines the number of bonds or notes that must be delivered per futures contract. Therefore, if the conversion factor is greater than one, the contract requires the delivery of a number of bonds or notes that is lower than the number of contracts. If the conversion factor is less than one, more bonds or notes must be delivered. As an example, assume a hedger sells 10 futures contracts on the 10-year U.S. Treasury note. This transaction requires the delivery of an equivalent note value of $1,000,000 in 6.00% 10-year U.S. Treasury notes. Using the deliverable grades and conversion factors from Exhibit 6.15, we can determine which of the bonds is the cheapest to deliver. Assuming P is the spot price of the U.S. Treasury note, the cost of delivering notes can be calculated as

Delivery Cost = (Number of Futures Contracts)(Size per Contract)$(1/CF)(P)$.

In Exhibit 6.16, delivery cost is calculated for each of the deliverable grades for the 10-year U.S. Treasury note contract as of November 13, 2003. The last entry, the 5 3/4 note due August 15, 2010, has the highest bond price but the lowest conversion factor and delivery cost. This particular note is the cheapest-to-deliver.

EXHIBIT 6.16

Calculation of Cheapest-to-Deliver for a $1,000,000 10-Year
U.S. Treasury Note Futures Contract

	Coupon	Maturity Date	Conversion Factor (CF)	1/CF	Approximate Note Price	Delivery Cost
1.)	3 5/8	05/15/13	0.8332	1.2002	97.05867	$1,164,890.48
2.)	3 7/8	02/15/13	0.8539	1.1711	99.03617	$1,159,809.94
3.)	4	11/15/12	0.8653	1.1557	99.99978	$1,155,666.03
4.)	4 1/4	08/15/13	0.8747	1.1432	101.9978	$1,166,088.42
5.)	4 1/4	11/15/13	0.8721	1.1467	102.0446	$1,170,102.31
6.)	4 3/8	08/15/12	0.8930	1.1198	102.7417	$1,150,523.38
7.)	4 7/8	02/15/12	0.9293	1.0761	106.0947	$1,141,662.38
8.)	5	02/15/11	0.9435	1.0599	106.2377	$1,125,996.19
9.)	5	08/15/11	0.9403	1.0635	106.6055	$1,133,739.30
10.)	5 3/4	08/15/10	0.9867	1.0135	110.2633	$1,117,495.63

Note: This exhibit contains conversion factors for all long-term U.S. Treasury notes eligible for delivery as of
November 13, 2003. The cost to deliver is equal to $1,000,000(1/CF)(*P*).
Source: www.CBOT.com.

INTEREST RATE FUTURES VALUATION

Many factors affect the price of an interest rate futures contract. Relative
levels of financing costs and the yield on the underlying bonds have an effect on the value of a futures contract. Earlier in the chapter we introduced
the concept of cost-of-carry. The price is also affected by the right to
choose which bond to deliver, or the *deliverability option*. We represent the
price of the contract based on these three valuation components: funding
costs, cash flow on the underlying bonds, and the deliverability option.

Consider the following example illustrating the cost-of-carry relationship for interest rate futures. A bank buys a $100 million block of the
cheapest-to-deliver on the 10-year U.S. Treasury note for 110.263 and finances the notes in the market at the prevailing repo rate.[4] Simultaneously, the bank sells 1,000 10-year U.S. Treasury note futures contracts
that expire in three months. The cash flows on this transaction are shown
in Exhibit 6.17.

---

4. Repo rate is the rate on a repurchase agreement which involves the commitment to sell
and then repurchase a specific bond issue.

EXHIBIT 6.17

Example Cash Flows on an Interest Rate
Futures Transaction

At Settlement		At Expiration	
Action	**Cash Flows**	**Action**	**Cash Flows**
Purchase Bonds	$-P_d$	Sell Bonds	$P_c + AI + C \sum\limits_{t=0}^{mn-1} \left(1 + \dfrac{r}{m}\right)^t$
Borrow Bond Price	P_d	Pay Back Loan	$-P_d\left(1 + \dfrac{r}{m}\right)^{mn}$
Sell Futures	0	Cover Futures	$F_0 - P_c$
Total	0	Total	$F_0 - P_d\left(1 + \dfrac{r}{m}\right)^{mn}$
			$+ AI + C \sum\limits_{t=0}^{mn-1} \left(1 + \dfrac{r}{m}\right)^t$

Initially the bank pays the dirty bond price, P_d, for the bonds and borrows an equal amount in the repo market at the prevailing repo rate r.[5] Over the holding period, the bank will receive coupon payments C, which are reinvested. At maturity in three months, the bank sells the bonds and repays the principal and interest on the borrowed funds. The bank receives three months of accrued interest (AI) when it sells the bonds. Given these expected cash flows adjusted for the conversion factor (CF) and including the value of the deliverability option, (DO) the value of the futures contract can be formulated as follows:

$$F_0 = \frac{P_d + \left\langle P_d(1 + \tfrac{r}{m})^{mn} - P_d \right\rangle - \left\langle AI + C \sum\limits_{t=0}^{mn-1} (1 + \tfrac{r}{m})^t \right\rangle}{CF} - DO$$

---

5. Recall from Chapter 4 that the dirty price of a bond includes accrued interest.

Since the future value of the coupons is equal to the present value of the coupons times $(1 + r/m)^{mn}$, the equation above can be simplified as follows:

$$F_0 = \frac{\left(P_\mathrm{d} - \left(c\sum_{t=1}^{mn} \frac{1}{\left(1 + \frac{r}{m}\right)^t} - \frac{\mathrm{AI}}{\left(1 + \frac{r}{m}\right)^{mn}}\right)\right)\left(1 + \frac{r}{m}\right)^{mn}}{\mathrm{CF}}$$

This pricing is typically expressed in continuous time. Since the bond pays a constant yield y, we can use the annual coupon payment relative to the bond price to represent a continuous cash flow to the investor. Therefore, the continuous time pricing model is simply

$$F_0 = \frac{P_\mathrm{d}e^{(r-y)n}}{\mathrm{CF}} - \mathrm{DO}$$

Example: Consider the cheapest-to-deliver from the example above with a current price of 110.263 and a coupon of 5 3/4%. The 10-year U.S. Treasury note futures contract has 90 days to maturity, and the 90-day repo rate is 3.00%. The annual coupon on the bond is 5 3/4%, and therefore y equals (0.0575)/1.10263 or 0.052148. If we assume the value of the delivery option is zero, the price of the futures contract is 110.855, as shown below:

$$F_0 = \frac{110.263e^{(0.02-0.052148)\frac{90}{360}}}{0.9867} = 110.85$$

DURATION

The values of a U.S. Treasury note or bond contract closely follow the values of the CTD. Therefore, for a particular contract, the volatility of the contract is determined by the price movements of the CTD. As discussed in Chapter 4, modified duration is used as a measure of price volatility. The modified duration of the futures contract D_{futures} is equal to the modified duration of the CTD, D_{CTD}, adjusted for the appropriate conversion factor, CF:

$$D_{\text{futures}} = \frac{D_{\text{CTD}}}{\mathrm{CF}}$$

Example: The CTD for the current 10-year U.S. Treasury futures contract is the 5 3/4 of August 15, 2010. The conversion factor we calculated earlier is 0.9867. If the current yield on the CTD is 4.00%, then the dollar price is 110.263 as of November 13, 2003. The modified duration of the CTD is 5.571. Therefore, the modified duration of the futures contract is

$$D_{futures} = \frac{5.571}{0.9867} = 5.646$$

THE EURODOLLAR FUTURES CONTRACT

Eurodollars are U.S. dollars deposited abroad. The eurodollar futures contract, which trades on the Chicago Mercantile Exchange, is one of the most popular short-term interest rate futures contracts. The eurodollar futures contract was designed as a proxy for changes in future short-term interest rates. It is based on the three-month eurodollar deposit rate. Since the underlying asset is a time deposit and not a security, the contract has cash settlement. These contracts are popular with market participants in the interest rate swap market who need to hedge the short end of the yield curve. They are also used by corporate treasurers and bank risk managers to control short-term interest rate risk.

Each eurodollars future contract has a face value of $1,000,000. Since it is a three-month contract, a one-point change in the value of the contract is worth $(1/4)(0.01)(\$1,000,000)$ or $2,500. The futures price is equal to 100% minus the annualized yield for a three-month eurodollar time deposit. For example, if the three-month eurodollar time deposit rate is 3.05%, the futures price would be approximately equal to $(100\% - 3.05\%)$ or 96.95%. As eurodollar deposit rates rise, the futures price declines. Exhibit 6.18 shows the terms for the eurodollar contract traded on the Chicago Mercantile Exchange.

MUNICIPAL FUTURES

The municipal market comprises thousands of bond issuers with varying credit ratings and sources of revenues. Interest on municipal bonds is generally exempt from federal and state taxes. Because of the tax exemption, the municipal market behaves differently than other taxable fixed-income markets. For this reason, traditional fixed-income hedges, such as U.S. Treasury futures, have proved to be a poor hedge for municipal bonds.

EXHIBIT 6.18

Terms of Eurodollar Futures Contract

Name	90-day Eurodollar Futures
Exchange	CME
Size	$1,000,000
Contract Grade	Eurodollar Time Deposit with a principal value of $1,000,000 with a three-month maturity. Prices quoted in terms of the IMM Three-month Eurodollar Index, 100 minus the yield on an annual basis for a 360-day year.
Settlement Procedure	Cash Settlement
Price Quotes	100 – yield
Tick Size and Value	0.005 of one point ($12.50)
Delivery Months	March, June, September, December

Margin Limits		Speculator	Hedger
	Initial	1080	800
	Secondary	800	800

The task of creating a contract that reflects changes in the value of the spot municipal market has been difficult for the exchanges. The original municipal futures contract was introduced in 1985. It was cash settled based on movements in the Bond Buyer 40 index (BB-40), a long-term municipal bond index created for the futures contract. The BB-40 is composed of 40 long-term general obligation and revenue bonds.[6] Although the contract was traded for many years, open interest and liquidity decreased dramatically over time because the contract did not adequately follow movements in the spot municipal market.

In March 2003, the CBOT introduced the 10-year municipal note index futures contract and eliminated the municipal bond futures contract. The new contract is based on the value of a synthetic 10-year municipal note with a par value of $100,000 that pays a fixed, semiannual coupon of 5.00%. The value of the hypothetical municipal note is based on a municipal index established for the contract. The index is composed of 100 to 250 municipal bonds. Eligible bonds have a minimum term size

---

6. Eligible bonds have a minimum term size of $50 million; an A rating or better by Moody's and an A– rating or better by Standard and Poor's; a remaining maturity of at least 19 years; at least seven years to first call date, if callable; an original issue price of between 85 and 105; and a fixed, semiannual coupon payment.

of $50 million from a municipal issuance that has a deal size of at least $200 million; a AAA rating by both Moody's and Standard and Poor's; a remaining maturity between 10 and 40 years; at least seven years to first call date, if callable; an original issue price of at least 90; and a fixed, semiannual coupon between 3.00% and 9.00%. The purpose of the expansion in the index was to track movements in the municipal spot market. The initial indication of the popularity of the new contract is favorable. Exhibit 6.19 describes the terms of the current municipal note index contract.

The cash settlement value is based on the value of a hypothetical 10-year municipal note with a 5.00% coupon. The yield on the hypothetical bond is measured by the average yield of the component bonds in the index. For a $100,000 contract, the cash settlement value is equal to

$$\text{Settlement Value} = \$100,000 \left[\frac{5}{r} + \left(1 - \frac{5}{r}\right)\left(1 + \frac{r}{200}\right)^{-20} \right]$$

where r represents the simple average yield-to-worst of the component bonds in the index for the last day of trading, expressed in percentage terms.[7] For example, if r equals 6.00%, the settlement value is

$$\text{Settlement Value} = \$100,000 \left[\frac{5}{6} + \left(1 - \frac{5}{6}\right)\left(1 + \frac{6}{200}\right)^{-20} \right] = \$92,561.26$$

DURATION

The duration of the municipal contract is equal to the duration of the hypothetical 10-year municipal note. The underlying note has a coupon of 5.00% and a yield equal to the average yield of the component bonds in the index. The price and duration of the municipal contract are easy to calculate, given the average yield on the index. For example, if the yield on the municipal note contract is 6.00%, the contract price is 92.561 and the modified duration is 7.665. Because the contract is based on a static coupon and maturity, the duration is affected only by changes in yield.

---

7. Previously, we use y to represent yield. In our discussion of municipal futures and swap futures, we use r to represent yield because it is consistent with the definition used by the CBOT.

EXHIBIT 6.19

Terms of a 10-Year Municipal Note Index Futures Contract

Name	10-Year Municipal Note Index Contract
Exchange	CBOT
Size	$100,000
Contract Grade	The notional price of a synthetic 10-year municipal note with a par value equal to $100,000 and paying a fixed, semiannual coupon of 5% based upon the Index.
	The Index is composed of 100 to 250 municipal bonds that are generally exempt from federal income taxation. Eligible bonds have a minimum term size of $50 million and are a component tranche of a municipal issuance that has a deal size of at least $200 million; a AAA rating by both Moody's and S&P; a remaining maturity between 10 and 40 years; at least seven years to first call date, if callable; an original issue price of at least 90; and a fixed, semiannual coupon between 3% and 9%. There are issuer, state, and insurer limits of 5, 15, and 40 percent, respectively.
Settlement Procedure	Cash settlement.
	The final settlement value is determined as:

$$\$100{,}000\left[\frac{5}{r} + \left(1 - \frac{5}{r}\right)\left(1 + \frac{r}{200}\right)^{-20}\right]$$

	where r represents the simple average yield-to-worst of the component bonds in the Index for the last day of trading, expressed in percentage terms. For example, if the simple average yield-to-worst for the last day of trading is 5 1/4%, then r is equal to 5.25. Bonds whose overnight price change exceeds one standard deviation of the mean Index bond change will be eliminated for final cash settlement calculations. The contract expiration price will be the final settlement value rounded to the nearest 1/32 of one point. FT Interactive Data Corporation shall calculate the final settlement value.
Price Quotes	Points and 32nds of a point
Tick Size and Value	1/32 of a point ($31.25)
Delivery Months	March, June, September, December

Margin Limits		Speculator	Hedger
	Initial	1485	1100
	Secondary	1100	1100

MUNICIPAL TO TREASURY BASIS

Basis is typically defined as the difference between spot prices and futures prices. The relationship between municipal bonds and U.S. Treasury bonds, sometimes called *municipal basis,* is important to municipal market participants. Municipal basis measures the spread between the tax-exempt and taxable markets. Although the municipal basis is constantly monitored in the cash market, it can be more effectively traded in the futures market as a *spread trade.* A spread trade consists of simultaneously buying one futures contract, such as the municipal note contract, and selling another contract, such as the U.S. Treasury note contract.

Under the old contract specification, the value of the contract was based on the 40 long-term bonds in the BB-40. Because the contract was a municipal bond contract, it was common to compare the level of the contract to that of the U.S. Treasury bond contract. The difference in the price of the two contracts in ticks was referred to as the *municipal-over-bond or MOB spread.* Since the introduction of the municipal note contract, a more relevant comparison is to the U.S. Treasury 10-year note contract. The difference between the two contracts is referred to as the *municipal-under-Treasury spread* or the *MUT spread.* Specifically, the MUT spread is equal to the price of the 10-year Treasury note futures contract minus the price of the 10-year municipal note index futures contract, in ticks. One tick is equal to 1/32 of a point on either contract.

Example: Assume the price of the nearest 10-year Treasury note futures contract is 112 2/32, and the price of the nearest 10-year municipal note index futures contract is 102 10/32. The difference in prices is equal to 112 2/32 minus 102 10/32 or 9 24/32. Therefore, the MUT spread in ticks is equal to 312.

The MUT spread can be used to hedge or speculate against changes in the relative values of tax-exempt and taxable notes. During periods of heavy municipal issuance, for example, market participants expect yields on municipal bonds to increase relative to U.S. Treasury yields. If U.S. Treasuries outperform municipal bonds, this will act to widen the MUT spread. If the MUT spread is expected to widen, a spread trader will buy the spread. This is accomplished by buying the municipal note contract and selling the U.S. Treasury note contract. If the MUT spread is expected to narrow, a spread trader will sell the spread. This is accomplished by selling the municipal note contract and buying the U.S. Treasury note contract. A true spread trade will not be accomplished with a one-to-one ratio of contracts. The number of contracts purchased or sold in each market is determined by the relative durations of the contracts.

SWAP FUTURES

The 10-year and five-year swap futures contracts were introduced by the Chicago Board of Trade in 2001 and 2002, respectively. The contracts have increased in popularity, with recent open interest in the 10-year swap futures reaching almost 40,000 contracts. Swap futures are an important tool for fixed-income market participants. Historically swap market yields have been highly correlated with municipal and corporate bond yields. The swap futures market allows hedgers to capitalize on the relationship between swaps and other markets without the burden and illiquidity of entering into an interest rate swap.

Ten-year swap futures are based on the price of a 10-year interest rate swap with a notional principal amount equal to $100,000. The underlying swap exchanges semiannual interest payments at a fixed rate of 6.00% per annum for floating interest rate payments based on three-month LIBOR. Exhibit 6.20 lists the details of the five-year and 10-year swap futures contracts. The pricing and hedging parameters of the swap contract are derived from the underlying interest rate swap. We discuss these concepts in detail in Chapter 7.

The cash value is based on the value of a hypothetical 10-year swap with a 6.00% coupon. The yield on the hypothetical swap is measured by using the average yield of the component bonds in the index. Per $100,000 contract, the cash settlement value equals

$$\text{Cash Settlement Value} = \$100,000\left[\left(\frac{6}{r}\right) + \left(1 - \frac{6}{r}\right)\left(1 + 0.01\frac{r}{2}\right)^{-20}\right],$$

where r represents the simple average yield-to-worst of the component swaps in the index for the last day of trading. For example, if r equals 3.00%, the settlement value is

$$\text{Cash Settlement Value} = \$100,000\left[\left(\frac{6}{3}\right) + \left(1 - \frac{6}{3}\right)\left(1 + 0.01\frac{3}{2}\right)^{-20}\right]$$

$$= \$125,752.96$$

EXHIBIT 6.20

Terms of Swap Futures Contracts

Name	5-Year Swap Futures	10-Year Swap Futures
Exchange	CBOT	CBOT
Size	$100,000	$100,000
Contract Grade	The Five-Year Swap Futures is based on the notional price of a five-year interest rate swap that has notional principal equal to $100,000 and that exchanges semiannual interest payments at a fixed rate of 6% per annum for floating interest rate payments based on three-month LIBOR.	The 10-Year Swap Futures is based on the notional price of a 10-year interest rate swap that has notional principal equal to $100,000 and that exchanges semiannual interest payments at a fixed rate of 6% per annum for floating interest rate payments based on three-month LIBOR.
Settlement Procedure	Cash settlement.	Cash settlement.
	The final settlement value will be determined as	The final settlement value will be determined as
	$$\$100,000\left[\left(\frac{6}{r}\right)+\left(1-\frac{6}{r}\right)\left(1+0.01\frac{r}{2}\right)^{-10}\right]$$	$$\$100,000\left[\left(\frac{6}{r}\right)+\left(1-\frac{6}{r}\right)\left(1+0.01\frac{r}{2}\right)^{-20}\right]$$
	where r represents the ISDA Benchmark Rate for a five-year U.S. dollar interest rate swap on the last day of trading, expressed in percentage terms. For example, if the ISDA Benchmark Rate were 5 1/4%, then r would be 5.25. The contract expiration price is the final settlement value rounded to the nearest one-quarter of 1/32 of one point.	where r represents the ISDA Benchmark Rate for a 10-year U.S. dollar interest rate swap on the last day of trading, expressed in percentage terms. For example, if the ISDA Benchmark Rate were 5 1/4%, then r would be 5.25. The contract expiration price is the final settlement value rounded to the nearest one-quarter of 1/32 of one point.
Price Quotes	Points and 32nds of a point	Points and 32nds of a point
Tick Size and Value	1/32 of a point ($31.25)	1/32 of a point ($31.25)
Delivery Months	March, June, September, December	March, June, September, December
Margin Limits	Speculator Hedger	Speculator Hedger
	Initial 1485 1100	Initial 2363 1750
	Secondary 1100 1100	Secondary 1750 1750

EQUITY FUTURES

Stock index futures are based on the value of equity indices. They are an effective way for hedgers to take a long or short position in the stock market. Stock index futures have cash settlement and are sized for institutional market participants. The S&P 500 futures contract has a contract size of $250 times the index. If the S&P 500 index is at 1,000, for example, the contract size is $250,000. The contract specifications for three popular stock index futures contracts are displayed in Exhibit 6.21.

EQUITY FUTURES VALUATION

As we discussed earlier in the chapter, a long equity position can be constructed by borrowing money and buying the underlying index. This position involves two sets of cash flows: a financing or opportunity cost and a dividend payment. The cost-of-carry on a futures contract where the underlying asset pays dividends depends on the relationship between the dividend yield and the cost of funding. Specifically, the cost-of-carry is equal to funding costs minus dividend income. A basic valuation model is

EXHIBIT 6.21

Terms of Equity Futures Contracts

Name	S&P 500 Futures	NASDAQ 100 Futures	NASDAQ 100 E-mini Futures
Exchange	CME	CME	CME
Size	250 times index	100 times index	20 times index
Contract Grade	The value of the S&P 500 index	The value of the NASDAQ 100 index	The value of the NASDAQ 100 index
Settlement Procedure	Cash Settlement	Cash Settlement	Cash Settlement
Price Quotes	Points and 1/10 points	Points and 1/2 points	Points and 1/2 points
Tick Size and Value	1/10 of a point ($25)	1/2 point ($50)	1/2 point ($10)
Delivery Months	March, June, September, December	March, June, September, December	March, June, September, December
Margin Limits	Speculator Hedger Initial 20000 16000 Secondary 16000 16000	Speculator Hedger Initial 18750 15000 Secondary 15000 15000	Speculator Hedger Initial 3750 3000 Secondary 3000 3000

developed based on this relationship. The price of the contract is equal to the spot price of the index grossed up by funding costs at the risk-free rate r less dividends received over the time period. Assuming the index currently pays a dividend of DIV_0, we can specify the fair value of an equity futures contract as follows:

$$F_0 = S_0 + \left\langle S_0(1 + \tfrac{r}{m})^{mn} - S_0 \right\rangle - \left\langle \text{DIV}_0 \sum_{t=0}^{mn-1} (1 + \tfrac{r}{m})^t \right\rangle$$

Notice that the basic valuation is a restatement of the cost-of-carry relationship. The first bracketed term represents the future value of funding costs, and the second bracketed term represents the future value of dividend payments. Since the future value of the dividends is equal to the present value of the dividends times $(1 + r/m)^{mn}$, the above equation can be simplified as

$$F_0 = \left(S_0 - \text{DIV}_0 \sum_{t=1}^{mn} \frac{1}{(1 + \tfrac{r}{m})^t} \right)(1 + \tfrac{r}{m})^{mn}$$

Dividend payments are often represented in continuous time. Although we cannot predict dividend payments on an equity index, we can assume that yields are constant and continuous.[8] We can represent the current dividend yield d as the ratio of the current dividend to the spot price, DIV_0/S_0. With this assumption, the equation above can be rewritten in continuous time as

$$F_0 = S_0 e^{(r-d)n}$$

Example: Suppose the S&P 500 index is currently at 1109.00. The continuously compounded risk-free rate is 4.00% per year, and the dividend yield is 2.00% per year. The maturity is equal to 0.25 years. Therefore, the futures price is

$$F_0 = 1109 e^{(0.04-0.02)0.25} = 1114.56$$

---

8. In reality dividends arrive at quarterly intervals based on each underlying firm's fiscal year. This will cause periodic inaccuracy when assuming continuous dividend payments.

SUMMARY

A futures contract is an agreement to exchange cash flows based on a predetermined purchase or sale price of an asset at a specified time in the future. Futures require a daily mark-to-market of positions. This effectively removes counterparty risk for market participants.

Futures were initially developed for the agricultural market but have grown to include many different commodities and financial instruments. The exchanges are continuously developing new contracts and eliminating outdated contracts. The CBOT recently introduced a new municipal note index futures contract, replacing the municipal bond contract that had been traded for more than 17 years, and two swap futures contracts. Meeting the needs of hedgers and speculators is an ongoing process in the futures market.

In this chapter, we discussed the structure and use of the futures markets. We reviewed the contract specification of the major contracts in the commodity, fixed-income, and equity markets. We discussed the cost-of-carry relationship between futures and spot prices and pricing models for futures contracts. An understanding of the pricing and mechanics of the futures market is important for effective hedging.

REFERENCES

Burghardt, Galen, Terrence Belton, Morton Lane, and John Papa. *The Treasury Bond Basis*. Chicago: Irwin, 1994.

Madura, Jeff. *International Financial Management*, 7th Ed. Cincinnati: Southwestern, 2003.

Stoll, Hans, and Robert Whaley. *Futures and Options: Theory and Applications*. Cincinnati: Southwestern, 1993.

Strong, Robert. *Derivatives: An Introduction*. Cincinnati: Southwestern, 2002.

CHAPTER 7

Swaps

The swap market is one of the largest and fastest growing derivative markets. According to a survey performed by the International Swaps and Derivatives Association, Inc. (ISDA), the outstanding volume of interest rate derivatives was $123.90 trillion as of mid-year 2003.[1] This was an increase of 21% from year-end 2002. In the survey, a total of 110 major swap market participants provided data on interest rate derivatives.

Swaps are over-the-counter transactions that are structured based on standard agreements established by the ISDA. Unlike exchange-traded derivatives, swaps have *counterparty risk*—the risk that one of the parties will fail to perform under the contract. Although counterparty risk is an important consideration, it can be managed through the diversification of counterparties. Overall, the swap market functions efficiently.

In this chapter, we describe the most popular swap contracts. We begin by describing interest rate swaps and cross-currency swaps. We explain swap contract structure, pricing, and volatility. We then describe other swap contracts, which include equity swaps, basis swaps, credit default swaps, and total rate of return swaps. All of these contracts are important to hedgers and are an integral part of the chapters on applied hedging that follow.

---

1. This includes interest rate swaps and options and cross-currency swaps.

VANILLA INTEREST RATE SWAPS

A *plain vanilla* interest rate swap is a contract under which two counter-parties, a floating-rate payer and a fixed-rate payer, agree to exchange net payments at a series of future points in time. A notional principal amount is used to calculate the amount of the net payments. An interest rate swap can have a maturity or *tenor* in excess of 30 years.

The fixed swap rate is set on the pricing date of the swap. The floating rate is established for the first payment based on market levels on the pricing date and reset periodically based on market levels. The floating rate on a plain vanilla swap is based on three-month LIBOR. Common floating-rate benchmarks include the commercial paper rate, the U.S. Treasury-bill rate, and one-month LIBOR.

SWAP QUOTES

Interest rate swaps are typically quoted in terms of the fixed swap rate. Quotes are given for the bid and ask sides of the market and mid market. The *bid* side of the market is the rate at which a counterparty is willing to pay the fixed rate and receive the floating rate. The *ask* side of the market is the level at which a counterparty is willing to receive the fixed rate and pay the floating rate. The bid–ask spread represents the potential profit for a swap dealer. Swaps are not always priced exactly on the bid or ask side of the market. Generally the fixed rate falls between the bid and ask rates.

Rates are also quoted in terms of a spread to U.S. Treasury cash rates. This is a market convention that holds in the corporate bond market and interest rate swap market. Exhibit 7.1 represents a typical quote page for closing swap rates as of December 22, 2003. The swap rates assume semiannual payments and the maturities as given.

Example: Consider a hedger who enters into a five-year swap and agrees to pay the fixed rate shown in Exhibit 7.1. The hedger pays fixed at 3.6140%, which is 41.75 basis points above the U.S. Treasury spot rate of 3.1965%. If instead the hedger wants to pay floating and receive fixed, the fixed swap rate is 3.574% or 39.75 basis points above the U.S. Treasury note spot rate of 3.0765%.

EXHIBIT 7.1

Example Quote Page for Interest Rate Swaps

	Bid		Ask		Mid	
Swap Tenor	Quote	Spread	Quote	Spread	Quote	Spread
2 yr	2.1600	35.75	2.2000	37.75	2.1800	36.75
3 yr	2.7490	43.25	2.7890	45.25	2.7690	44.25
4 yr	3.2070	46.00	3.2470	48.00	3.2270	47.00
5 yr	3.5740	39.75	3.6140	41.75	3.5940	40.75
6 yr	3.8480	47.50	3.8880	49.50	3.8680	48.50
7 yr	4.0660	49.50	4.1060	51.50	4.0860	50.50
8 yr	4.2490	48.00	4.2890	50.00	4.2690	49.00
9 yr	4.4020	45.50	4.4420	47.50	4.4220	46.50
10 yr	4.5380	38.00	4.5780	40.00	4.5580	39.00
15 yr	4.9880	63.00	5.0280	65.00	5.0080	64.00
20 yr	5.1880	62.75	5.2280	64.75	5.2080	63.75
30 yr	5.2660	30.00	5.3060	32.00	5.2860	31.00

Source: Bloomberg, December 22, 2003.

SWAP PAYMENTS

Interest rate swaps require periodic interest payments. The payments may be made monthly, quarterly, or semiannually on a net basis. The fixed payment is the fixed rate times the notional amount adjusted for the number of days in the period. The floating payment is equal to the average of the floating-rate index over the payment period times the notional amount adjusted for the number of days in the time period. In general, the fixed payment is based on a 30/360 day basis. We refer to this in notation as *days*(360). The floating payment is based on the actual number of days in the time period. The formulas for the fixed-rate and floating-rate payments are

$$\text{Fixed Payment} = \left(\begin{array}{c}\text{Notional} \\ \text{Amount}\end{array}\right) \times \left(\text{days}(360)/360\right) \times \left(\begin{array}{c}\text{Fixed} \\ \text{Rate}\end{array}\right)$$

$$\text{Floating Payment} = \left(\begin{array}{c}\text{Notional} \\ \text{Amount}\end{array}\right) \times \left(\text{days}/(365\,\text{or}\,366)\right) \times \left(\begin{array}{c}\text{Floating} \\ \text{Rate Index}\end{array}\right)$$

The net payment at the end of a time period is equal to the difference between the fixed payment and the floating payment. One party is a net payer in each period and one party is a net receiver.

Example: Consider a 10-year swap with a fixed rate of 4.50% and a floating rate equal to three-month LIBOR. Assume the swap makes semiannual payments in arrears based on the average of three-month LIBOR over the previous six months. The six-month period has 182 days and 180 *days* (360). The swap has a notional amount of $10 million. If three-month LIBOR averaged 2.50% over the six-month time period, the fixed, floating, and net payments would be calculated as

$$\text{Fixed Payment} = (\$10{,}000{,}000) \times (180/360) \times (4.50\%) = \$225{,}000.00$$
$$\text{Floating Payment} = (\$10{,}000{,}000) \times (182/365) \times (2.50\%) = \$124{,}657.53$$
$$\text{Net Payment} = (\$225{,}000.00) - (\$124{,}657.53) = \$100{,}342.47$$

HEDGING EXAMPLES

Swaps are an important tool for hedgers. In the interest rate market there are many types of synthetic interest rate swaps. For example, commercial banks exchange floating and fixed payments when they issue floating-rate mortgages and fund them with time deposits. Corporations create synthetic swaps when they finance securities in the floating-rate market. Swaps allow hedgers to replicate these cash flows. Since swaps are structured in the over-the-counter market, they can be constructed to match any set of expected cash flows.

Short Hedge Example

A corporation that buys a Treasury bond will receive a fixed coupon payment. If the purchase is financed in the short-term floating-rate market, the combined transactions represent a synthetic swap for the corporation. Under the synthetic swap, the corporation receives a fixed rate and pays a floating rate, such as three-month LIBOR. To hedge this transaction, the corporation can enter into an interest rate swap under which it pays the fixed swap rate and receives three-month LIBOR. The cash flows are shown in Exhibit 7.2.

Cash Flows on a Short Hedge with an Interest Rate Swap

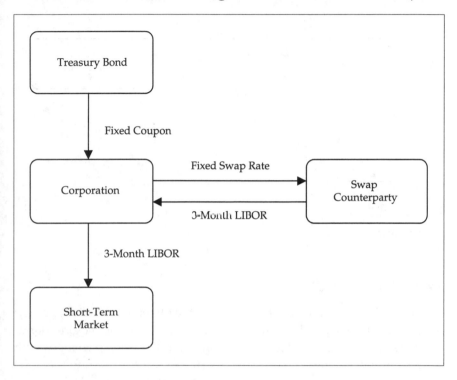

Long Hedge Example

Consider a corporation that issued fixed-rate bonds several years ago. The CFO has decided that the corporation needs additional floating-rate exposure and believes that short-term interest rates will remain below the current fixed rate on the bonds in the future. Using an interest rate swap, the corporation can synthetically change the fixed-rate bonds into floating-rate bonds. Assume the fixed-rate bonds were issued at par and pay interest at 8.00% semiannually. The bonds mature in 10 years. The current 10-year fixed versus three-month LIBOR swap rate is 6.00%. The corporation can match the timing of the cash flows. In this scenario, the corporation will pay the floating rate and receive the 6.00% fixed rate. The net result is a synthetic floating-rate bond where the corporation pays LIBOR + 2.00%. The cash flows are shown in Exhibit 7.3.

EXHIBIT 7.3

Cash Flows for a Long Hedge with an Interest Rate Swap

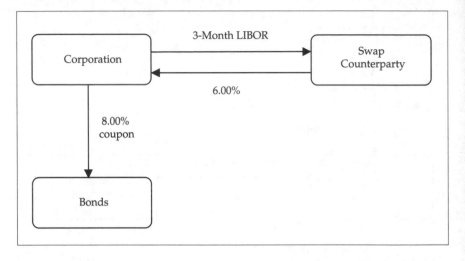

SWAP VALUATION

In a swap, the fixed-rate payer is said to be the buyer and the floating-rate payer is said to be the seller; however, from an economic or hedging standpoint the opposite is true. The value of an interest rate swap changes with changes in interest rates. For the fixed-rate payer (floating-rate receiver) the value of the swap increases when interest rates increase. This is similar to the relationship between short interest rate futures and interest rates. For the floating-rate payer (fixed-rate receiver) the value of the swap increases when interest rates decrease. This is similar to the relationship between long interest rate futures and interest rates. Exhibit 7.4 shows the change in the value of a swap relative to changes in interest rates.

Valuation models typically begin the construction of a yield curve by following the process described in Chapter 5. In this section, we begin with a simple valuation model for interest rate swaps. Recall that the value of a fixed rate bond is equal to the present value of the expected future cash flows discounted at the market yield. Similarly, the value of the fixed leg of an interest rate swap, PV_{fixed}, is equal to the present value of the fixed payments,

$$PV_{fixed} = \sum_{t=1}^{mn} \frac{\dfrac{C}{m}}{\left(1 + \dfrac{r_t}{m}\right)^t}$$

EXHIBIT 7.4

Value of an Interest Swap Contract

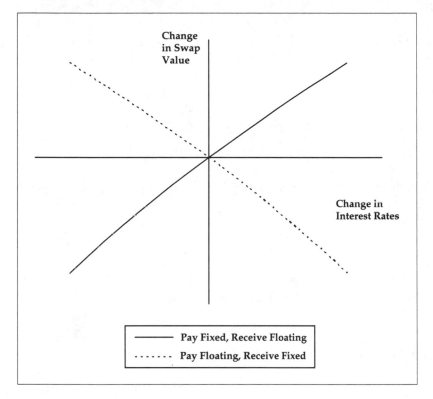

where C is the fixed annual swap payment and r_t is the discount rate at time t.

The floating leg of the swap is similar to a floating-rate bond that pays no principal. Recall that a floating-rate bond always sells for its face value because the coupon payments adjust to market rates in each time period. The price of a floating-rate bond P is equal to the present value of its expected cash flows. If we define I_t as the expected floating coupon at time t, then the value of a floating-rate bond with face value F is equal to

$$P = \sum_{t=1}^{mn} \frac{\dfrac{I_t}{m}}{\left(1 + \dfrac{r_t}{m}\right)^t} + \frac{F}{\left(1 + \dfrac{r_{mn}}{m}\right)^{mn}}$$

The only unknowns in the pricing formula are the expected floating-rate payments in each time period I_t. Since interest rate swaps do not require the payment of principal, the first term on the right side of the equation is the value of the floating-rate leg of the swap. If we rearrange the equation above and replace P with F (since the bond always sells for its face value), the pricing formula can be expressed as

$$F - \frac{F}{\left(1 + \frac{r_{mn}}{m}\right)^{mn}} = \sum_{t=1}^{mn} \frac{\frac{I_t}{m}}{\left(1 + \frac{r_t}{m}\right)^t}$$

Therefore, the value of the floating leg of the swap, $PV_{floating}$, is equal to

$$PV_{floating} = F - \frac{F}{\left(1 + \frac{r_{mn}}{m}\right)^{mn}}$$

The value of the swap for the fixed-rate payer V_{fixed} is

$$V_{fixed} = PV_{floating} - PV_{fixed}$$

and the value of the swap for the floating-rate payer $V_{floating}$ is

$$V_{floating} = PV_{fixed} - PV_{floating}$$

Example: A $10,000,000 interest rate swap has semiannual payments based on average three-month LIBOR. The swap matures in five years and has a fixed payment rate of 4.00%. The value of the swap for both the fixed-rate and floating-rate payers can be calculated from the zero-coupon discount rates in Exhibit 7.5. DF refers to the discount factor and is calculated as $1/(1 + r_r / 2)^t$.

We begin by calculating the value of the fixed leg of the swap as shown in Exhibit 7.6. The semiannual payment is $10,000,000(0.04)(1/2)$ or $200,000. Therefore, the value of the fixed leg is the present value of the stream of $200,000 payments, which is equal to $1,809,445.

From the equation derived above, the value of the floating leg of the swap is

$$PV_{floating} = \$10,000,000 - (\$10,000,000)(0.80051) = \$1,994,899$$

EXHIBIT 7.5

Sample Discount Rates and Factors

t	r_t	$\dfrac{r_t}{2}$	DF
1	2.00%	1.00%	0.99010
2	2.50%	1.25%	0.97546
3	2.80%	1.40%	0.95915
4	3.00%	1.50%	0.94218
5	3.20%	1.60%	0.92370
6	3.60%	1.80%	0.89849
7	3.80%	1.90%	0.87656
8	4.00%	2.00%	0.85349
9	4.25%	2.13%	0.82758
10	4.50%	2.25%	0.80051

Therefore, the value of the swap to the fixed-rate payer is

$$V_{\text{fixed}} = \$1,994,899 - \$1,809,445 = \$185,454$$

and the value of the swap to the floating-rate payer is

$$V_{\text{floating}} = \$1,809,445 - \$1,994,899 = -\$185,454$$

EXHIBIT 7.6

Valuation of the Fixed Leg of a Swap

t	r_t	$\dfrac{r_t}{2}$	DF	($200,000)(DF)
1	2.00%	1.00%	0.99010	$198,019.80
2	2.50%	1.25%	0.97546	$195,092.21
3	2.80%	1.40%	0.95915	$191,829.83
4	3.00%	1.50%	0.94218	$188,436.85
5	3.20%	1.60%	0.92370	$184,740.22
6	3.60%	1.80%	0.89849	$179,698.03
7	3.80%	1.90%	0.87656	$175,311.62
8	4.00%	2.00%	0.85349	$170,698.07
9	4.25%	2.13%	0.82758	$165,516.53
10	4.50%	2.25%	0.80051	$160,102.03
Total				$1,809,445

In the example above, interest rates have risen since the issuance of the swap—the swap has a fixed rate of 4.00% and the current five-year market rate is 4.50%. For this reason, the value for the fixed-rate payer has increased to $185,454, and the value for the floating-rate payer has decreased to −$185,454.

TERM STRUCTURE OF INTEREST RATES

Although it is simple and accurate, the valuation methodology described above has limitations. Complex swaps cannot be valued with a simple model. For complex swap structure we use a more flexible valuation methodology.

In Chapter 5, we discussed the term structure of interest rates. The term structure has important information concerning expectations of forward interest rates. We showed how the yield curve, made up of zero-coupon rates observed in the market, can be used to construct a series of implied forward rates. If the yield curve is upward sloping, implied forward rates are higher than spot rates. If the yield curve is downward sloping, implied forward rates are lower than spot rates. And if the yield curve is flat, implied forward and spot rates are the same in all time periods. Implied forward rates are important to swap valuation because they are estimates of the level of expected future floating rates.

An alternative swap valuation method uses implied forward rates. The floating-rate leg is valued as the present value of expected cash flows, with the implied forward rates $_{t-1}f_1$ used to calculate the expected cash flows. By this method, the value of a swap to the floating-rate payer is

$$V_{\text{floating}} = \sum_{t=1}^{mn} \frac{\frac{C}{m}}{\left(1 + \frac{r_t}{m}\right)^t} - \sum_{t=1}^{mn} \frac{\frac{t-1f_t}{m}F}{\left(1 + \frac{r_t}{m}\right)^t}$$

and the value of a swap to the fixed-rate payer is

$$V_{\text{fixed}} = \sum_{t=1}^{mn} \frac{\frac{t-1f_t}{m}F}{\left(1 + \frac{r_t}{m}\right)^t} - \sum_{t=1}^{mn} \frac{\frac{C}{m}}{\left(1 + \frac{r_t}{m}\right)^t}$$

In the previous example, the fixed rate on the swap is 4.00% and the notional amount of the swap is $10,000,000. Using the information from

EXHIBIT 7.7

Swap Valuation Calculated with Implied Forward Rates

t	$\dfrac{r_t}{2}$	$\dfrac{t-1f_t}{2}$	DF	$PV_{floating}$	PV_{fixed}	Net Payment (Fixed Leg)
1	1.00%	1.00%	0.99010	0.990%	1.98%	−0.99010%
2	1.25%	1.50%	0.97546	1.464%	1.95%	−0.48713%
3	1.40%	1.70%	0.95915	1.631%	1.92%	−0.28710%
4	1.50%	1.80%	0.94218	1.696%	1.88%	−0.18788%
5	1.60%	2.00%	0.92370	1.848%	1.85%	0.00091%
6	1.80%	2.81%	0.89849	2.521%	1.80%	0.72411%
7	1.90%	2.50%	0.87656	2.193%	1.75%	0.44009%
8	2.00%	2.70%	0.85349	2.307%	1.71%	0.59979%
9	2.13%	3.13%	0.82758	2.591%	1.66%	0.93561%
10	2.25%	3.38%	0.80051	2.707%	1.60%	1.10623%
Total				19.949%	18.09%	1.85453%

Exhibit 7.5, we can calculate implied forward rates. Exhibit 7.7 shows the implied forward rates and the present values of the implied forward rates and fixed-rate payments. For simplicity, we ignore the notional amount and calculate values based on percentage. The present value of the floating-rate payments is calculated as the sum of the discounted values of the implied forward rates. The present value of the fixed-rate payments is the sum of the discounted value of the 2.00% fixed-rate payments. The value of the fixed leg of the swap is the sum of the net payments as a percentage of notional principal. The value of the fixed leg of the swap is 1.85453% of the notional principal amount. Multiplying this value by $10,000,000, we get a swap value of $185,453. The same value is calculated with the previous model.[2]

AT-MARKET SWAP

Generally, at the time an interest rate swap is settled, the present value of the expected net payments has a value of zero. Neither party expects to have zero payments in every period. If the yield curve is upward sloping, the fixed-rate payer expects to make positive swap payments in the early

---

2. The slight difference is due to rounding.

years and receive positive swap payments in the later years. If the yield curve is downward sloping, the fixed-rate payer will expect to receive positive swap payments in the early years and make positive swap payments in the later years. In a flat yield-curve environment, the expected future payments for both the fixed-rate and floating-rate payers are zero. In any interest rate environment, the fixed rate that makes the present value of the expected net payments equal to zero is known as the *at-market swap rate*.

Recall from the foregoing explanations that the value of a swap is based on implied forward rates. When one is solving for the at-market swap rate, all of the valuation inputs are known, except for the fixed swap rate. For an at-market swap, the following must hold:

$$\sum_{t=1}^{mn} \frac{\frac{c}{m}F}{\left(1+\frac{r_t}{m}\right)^t} = \sum_{t=1}^{mn} \frac{\frac{t-1f_t}{m}F}{\left(1+\frac{r_t}{m}\right)^t}$$

Solving the equation for the at-market swap rate c we get

$$c = \frac{\displaystyle\sum_{t=1}^{mn} \frac{\frac{t-1f_t}{m}}{\left(1+\frac{r_t}{m}\right)^t}}{\displaystyle\sum_{t=1}^{mn} \frac{1}{\left(1+\frac{r_t}{m}\right)^t}}(m)$$

The at-market swap rate is equal to the present value of the implied forward rates divided by the sum of the discount factors times the number of payment periods per year.

Example: Using the data from above, we calculate the at-market swap rate. The sum of the implied forward rates is 19.949%. The sum of the discount factors is 9.0472; therefore the at-market swap rate is (19.949%/ 9.0472)(2) = 4.4099%. Exhibit 7.8 summarizes the calculations of the at-market swap rate. The last two columns are included to show that the pricing relationship holds. The sum of the net payments expected on the swap at the at-market swap rate is zero since PV_{fixed} and $PV_{floating}$ are both equal to 19.949%.

EXHIBIT 7.8

Calculation of at-Market Swap Rate

t	$\dfrac{t-1f_t}{2}$	$PV_{floating}$	DF	PV_{fixed}	Net Payment (Fixed Leg)
1	1.00%	0.990%	0.99010	2.183%	−1.193%
2	1.50%	1.464%	0.97546	2.151%	−0.687%
3	1.70%	1.631%	0.95915	2.115%	−0.484%
4	1.80%	1.696%	0.94218	2.077%	−0.381%
5	2.00%	1.848%	0.92370	2.037%	−0.188%
6	2.81%	2.521%	0.89849	1.981%	0.540%
7	2.50%	2.193%	0.87656	1.933%	0.260%
8	2.70%	2.307%	0.85349	1.882%	0.425%
9	3.13%	2.591%	0.82758	1.825%	0.766%
10	3.38%	2.707%	0.80051	1.765%	0.942%
Total		19.949%	9.04722	19.949%	0.0000%

A graphical representation of the valuation components over the 10 time periods is presented in Exhibit 7.9.[3] As shown in the graph, the net payment is not expected to be zero in each time period. The present value of the floating-rate cash flows is equal to the present value of the fixed-rate cash flows.

DURATION OF A SWAP

For interest rate swaps, volatility is measured with duration. The duration of a swap is equal to the difference between the durations of the two legs of the swap. In Chapter 4 we calculate the durations of fixed-rate and floating-rate bonds. The same techniques are used to calculate the duration of an interest rate swap. Since payments on the fixed leg of an interest

---

3. As we discussed in Chapter 4, a convexity bias is introduced by deriving forward rates from a zero-coupon curve constructed in part from eurodollar futures. For this reason, a convexity adjustment must be made to the implied forward rate to account for this bias. In this chapter, for simplicity we ignore the convexity adjustment. We assume that the appropriate convexity adjustment is included when a swap is priced.

EXHIBIT 7.9

Valuation Components of an at-Market Swap

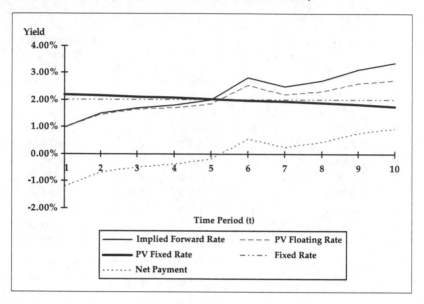

rate swap are the same as the payments on a fixed-rate bond without a principal payment, the modified duration of the fixed leg D_m^{fixed} can be calculated as

$$D_m^{\text{fixed}} = \frac{\displaystyle\sum_{t=1}^{mn} \left(\frac{\dfrac{\left(\dfrac{C}{m}\right)}{\left(1 + \dfrac{r_t}{m}\right)^t}}{\text{PV}_{\text{fixed}}} \right)\left(\frac{t}{m}\right)}{\left(1 + \dfrac{r_{mn}}{m}\right)}$$

The duration of the floating leg can be calculated with two methods. We have shown that the value of the swap is equal to the notional principal amount minus the present value of the notional principal amount. We can use this relationship to calculate the duration of the floating leg.[4] The modified duration for the floating leg of a swap $D_m^{floating}$ is

$$D_m^{floating} = - \left(\frac{mn}{m\left(1 + \dfrac{r_{mn}}{m}\right)^{mn+1}} \right) \left(\frac{1}{PV_{floating}} \right)$$

The duration of a swap is equal to a value-weighted average of the durations of individual legs of the swap. Therefore, the modified duration of a swap for a fixed-rate payer D_{fixed}^{swap} can be written as

$$D_{fixed}^{swap} = \frac{PV_{floating}}{V_{fixed}} D_m^{floating} - \frac{PV_{fixed}}{V_{fixed}} D_m^{fixed}$$

Example: Consider the swap example from the valuation section above. The fixed swap rate is 4.00% paid semiannually, and the tenor is five years. The notional principal amount of the swap is $10 million. The value of the fixed leg, PV_{fixed}, is equal to 18.094%. From the duration formula for the fixed-leg cash flows, the duration of the fixed leg D_m^{fixed} is equal to 2.5951. Exhibit 7.10 lists the results of the duration calculations.
The duration of the floating leg is calculated as

$$D_m^{floating} = - \left[\frac{(10)}{2(1.0225)^{11}} \right] \left(\frac{1}{0.1994899} \right) = -19.6224$$

The floating leg of the swap has almost 8 times the volatility of the fixed leg.
Alternatively, we can calculate the duration of the floating leg of the swap based on implied forward rates. The value of the floating leg of the swap is equal to the sum of the present values of the expected cash flows

---

4. We begin with the partial derivative of the price, $PV_{floating}$, with respect to the discount rates r_t and adjust for the price. The partial derivative of the price of the floating rate with respect to r_t is equal to

$$\frac{\partial PV_{floating}}{\partial r_t} = \frac{mn}{m\left(1 + \dfrac{r_{mn}}{m}\right)^{mn+1}}$$

EXHIBIT 7.10

Duration Calculation for the Fixed Leg of a Swap

(1) t	(2) t/2	(3) c/2	(4) DF	(5) (3)×(4)	(6) (2)×(5)	(7) (6)/PV$_{fixed}$
1	0.5	2.00%	0.99010	0.020	0.010	0.0547
2	1.0	2.00%	0.97546	0.020	0.020	0.1078
3	1.5	2.00%	0.95915	0.019	0.029	0.1590
4	2.0	2.00%	0.94218	0.019	0.038	0.2083
5	2.5	2.00%	0.92370	0.018	0.046	0.2552
6	3.0	2.00%	0.89849	0.018	0.054	0.2979
7	3.5	2.00%	0.87656	0.018	0.061	0.3391
8	4.0	2.00%	0.85349	0.017	0.068	0.3773
9	4.5	2.00%	0.82758	0.017	0.074	0.4116
10	5.0	2.00%	0.80051	0.016	0.080	0.4424
Total				0.18094		2.6535
				Modified Duration		2.5951

estimated from the implied forward rates.[5] The duration formula based on implied forward rates is

$$D_m^{\text{floating}} = -\sum_{t=1}^{mn} \left(\frac{1-t}{\left(1+\frac{r_{t-1}}{m}\right)^t} + \frac{t}{\left(1+\frac{r_t}{m}\right)^{(t+1)}} \right) \left(\frac{1}{m}\right) \left(\frac{1}{PV_{\text{floating}}}\right)$$

Example: Using the previous example, we can create a table to apply the formula above. Exhibit 7.11 lists the calculations required to apply this duration methodology. The modified duration based on this method is equal to –19.6224. The duration calculations are the same for either method.

---

5. We calculate the modified duration of the floating leg by taking the partial derivative of the floating leg pricing formula based on implied forward rates, PV$_{\text{floating}}$, with respect to the discount rates r_t and adjusting for the price of the floating leg. The partial derivative of the floating-rate price formula with respect to r_t in this case is equal to

$$\frac{\partial PV_{\text{floating}}}{\partial r_t} = \sum_{t=1}^{mn} \left(\frac{1-t}{\left(1+\frac{r_{t-1}}{m}\right)^t} + \frac{t}{\left(1+\frac{r_t}{m}\right)^{(t+1)}} \right) \left(\frac{1}{m}\right)$$

Given the duration values of each leg and the swap, the duration of the swap for the fixed-rate payer is equal to

$$D_{\text{fixed}}^{\text{swap}} = \frac{1,994,899}{185,454}(-19.6224) - \frac{1,809,445}{185,454}2.5951 = -236.39$$

The duration implies that a fixed-rate payer expects the value of the swap to change by (236.39)($185,454)(0.0001) or $4,384.95 for an increase in rates of one basis point. The floating-rate payer expects the value of the swap to change by (236.39)(−$185,454)(0.0001) or −$4,384.95 for an increase in interest rates of one basis point.[6]

EXHIBIT 7.11

Duration Calculation for the Floating Leg of a Swap

(1)	(2)	(3)	(4)	(5)
t	$\dfrac{r_t}{2}$	$\dfrac{1-t}{\left(1+\dfrac{r_{t-1}}{2}\right)^t}$	$\dfrac{t}{\left(1+\dfrac{r_t}{2}\right)^{(t+1)}}$	(3) + (4)
1	1.000%	—	0.980	0.98
2	1.250%	(0.980)	1.927	0.95
3	1.400%	(1.927)	2.838	0.91
4	1.500%	(2.838)	3.713	0.88
5	1.600%	(3.713)	4.546	0.83
6	1.800%	(4.546)	5.296	0.75
7	1.900%	(5.296)	6.021	0.73
8	2.000%	(6.021)	6.694	0.67
9	2.125%	(6.694)	7.293	0.60
10	2.250%	(7.293)	7.829	0.54
Total				**7.83**
Modified Duration = −(Total)(1/m)(1/PV$_{\text{floating}}$)				**−19.6224**

---

6. The modified duration of the swap is the same for the fixed-rate payer and the floating-rate payer. For this reason we present only duration for the fixed-rate payer. Although this result is counterintuitive, it occurs because one side of the swap has a negative value. The interpretation of the duration of a negative asset value is not clear. However, since the expected change in swap value, or PV01 of the swap, is found by multiplication of the modified duration by the value of the swap, the sign of the expected change in the value of the swap is correct.

COST OF CARRY

Cost of carry refers to the cost of hedging in the absence of a change in market rates. As in all interest rate markets, the slope of the yield curve determines the carrying cost. The slope of the yield curve determines the levels of implied forward rates and the level of the at-market swap rate. If the yield curve is upward sloping, the at-market swap rate exceeds the current floating rate. If a swap is used to hedge a bond and interest rates remain the same over a period of time, the value of the bond will not change, but the swap will incur carrying costs equal to the fixed rate minus the floating rate.

FORWARD-DELIVERY INTEREST RATE SWAPS

Interest rate swaps typically settle two business days after the trade date. In some cases, a hedger will want to establish a swap based on current market conditions and have the swap begin accruing interest at a future date. This is referred to as a *forward-delivery swap*. The fixed swap rate associated with a delayed settlement is referred to as the *forward swap rate*. If the yield curve is upward sloping, the forward swap rate is higher than a current delivery swap rate. If the yield curve is downward sloping, the forward swap rate is lower than a current delivery swap rate.

     We can value a forward delivery swap with the use of implied forward rates. As shown in Exhibit 7.8, the calculated value of the five-year at-market swap rate is 4.4099% annually (2.20495% semiannually). The at-market swap rate is based on a series of implied forward rates derived from the zero-coupon curve. The implied forward rates are the short-term rates expected to prevail in the future. To calculate the at-market swap rate for a forward delivery swap, the implied forward rates must be matched to the expected cash flows of the swap. This requires the removal of an early swap payment and the inclusion of a later swap payment. For example, if the swap is for delivery six months from today, the second six-month forward rate represents the first expected cash flow. An additional six-month forward rate must be added to the end since the swap tenor extends by six months. Once the correct forward rates are established, the valuation is computed in the same manner as above.

Example: Consider a portfolio manager who is about to purchase forward-delivery corporate bonds. The bonds will be priced today but will not settle for six months. The portfolio manager wants to hedge the interest rate risk associated with these bonds with an interest rate swap. The fixed rate on the swap will be established today, but the swap will not begin to accrue interest for six months. The portfolio manager will pay fixed and receive three-month LIBOR. The swap has a five-year tenor and is based on the market rates shown in Exhibit 7.12.

Since the swap starts accruing interest in six months, the first implied forward rate is not needed. The initial forward rate that is relevant is the forward rate in period two, $_1f_2$. This represents the first reset of three-month LIBOR six months hence. The tenor of the swap is 5.5 years from today. Therefore, we have added an eleventh period to the calculation. These calculations are shown in Exhibit 7.13. The value of the floating leg of the swap is 21.765%, and the sum of the discount factors is 8.8296. The at-market swap rate for the six-month forward delivery swap is 4.9300%. The swap rate is 52 basis points higher than the current delivery swap rate of 4.4099%, because the yield curve is upward sloping in this example.

MUNICIPAL SWAPS

The municipal swap market is a rapidly growing segment of the interest rate swap market. State and local governments, hospitals, school districts,

EXHIBIT 7.12

Sample Yield Curve

Period	$\dfrac{r_t}{2}$	$\dfrac{t-1f_t}{2}$
1	—	—
2	1.250%	2.51563%
3	1.400%	1.70067%
4	1.500%	1.80059%
5	1.600%	2.00099%
6	1.800%	2.80592%
7	1.900%	2.50207%
8	2.000%	2.70275%
9	2.125%	3.13053%
10	2.250%	3.38191%
11	2.375%	3.63344%

EXHIBIT 7.13

Calculation of a Forward-Delivery at-Market Swap Rate

t	$\dfrac{t-1f_t}{2}$	PV$_{floating}$	DF	PV$_{fixed}$	Net Payment (Fixed Leg)
1	—	—	—	—	—
2	1.50%	1.464%	0.9755	2.405%	−0.941%
3	1.70%	1.631%	0.9591	2.364%	−0.733%
4	1.80%	1.696%	0.9422	2.323%	−0.626%
5	2.00%	1.848%	0.9237	2.277%	−0.429%
6	2.81%	2.521%	0.8985	2.215%	0.306%
7	2.50%	2.193%	0.8766	2.161%	0.032%
8	2.70%	2.307%	0.8535	2.104%	0.203%
9	3.13%	2.591%	0.8276	2.040%	0.551%
10	3.38%	2.707%	0.8005	1.973%	0.734%
11	3.63%	2.807%	0.7724	1.904%	0.902%
Total		21.765%	8.8296	21.765%	0.000%

transportation authorities, and many other entities issue bonds that are exempt from federal taxes and, in many cases, state taxes. Because of the tax exemption, municipal bonds have unique pricing and volatility characteristics. Municipal swaps allow issuers and investors in the municipal market to hedge their exposure to interest rate risk.

Municipal swaps can be structured in many ways. The two most popular structures are shown in Exhibit 7.14. In the top panel, an interest rate swap is structured under which the floating rate is a percentage of LIBOR plus or minus a spread. The percentage of LIBOR b is set to approximate short-term municipal rates as a percentage of LIBOR. The Bond Market Association publishes a weekly survey of short-term tax-exempt rates referred to as the *BMA rate*. The BMA rate serves as the benchmark for weekly tax-exempt rates. The ratio of BMA to LIBOR has averaged approximately 68% over the past 10 years. This ratio can change considerably around quarterly tax payment dates and is a function of the absolute level of interest rates.

The pricing of a percentage of LIBOR swap uses the same techniques as discussed above. Since the percentage adjustment is linear, the at-market

EXHIBIT 7.14

Example Municipal Swap Structures

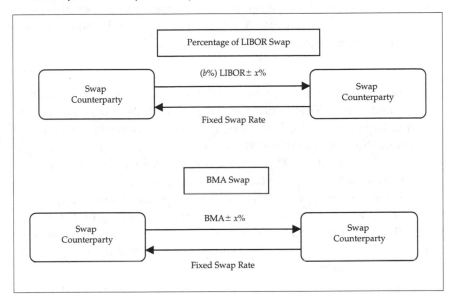

swap rate is equal to the percentage of LIBOR times the at-market swap rate for a plain vanilla swap. For example, the at-market swap rate calculated in Exhibit 7.8 is 4.4099% (2.20495% semiannually). The at-market swap rate for a 65% of three-month LIBOR swap that is otherwise identical is (0.65)(4.4098) or 2.8664%. If there is a spread in addition to the percentage, the spread is added to calculate the at-market swap rate.

The lower panel of Exhibit 7.14 shows an alternative municipal swap structure, a *BMA swap*. Under this structure the floating rate is based on the weekly reset of the BMA rate. Both markets are used by market participants and are generally monitored simultaneously because of the tendency for the short-term ratio to change. Because of its size, the LIBOR-based swap market is more liquid than the BMA swap market. For this reason, a hedger may find it more efficient to transact in percentage of LIBOR swaps.

The pricing of BMA swaps is more complex than the pricing of LIBOR-based swaps. While BMA swaps are meant to represent expected tax-exempt cash flows, the cash flows are taxable. Because of this, the pricing involves an additional step. Starting with a tax-exempt spot yield curve, tax-exempt implied forward rates are determined.[7] The tax-exempt implied forward rates are used to form expectations of the forward BMA rate. However, since the expected cash flows are taxable, they are generally discounted at a taxable rate. Therefore the pricing is based on the tax-exempt and taxable yield curves.

Example: Consider a municipality that has $100 million in tax-exempt floating-rate bonds. The bonds reset weekly at BMA + 20 basis points. The municipality would like to hedge the exposure to interest rate changes by creating a synthetic fixed-rate bond in the swap market. The maturity of the bonds is 30 years. Exhibit 7.15 shows the structure of a BMA swap used to create synthetic fixed-rate bonds for an issuer.

Under the terms of the swap, the municipality agrees to pay the at-market swap rate of 4.50% and will receive the BMA rate plus 20 bps. The cash inflows on the swap are sufficient to pay the interest payments on the bonds. The net result for the municipality is a fixed interest payment of 4.50% on its bonds.

CURRENCY SWAPS

A common risk exposure for corporations, banks, and institutional investors is exchange rate risk. Many corporations fund foreign projects domestically and must convert foreign revenues into domestic currency to make interest payments. Banks have exposure to exchange rates from foreign currency–denominated loans or investments. Fund managers may invest in foreign-denominated investments such as eurobonds. In each case, a change in exchange rates will adversely affect the expected return on investment or funding costs.

---

7. Recall that implied forward rates are based on expectations. Implied forward rates are calculated based on the pure expectations model of the yield curve, which argues that forward rates are forced into equilibrium by no-arbitrage conditions. In the municipal market, in the short term, it is difficult to make the same argument. Because of the tax exemption of interest payments, it is not possible to short a municipal bond effectively. Therefore, it is often not possible to arbitrage in the municipal market. For this reason, implied tax-exempt forward rates generated from the municipal curve do not have the same interpretation and are not as well grounded in theory as taxable implied forward rates.

EXHIBIT 7.15

Synthetic Fixed-Rate Bonds using Municipal Swap

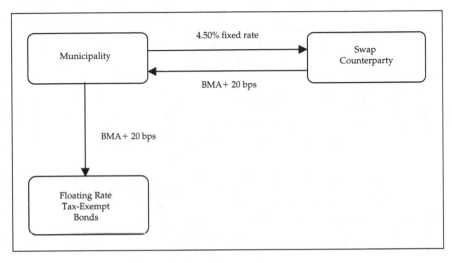

For institutions with exposure to exchange rates, currency swaps are an important hedging tool. Like an interest rate swap, a currency swap requires the exchange of cash flows. The floating-rate and fixed-rate cash flows, however, are denominated in different currencies. Unlike interest rate swaps, currency swaps generally require the exchange of principal at the settlement date of the swap and at tenor. Principal is exchanged initially in each currency and then exchanged back into each currency at tenor. Over the term of the swap, floating-rate and fixed-rate cash flows are exchanged in each currency. Exhibit 7.16 shows the cash flows for a typical currency swap.

Example: Consider a multinational corporation that has five-year bonds that pay interest in U.S. dollars. The corporation has several subsidiaries that remit cash flows in euros (€). Because the cash flows are in euros and the interest payments are in U.S. dollars, the corporation has exposure to exchange rate movements on its funding. To hedge this risk, the corporation can enter into a five-year currency swap under which it pays a variable rate in euros and receives fixed payments in U.S. dollars. The company wishes to protect $10 million in exposure. The exchange rate is $1.10 (one

EXHIBIT 7.16

Cash Flows for a Typical Currency Swap

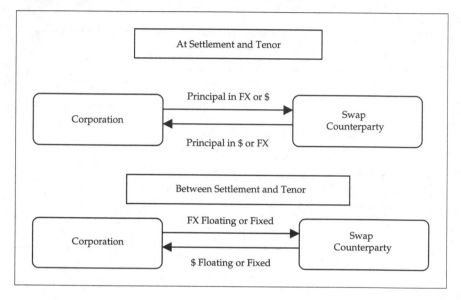

U.S. dollar buys 0.9091 euros). Initially, the corporation will pay $10,000,000 and receive €9,090,909. At tenor, the opposite principal exchange will take place. Semiannually, starting six months after settlement, the corporation will pay Euribor, a euro-denominated lending rate. The fixed rate on the swap is set in U.S. dollars. Under this swap, the corporation has effectively swapped its euro cash flows for U.S. dollar cash flows that can be used to pay its debt service. Exhibit 7.17 shows the cash flows for the example currency swap.

PRICING OF CURRENCY SWAPS

The valuation of currency swaps is similar to the valuation of plain vanilla swaps. Expected cash flows on a currency swap are determined from implied forward rates of the two currencies involved in the swap. The expected cash flows are converted into a common currency, and the value of the swap is the difference between the resulting cash flows. Currency swaps are typically structured so that the price at settlement is zero.

EXHIBIT 7.17

Cash Flows for Currency Swap Hedge

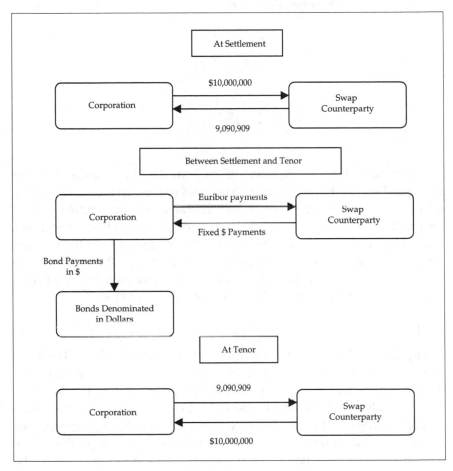

The value of the swap to the fixed-rate payer is equal to the value of the floating leg less the value of the fixed leg:

$$V_{\text{fixed}} = \sum_{t=1}^{mn} \left(\frac{\frac{t-1f_t}{m} F_2}{\left(1 + \frac{r_t(2)}{m}\right)^t} \right) (\text{er}_1) - \sum_{t=1}^{mn} \frac{\frac{cF_1}{m}}{\left(1 + \frac{r_t(1)}{m}\right)^t}$$

where F_1 and F_2 are the principal amounts in terms of currency 1 and currency 2, respectively; er_1 is the exchange rate in terms of currency 1; and

$r_t(1)$ and $r_t(2)$ are the discount rates at time t in terms of currency 1 and currency 2, respectively. Since the initial value of the swap is zero, the at-market swap rate is chosen such that

$$c = \frac{\displaystyle\sum_{t=1}^{mn} \frac{\frac{t-1 f_t}{m}}{\left(1 + \frac{r_t(2)}{m}\right)^t}}{\displaystyle\sum_{t=1}^{mn} \frac{1}{\left(1 + \frac{r_t(1)}{m}\right)^t}}(m)$$

The at-market currency swap rate differs from the plain vanilla at-market swap rate because the discount rates are different for each leg; otherwise, the calculations are the same. When an at-market swap is structured, the ratio of the principal amounts F_2/F_1 equals the reciprocal of the exchange rate, $1/er_1$. The principal amounts and exchange rate can be cleared from the formula, implying that the at-market swap rate is not a function of the exchange rate. The exchange of principal offsets the impact of exchange rates on expected cash flows. This relationship holds only on the settlement date.

Example: Consider the currency swap hedging example above. We begin by showing that the fixed rate is an at-market swap rate. We need to introduce a Euribor yield curve. For the U.S. dollar-denominated yield curve, we use the discount rates from Exhibit 7.5. Exhibit 7.18 outlines the valuation of the 10-period swap. The second and third columns represent the Euribor-based discount and implied forward rate curves, respectively. The present value of the floating rate payments is in the fourth column. The fifth, sixth, and seventh columns are use to calculate the value of the fixed leg of the bond. The last column represents the value of the swap at settlement. The at-market swap rate is equal to the sum of the present values of the expected floating-rate payments divided by the sum of the discount factors in U.S. dollars times 2. The at-market swap rate is 5.657%. The last two columns of Exhibit 7.18 are added for comparison. Notice that using the at-market rate in column seven results in an initial swap value of zero.

The value of a swap over time will be affected by changes in interest rates and the exchange rate. We now examine the valuation of the swap

EXHIBIT 7.18

Calculation of an at-Market Currency Swap Rate

t	$\frac{r_t}{2}$ (€)	$\frac{t-1f_t}{2}$ (€)	PV$_{floating}$	$\frac{r_t}{2}$ ($)	DF	PV$_{fixed}$	Net Payment (floating leg)
1	1.200%	1.200%	1.186%	1.000%	0.9901	2.801%	1.615%
2	1.400%	1.600%	1.557%	1.250%	0.9755	2.759%	1.203%
3	1.600%	2.001%	1.908%	1.400%	0.9591	2.713%	0.805%
4	1.850%	2.604%	2.420%	1.500%	0.9422	2.665%	0.245%
5	2.100%	3.106%	2.800%	1.600%	0.9237	2.613%	−0.187%
6	2.200%	2.701%	2.371%	1.800%	0.8985	2.541%	0.171%
7	2.400%	3.608%	3.056%	1.900%	0.8766	2.479%	−0.577%
8	2.600%	4.011%	3.266%	2.000%	0.8535	2.414%	−0.852%
9	2.800%	4.414%	3.443%	2.125%	0.8276	2.341%	−1.102%
10	3.000%	4.818%	3.585%	2.250%	0.8005	2.264%	−1.320%
Total			25.591%		9.0472	25.591%	0.000%

when the market has changed. Assume that a full six-month period has passed and interest rates in both countries have fallen by 10 basis points. The current exchange rate is \$1.12/€. Exhibit 7.19 shows the updated implied forward rates and the valuation of the swap. The corporation in the example above is the floating-rate payer, so the value of the floating-rate leg is shown. To calculate the value of the swap, we begin by calculating the expected payoffs on each leg of the swap. For the floating leg, the present values of the implied forward rates are multiplied by the principal amount of €9,090,909 and converted to U.S. dollars, based on the new exchange rate. For the fixed leg, the fixed swap rate of 2.829% semiannually is multiplied by \$10,000,000 and discounted. The value for the floating-rate payer is PV$_{fixed}$ minus PV$_{floating}$. The swap has increased in value by \$173,061 for the floating-rate payer. A decrease in interest rates increases the value of the swap, and an increase in the exchange rate decreases the value of the swap. In this example, the valuation effects from the decrease in interest rates outweigh the loss of value from the increase in exchange rates.

EQUITY SWAPS

An *equity swap* involves the exchange of cash flows where a counterparty pays the change in value of an underlying stock or stock index. In exchange

EXHIBIT 7.19

Calculation of Currency Swap Value

t	$\dfrac{t-1f_t}{2}$ (€)	PV$_{floating}$	PV$_{floating}$ (€)	PV$_{floating}$ ($)	PV$_{fixed}$	Net Payment (floating leg)
1	1.100%	1.088%	98,911	110,781	280,332	169,551
2	1.500%	1.462%	132,921	148,871	276,460	127,589
3	1.901%	1.818%	165,284	185,119	272,105	86,986
4	2.504%	2.336%	212,349	237,831	267,555	29,723
5	3.006%	2.723%	247,524	277,226	262,563	−14,663
6	2.601%	2.296%	208,771	233,824	255,6467	21,821
7	3.508%	2.992%	271,999	304,639	249,649	−54,989
8	3.911%	3.210%	291,811	326,828	243,316	−83,512
9	4.314%	3.394%	308,576	345,606	236,159	−109,446
Total				2,170,729	2,343,789	173,061

for the equity-based payment, a counterparty pays a fixed or floating rate. Equity swaps are a useful alternative to futures and options for hedgers because they provide tax advantages and flexibility and can be structured with custom terms.

Exhibit 7.20 shows the cash flows for an equity swap. The portfolio manager in this example agrees to exchange three-month LIBOR plus a spread for the total return, capital gains plus dividends, on an underlying stock or equity index. The spread adjustment to the floating rate is set to make the expected cash flows equal. The floating rate including the spread is the at-market swap rate for the equity swap.

Example: Consider a portfolio manager with a $10 million investment in IBM common stock. The manager does not want to sell the position because of tax concerns, but wants to protect the value over the next three years. The portfolio manager can establish a short hedge to protect the value of the stock. Under the terms of the swap, the portfolio manager agrees to pay the total return on IBM stock annually for the next three years in exchange for a fixed rate of 7.00%. If the total return on IBM stock exceeds 7.00%, the portfolio manager makes a net payment to the swap counterparty. If the total return on IBM stock is negative in a given year,

EXHIBIT 7.20

Cash Flows for a Typical Equity Swap

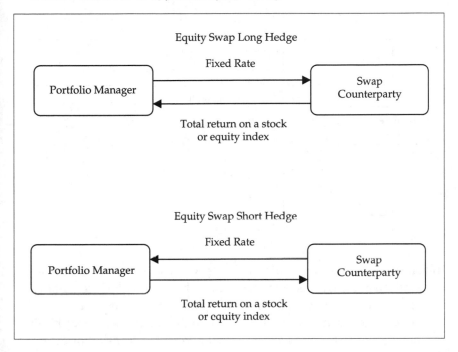

the portfolio manager will receive a payment in excess of the floating rate. In any case, the change in value of IBM stock in the portfolio is offset by the swap payment. In this way the portfolio manager has preserved the value of IBM stock. Notice that the portfolio manager must fund all gains on the stock. If the value of the stock increases, the gains will be unrealized in the portfolio but must be monetized under the terms of the swap. The floating rate received on the swap will offset funding costs associated with paying unrealized capital gains. The cash flows for this swap are shown in Exhibit 7.21.

BASIS SWAPS AND CREDIT DEFAULT SWAPS

Credit derivatives include *basis swaps* and *credit default swaps*. The credit derivative market has grown rapidly in recent years. According to ISDA, the credit derivatives market grew 25% in the first six months of 2003 to $2.69

EXHIBIT 7.21

Cash Flows for a Equity Swap Short Hedge

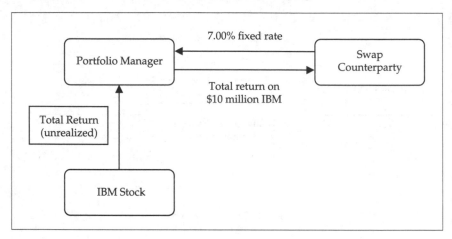

trillion after growing at a similar rate the previous six months. Credit derivatives are an important risk management tool for bond portfolio managers.

Basis swaps allow market participants to speculate on or hedge against changes in the credit spread. A credit spread is a risk premium that changes over time based on market perception of risk. For example, the yields on corporate bonds include a risk premium relative to U.S. Treasury bonds.

Exhibit 7.22 shows the cash flows on a typical basis swap. The swap involves an exchange of the corporate bond yield (the floating rate) for the U.S. Treasury yield plus a corporate bond spread (the fixed rate) established on the pricing date. A portfolio manager that expects credit spreads

EXHIBIT 7.22

Typical Basis Swap

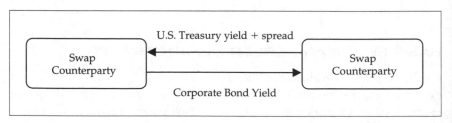

to tighten can enter into a credit swap to capitalize on the expected change. Under the terms of the swap, the portfolio manager would want to pay the corporate bond yield and receive the fixed rate. If credit spreads tighten, the swap will increase in value.

Example: Consider a corporate bond portfolio manager who recently purchased $30 million of WalMart, Inc. fixed-rate bonds that mature in five years. The bonds are currently trading at U.S. Treasuries plus 2.00%, and the portfolio manager expects the credit spread to widen over the next five years. The portfolio manager can enter into a five-year basis swap. Under the terms of the swap, the portfolio manager will pay the U.S. Treasury yield plus 2.00% and receive the corporate bond yield. Assume that the five-year U.S. Treasury yield is 3.19% and the fixed rate on the swap is 5.19%. Exhibit 7.23 shows the cash flows for the basis swap. Over the tenor of the swap, the portfolio manager will be protected against changes in credit spreads.

Credit default swaps protect a counterparty against a negative credit event in exchange for the payment of a credit premium. Under a credit default swap, the counterparty seeking credit protection pays a fixed

EXHIBIT 7.23

Example Basis Swap Hedge

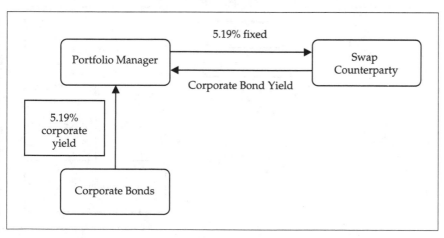

credit premium over the tenor of the swap in exchange for the credit protection. If there is no credit event, the party will receive no payments. If, however, there is a credit event, the party will receive interest or principal payments as specified in the swap agreement. Credit events vary but may include a downgrade below investment grade or a default on the underlying bonds. Credit default swaps provide protection against adverse credit events and may act to release capital reserves.

TOTAL RATE OF RETURN SWAPS

Total rate of return (TROR) swaps effectively transfer all credit and market risk exposure of an asset. Under a TROR swap, the owner of an asset agrees to pay the total rate of return in exchange for a floating rate. The TROR is equal to all interest or dividends plus the change in asset value. If the change in asset value is negative, the TROR receiver pays the absolute value of the change back to the counterparty. The floating rate can be viewed as compensation to the owner for funding the asset on the balance sheet. Exhibit 7.24 shows the cash flows for a TROR swap.

EXHIBIT 7.24

Typical Total Rate of Return (TROR) Swap

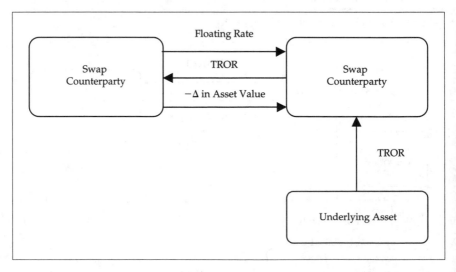

SUMMARY

Swaps are an important hedging tool. In this chapter, we described the most popular swap contracts. We began by discussing plain vanilla interest rate swaps. We explained two alternative pricing models, calculated at-market swap rates, and calculated duration for interest rate swaps.

Municipal swaps allow issuers and investors in the municipal market to hedge their exposure to interest rate risk. Under a BMA swap, a counterparty pays the BMA rate, a short-term tax-exempt rate, in exchange for a fixed rate. Alternatively, municipal swaps can be structured so that the floating rate is based on a percentage of LIBOR.

Currency swaps are used by corporations with exchange rate risk. Like interest rate swaps, a currency swap requires an exchange of cash flows. The floating-rate and fixed-rate cash flows, however, are denominated in different currencies. Unlike interest rate swaps, currency swaps generally require the exchange of principal at the settlement date of the swap and at tenor.

An equity swap involves the exchange of cash flows where a counterparty pays the change in value of an underlying stock or stock index. In exchange for the equity-based payment, a counterparty pays a fixed or floating rate. Equity swaps allow for custom terms and are more flexible than exchange-traded hedges.

Credit derivatives include basis swaps and credit default swaps. Basis swaps allow market participants to speculate on or hedge against changes in the credit spread. Credit default swaps protect a counterparty against a negative credit event in exchange for the payment of a credit premium. Under a credit default swap, the counterparty seeking credit protection pays a fixed credit premium over the tenor of the swap in exchange for the credit protection.

Total rate of return (TROR) swaps transfer all credit and market risk exposure of an asset. Under a TROR swap, the owner of an asset agrees to pay the total rate of return in exchange for a floating rate. TROR swaps may be used by investors to gain or remove risk exposure to an asset for a period of time.

REFERENCES

Chance, Don M. *An Introduction to Derivatives and Risk Management*, 6th Ed. Cincinnati: Southwestern, 2004.

Young, Andrew R. *A Morgan Stanley Guide to Fixed Income Analysis*. New York: Morgan Stanley, 1997.

CHAPTER 8

Options

In this chapter we discuss options as a risk management tool for hedgers. A hedger who uses options to protect positions is not obligated to perform at the maturity date of the option. For this reason, an options contract is more valuable than a forward, futures, or swap contract, other things being equal. Since options are more valuable than other hedging instruments, they are the most expensive.

Call options give the buyer the right to buy an underlying asset at a prespecified price, the strike price. *Put options* give the buyer the right to sell an underlying asset at the strike price. As in the futures and swaps markets, two parties combine to complete the market. The options market is referred to as a zero-sum game since gains on an option position are equaled by losses on the opposite option position.

THE OPTIONS MARKET

Options are traded on organized exchanges or in the over-the-counter market. In the United States, equity, U.S. Treasury, and currency options are exchange traded. Other options, such as interest rate options, options on swaps (*swaptions*), and embedded bond options, are strictly over-the-counter transactions. In this section, we describe the exchange-traded and over-the-counter options markets.

EXCHANGE-TRADED OPTIONS

Most options are traded on organized exchanges. Exchange-traded option contracts are issued, guaranteed, and cleared by the Options Clearing Corporation (OCC). Options are traded primarily on the Chicago Board Options Exchange (CBOE), the American Stock Exchange (AMEX), the Pacific Exchange (PE), and the Philadelphia Stock Exchange (PHLX). The CBOE lists equity options on approximately 1,500 stocks and American Depository Receipts (ADRs). Exchange-traded options include options on currencies (PHLX) and U.S. Treasuries (CBOE). Options are also traded on futures contracts, generally on the exchange where the underlying futures contracts are traded. For example, futures options are traded on corn, wheat, and U.S. Treasury notes at the Chicago Board of Trade. Exhibit 8.1 shows total volume and open interest statistics for CBOE-traded options in 2001.

The terms of most exchange-traded options are standardized. The expirations include the two near-term months plus two additional months, as appropriate, from the January, February, or March quarterly cycles. The expiration date is the Saturday immediately following the third Friday of the expiration month. Strike prices are set in 2 1/2-point increments if the strike price is between $5 and $25, five-point increments when the strike price is between $25 and $200, and 10-point increments if the strike price exceeds $200.

Exhibit 8.2 shows sample option prices for Intel Corporation (INTC) common stock as of the close of business on January 9, 2004. The closing price of INTC stock was $34.00. Included in the exhibit are the most popular

E X H I B I T   8.1

CBOE Options: Summary Statistics, 2001 Annual

	Calls	Puts	Total
Number of Contracts	117,139,776	189,528,075	306,667,851
Average Daily Volume (contracts)	472,338	764,226	1,236,564
Dollar Volume (billions of dollars)	$83.694	$111.358	$195.052
Open Interest (contracts)	57,328,177	31,433,705	88,761,882
Total Number of Transactions	12,416,964	6,515,781	18,929,450

Source: www.CBOE.com.

contracts, by volume, on that date. Each option has its own symbol, which signifies the expiration of the option and the strike price of the option. Also listed are the closing prices and the bid and ask prices. The bid price is the price at which the option can be sold and the ask price is the price at which the option can be bought. Finally, the table lists the volume in contracts. Each contract represents 100 shares of the underlying stock.

Long-Term Equity AnticiPation Securities (LEAPS) are long-term options with maturities as long as three years. They trade on approximately 450 equities and 10 indices. LEAPS allow investors to take a long-term view of the market without rolling option positions.

Index options give buyers the right to buy or sell an underlying index at a strike price. Since the underlying asset covered by index options is an equity index, such as the S&P 500, the options are cash-settled. Index options are intended for institutional traders and are typically structured based on the value of the underlying index multiplied by 100 or 250. The CBOE currently trades cash-settled index options on approximately 40 indices.

OVER-THE-COUNTER OPTIONS

The largest OTC options markets include those on interest rates, currencies, equities, and commodities. The total notional amount of interest rate options, including swaptions and interest rate caps and floors, was over $16.9 trillion as of June 2003. Exhibit 8.3 summarizes the growth in the OTC options markets.

EMBEDDED OPTIONS

An understanding of options is important for market participants because of the occurrence of embedded options in many assets. For example, many corporate and municipal bonds include an issuer call option. Some corporate bonds include a put option that allows an investor to sell bonds back to the issuer at a predetermined price. Call features on bonds are structured at the time of pricing of the new issue, and the value of the option is reflected in the initial price. The option generally cannot be separated from the bond, and its value continually affects the value of the bond.

EXHIBIT 8.2

Sample Call and Put Prices for Intel (INTC)

Call Options on INTC						
Symbol	Expiration	Strike	Last Price	Bid	Ask	Volume
INQAY	Jan 04	27.50	6.50	6.40	6.50	428
INQAF	Jan 04	30.00	4.00	3.90	4.00	10,238
INQAZ	Jan 04	32.50	1.65	1.65	1.70	8,014
INQAG	Jan 04	35.00	0.35	0.30	0.35	21,727
INQAU	Jan 04	37.50	0.05	0.05	0.05	850
INQBY	Feb 04	27.50	6.70	6.40	6.60	12
INQBF	Feb 04	30.00	4.30	4.20	4.30	6,128
INQBZ	Feb 04	32.50	2.30	2.30	2.30	5,000
INQBG	Feb 04	35.00	1.00	0.95	1.00	12,019
INQBU	Feb 04	37.50	0.35	0.30	0.35	1,532
INQBH	Feb 04	40.00	0.05	0.05	0.10	1,115
INDDY	Apr 04	27.50	6.90	6.70	6.90	65
INQDF	Apr 04	30.00	4.80	4.70	4.80	1,177
INQDZ	Apr 04	32.50	2.95	2.95	3.00	3,919
INQDG	Apr 04	35.00	1.65	1.65	1.70	2,259
INQDU	Apr 04	37.50	0.90	0.85	0.90	1,192
INQDH	Apr 04	40.00	0.40	0.40	0.45	725
INQGY	Jul 04	27.50	7.40	7.20	7.40	61
INQGF	Jul 04	30.00	5.40	5.40	5.50	67
INQGZ	Jul 04	32.50	3.90	3.70	3.90	814
INQGG	Jul 04	35.00	2.55	2.40	2.50	984
INQGU	Jul 04	37.50	1.55	1.50	1.55	3,543
INQGH	Jul 04	40.00	0.95	0.85	0.95	1,256
						(continued)

CALL OPTIONS

A *call option* is the right to buy an underlying asset at a specific price, the *strike price*, within a predetermined time, the *term* of the option. The buyer of the call option pays a *call premium* to the seller or writer of the call option. A long call option is *in-the-money* if the spot price of the underlying asset S_t is greater than the exercise price X_c at time t. If the spot price is equal to the strike price, $S_t = X_c$, the option is said to be *at-the-money*; otherwise, the option is *out-of-the-money*.

The buyer pays a call premium equal to the value of the call option $V_0(c)$ to the seller of the call. If the price of the underlying asset increases,

E X H I B I T   8.2

Sample Call and Put Prices for Intel (INTC) (Continued)

			Put Options on INTC			
Symbol	Expiration	Strike	Last Price	Bid	Ask	Volume
INQMY	Jan 04	27.50	0.05	0.05	0.05	20
INQMF	Jan 04	30.00	0.05	0.05	0.05	1,389
INQMZ	Jan 04	32.50	0.25	0.20	0.25	10,096
INQMG	Jan 04	35.00	1.35	1.35	1.40	5,214
INQMU	Jan 04	37.50	3.60	3.50	3.70	300
INQNY	Feb 04	27.50	0.10	0.05	0.15	3
INQNF	Feb 04	30.00	0.30	0.25	0.35	3,760
INQNZ	Feb 04	32.50	0.85	0.80	0.85	4,924
INQNG	Feb 04	35.00	1.95	2.00	2.05	1,229
INQNU	Feb 04	37.50	3.60	3.80	3.90	5
INDPY	Apr 04	27.50	0.30	0.30	0.35	536
INQPF	Apr 04	30.00	0.75	0.70	0.75	1,779
INQPZ	Apr 04	32.50	1.50	1.45	1.55	1,979
INQPG	Apr 04	35.00	2.60	2.65	2.75	373
INQPU	Apr 04	37.50	4.20	4.30	4.40	38
INQSY	Jul 04	27.50	0.75	0.75	0.85	95
INQSF	Jul 04	30.00	1.35	1.30	1.40	503
INQSZ	Jul 04	32.50	2.20	2.20	2.20	190
INQSG	Jul 04	35.00	3.30	3.40	3.50	4,260
INQSU	Jul 04	37.50	4.70	4.90	5.10	55

Source: Smith Barney.com, January 9, 2004.

a hedger benefits who is long a call. The gross payoff to the option at maturity n is the asset price S_n minus the exercise price X_c if the difference is a positive number. Otherwise the payoff is zero. An investor will only exercise a call option at expiration when $S_n > X_c$. The net payoff or profit is simply the gross payoff minus the call premium.

Example: Consider an investor who buys an INTC February 2004 call option with a strike price of 30.00, shown in Exhibit 8.2. The investor pays the ask price of $4.30 per contract. The option is out-of-the-money if the stock price is below 30.00, at-the-money if the stock price equals 30.00,

EXHIBIT 8.3

Growth in the OTC Options Markets (billions of $)

	Notional Amounts		Market Values	
	Mid-Year 2002	Mid-Year 2003	Mid-Year 2002	Mid-Year 2003
Interest Rate	12,575	16,946	235	434
Foreign Exchange	3,427	4,597	97	101
Equity-linked	1,828	2,311	181	193
Commodity	208	279	...	...

Source: Bank for International Settlements (bis.org). Notes: Notional amounts outstanding have been adjusted by halving positions versus other reporting dealers. Gross market values have been calculated as the sum of the total gross positive market value of contracts and the gross negative market value of contracts with nonreporting counterparties. Interest rate contracts represent single-currency contracts only.

and in-the-money if the stock price exceeds 30.00. The gross and net payoffs for this option are shown in Exhibit 8.4.

Writing or selling a call is sometimes referred to as a *naked call option*. The seller of a call receives a premium equal to the value of the call option $V_0(c)$ from the buyer of the call. The seller benefits if the price of the underlying asset decreases. The gross payoff at the expiration date of the option is $MIN[0, X_c - S_n]$. The net payoff is the gross payoff plus the call premium.

Example: Consider an investor who sells an INTC February 2004 call option with a strike price of 30.00, listed in Exhibit 8.2. The investor receives the bid price of $4.20 per contract. The seller of the option will earn a maximum profit of $4.20 per contract if the long option is at-the-money or out-of-the-money. Otherwise, the option seller will lose some or all the option premium. The gross payoff to the option seller is the opposite of the payoff to the option buyer. However, the net payoffs differ by the bid–ask spread. The gross and net payoffs for this option are shown in Exhibit 8.5.

PUT OPTIONS

A *put option* is the right to sell an underlying asset at a specific price, the strike price, within a predetermined time, the term of the option. The buyer of the put option pays a fee or *put premium* to the seller or writer of

EXHIBIT 8.4

Payoff at Expiration on a Long Call Option

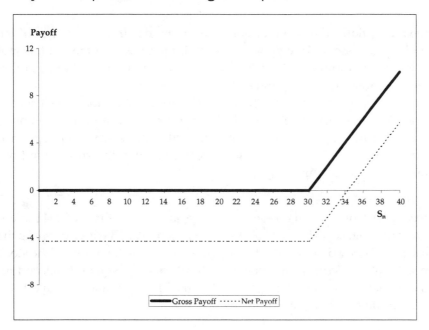

EXHIBIT 8.5

Payoff at Expiration on a Short Call Option

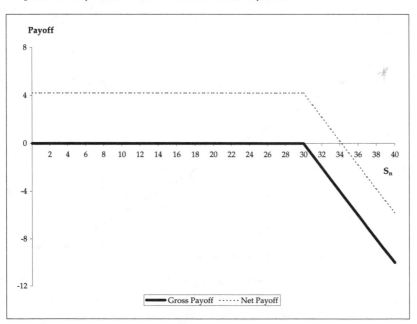

the put option. A long put option is in-the-money if the spot price of the underlying asset S_t is less than the exercise price X_p at time t. If the spot price is equal to the strike price, $S_t = X_p$, the option is said to be at-the-money; otherwise, the option is out-of-the-money.

The gross payoff at the maturity of a long put option is the exercise price X_p minus the asset price S_n if the difference is a positive number; otherwise the payoff is zero. An investor will only exercise a put option at expiration when $S_n < X_p$. The net payoff is equal to the gross payoff minus the option premium $V_0(p)$.

Example: Consider an investor who buys an INTC February 2004 put option with a strike price of 35.00, listed in Exhibit 8.2. The investor pays the ask price of $2.05 per contract. The option is out-of-the-money if the stock price is above 35.00, at-the-money if the stock price equals 35.00, and in-the-money if the stock price is below 35.00. The gross and net payoffs for this option are shown in Exhibit 8.6.

EXHIBIT 8.6

Payoff at Expiration on a Long Put Option

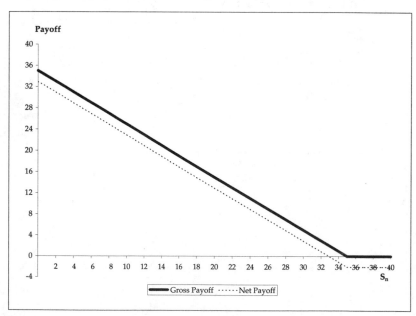

The seller of a put receives a premium equal to the value of the put option $V_0(p)$ from the buyer of the put. A short put is also referred to as a naked put option. The seller benefits if the price of the underlying asset increases. The gross payoff at the expiration date for the short put option is MIN$[0, S_n - X_p]$. The net payoff is the gross payoff plus the call premium.

Example: Consider an investor who sells the INTC February 2004 put option with a strike price of 35.00, listed in Exhibit 8.2. The investor receives the bid price of $2.00 per contract. The seller of the option will earn a maximum profit of $2.00 per contract if the long option is at-the-money or out-of-the-money. Otherwise, the option seller will lose some or all of the option premium. As with a call option, the gross payoff to the put seller is the opposite of the payoff to the option buyer. However, the net payoff differs by the bid–ask spread. The gross and net payoffs for this option are shown in Exhibit 8.7.

EXHIBIT 8.7

Payoff at Expiration on a Short Put Option

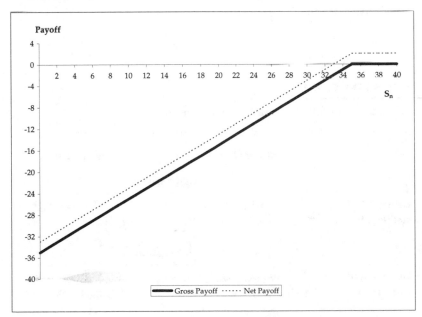

GROSS AND NET PAYOFFS

We can generalize the gross and net payoffs described above. We use the notation MAX[·] and MIN[·] to denote, respectively, the maximum and minimum of the values in the parentheses. The payoffs can be abbreviated as shown in Exhibit 8.8.

EXERCISE PROVISIONS

There are three common types of exercise provisions: American, European, and Bermudan. *American options* can be exercised on any business day prior to or including the expiration date of the option. Most equity options are American options. *European options* can be exercised only on a specific date. Most bond options and swaptions are European options. For example, a typical call option on a corporate bond cannot be exercised until the first call date. After the first call date, bond options can generally be exercised on any coupon payment date. Therefore, a corporate bond option is European to the first call date. *Bermudan options* are a combination of European and American options. Bermudan options can be exercised on a series of specific dates. Bermudan options are common in the interest rate options market.

E X H I B I T   8.8

Gross and Net Payoffs to Option Parties

	Buyer (*Long*)	Seller (*Short*)
	Call Option	
Gross Payoff	$\text{MAX}[S_n - X_c, 0]$	$\text{MIN}[0, X_c - S_n]$
Net Payoff	$\text{MAX}[S_n - X_c - V_0(c), - V_0(c)]$	$\text{MIN}[V_0(c), X_c - S_n + V_0(c)]$
	Put Option	
Gross Payoff	$\text{MAX}[X_p - S_n, 0]$	$\text{MIN}[0, S_n - X_p]$
Net Payoff	$\text{MAX}[X_p - S_n - V_0(p), - V_0(p)]$	$\text{MIN}[V_0(p), S_n - X_p + V_0(p)]$

OPTION STRATEGIES

The payoffs we described above are for stand-alone or naked option positions. Options can also be used to manage the risk of an underlying asset. In this section, we discuss popular option hedging strategies. The strategies involve the combination of the underlying asset, calls, and puts. Combining options and the underlying asset can significantly change payoff profiles.

COVERED CALL

The most basic option strategy is the covered call. A covered call involves buying the underlying asset and selling a call. Covered calls limit the upside performance of the asset in exchange for the premium. This strategy is typically used by investors who want to improve on the current market price and do not believe the asset price will decrease significantly over the term of the option.

Example: Consider an investor who buys 100 shares of INTC on January 9, 2004 for $34.00 per share and simultaneously sells an April 2004 call option with a strike price of 35.00. The investor receives the bid price of $1.65 per contract. The net position is a covered call. Assuming no dividends are received and no transaction costs are paid, the investor's maximum profit is $2.65 ($1.00 in capital gains plus the option premium of $1.65). The break-even price on the covered call is $32.35 ($34.00 − $1.65). If the stock price goes to zero, the investor loses the purchase price of the stock net of the option premium. Therefore, the maximum loss on the investment is $32.35. The net payoff for this covered call is shown in Exhibit 8.9.

PROTECTIVE PUT (SYNTHETIC CALL)

If an investor is long an asset, purchasing a put protects the value of the asset. The combination of a long asset and a long put is referred to as a *protective put*. This strategy protects the value of the investment for the cost of the option premium while keeping the upside of the investment unlimited. The payoff profile of a protective put is similar to that of a long call option. Therefore it is sometimes referred to as a *synthetic call option*.

EXHIBIT 8.9

Net Payoff at Expiration on a Covered Call

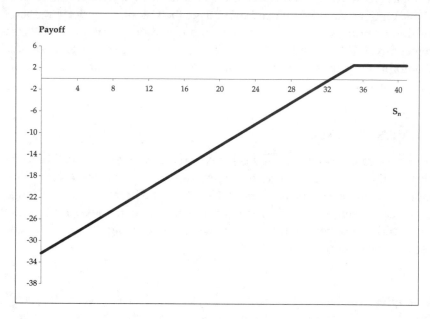

Example: Consider an investor who buys 100 shares of INTC on January 9, 2004 for $34.00 per share and simultaneously buys an April 2004 put option with a strike price of 32.50. The investor pays the ask price of $1.55 per contract. The net position is a protective put. Assuming no dividends are received and no transaction costs are paid, the investor's maximum loss is $3.05 ($1.50 in capital loss and the option premium of $1.55). The breakeven price on the protective put is $35.55. The investor maintains maximum upside exposure on the stock while lowering the gain by the option premium. The net payoff for this protective put is shown in Exhibit 8.10.

SYNTHETIC PUT (REVERSE HEDGE)

A portfolio manager with a short position in an asset can decrease the risk of the position by buying a call option. The resulting hedged portfolio has a payoff profile similar to that of a long put option and is referred to as a *synthetic put option* or a *reverse hedge*. The strike price of the call option is

E X H I B I T   8.10

Net Payoff at Expiration on a Protective Put

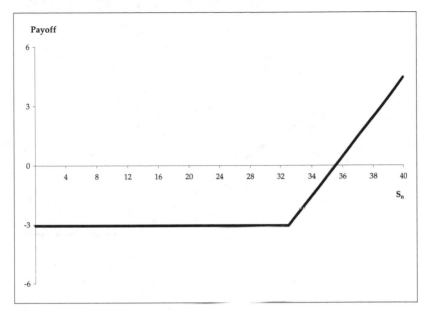

set at a level determined by the risk tolerance of the portfolio manager and determines the maximum risk of the portfolio.

Example: Consider an investor who shorts INTC common stock at $34.00. To hedge the value of the investment, the investor buys an INTC February 2004 call option with a strike price of $35.00 for the ask price of $1.00 per contract. The net position is a synthetic put option or a reverse hedge. Assuming no dividends are received and no transaction costs are paid, the investor's maximum loss is $2.00 and the breakeven price on the synthetic put is $33.00. The maximum gain is $33.00 and occurs at an asset price of $0.00. The net payoff for a synthetic put is shown in Exhibit 8.11.

OPTION COLLAR

An investor with a long position in an asset can protect the value of the asset by using an *option collar*. An investor establishes a long option

EXHIBIT 8.11

Net Payoff at Expiration on a Synthetic Put Option

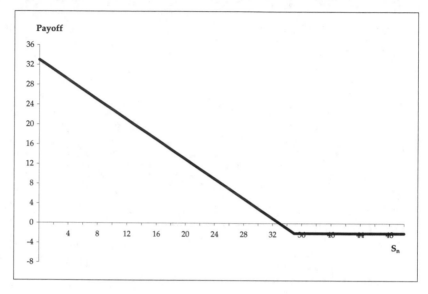

collar by writing a covered call and simultaneously buying a put on the underlying asset. The proceeds from the call are used to fund the cost of the put. A collar limits the upside and downside performance of an asset. For this reason, it is appropriate for hedging short-term changes in an asset.

Example: Consider an investor who owns INTC common stock at a price of $30.00. The investor expects a temporary decrease in the price of the stock, but does not want to sell. To hedge the position, the investor sells an April 2004 call option with a strike price of $40.00 and simultaneously buys an April 2004 put with a strike price of 35.00. The investor receives the bid price of $0.40 per contract for the call option and pays the ask price of $1.70 for the put option. The net position is an option collar with a net cost of $1.30. Assuming no dividends are received and no transaction costs are paid, the investor has a minimum gain of $3.70 and a maximum gain of $8.70. The net payoffs for the option collar are shown in Exhibit 8.12.

EXHIBIT 8.12

Net Payoff at Expiration on a Long Option Collar

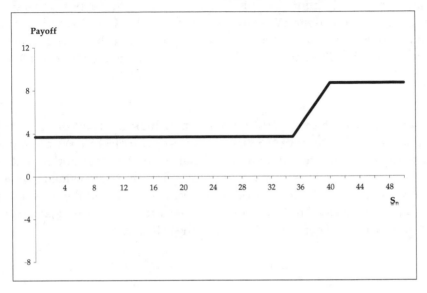

PUT-CALL PARITY

We have shown that combining puts, calls, and the underlying asset can significantly change a payoff profile. In this section we show that the payoff profiles of a call, a put, or the underlying asset can be replicated. This relationship between the payoffs of calls and puts is known as *put-call parity*. The concept is based on a portfolio consisting of three of the following: the underlying asset, a call option or a put option with the same strike price and maturity date, and a discount bond. Any three of these assets can be combined to form the expected payoff of the fourth.

Put-call parity states that an investor can replicate the value of a long call option $V_0(c)$ with strike price X by buying a put with the same strike price and maturity for $V_0(p)$, buying the underlying asset S_t, and borrowing the present value of the strike price until the maturity date of the option n. It is assumed that the investor can borrow at the risk-free rate of interest r. Therefore the value of the call can be represented as

$$V_t(c) = V_t(p) + S_t - Xe^{-rn}$$

If we examine the payoff on the portfolio of assets on the right side of the equation, we find that the payoff at maturity is the same as the payoff on a call option. Exhibit 8.13 summarizes the payoffs on a replicated call option, assuming a strike price of $20.00. The dotted and dashed lines represent the payoff on the stock, the put, and the borrowed value of the strike price. The sum of the three lines adds to the payoff on a call option.

Example: Consider the INTC options from Exhibit 8.2. The April 2004 call option with a strike price of $30.00 has an ask price of $4.80. We can replicate the value of that option by buying an April 2004 put option with a strike price of $30.00, buying the stock for $34.00, and borrowing the present value of $30.00. The ask price of the put is $0.75, and the option has 99 days to maturity. The three-month U.S. Treasury bill rate as of January 9, 2004 was 0.87%. Therefore, the value of the call is equal to

$$V_t(c) = 0.75 + 34.00 - 30e^{-0.0087\left(\frac{99}{360}\right)} = \$4.822$$

EXHIBIT 8.13

Put-Call Parity Payoffs

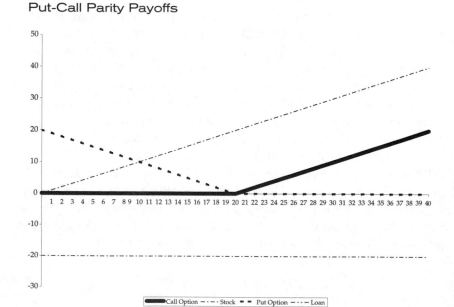

| Call Option —·—· Stock ■ ■ Put Option —··— Loan |

The value of the call option based on replication with put-call parity is $4.822, which is $0.022 higher than the market price of $4.80. Transaction costs would exceed the difference in prices, so no arbitrage opportunity exists. We can rearrange the formula above and similarly replicate the value of a put option or the underlying asset.

OPTION VALUATION

In this section we discuss the basics of option valuation. For a hedger, an understanding of option pricing is important, as is an understanding of option hedge ratios. Because of the unique characteristics of the different option markets, many option pricing models exist. It is important for a hedger to understand the strengths and weaknesses of the many models and to know which option pricing model is appropriate for a particular option.

The value of an option has two components: intrinsic value and time value. Intrinsic value is the difference between the current asset price and the strike price of the option. This is also referred to as the *moneyness* of the option. It represents the amount the option is worth if it is exercised today, regardless of option exercise provisions. If an option is out-of-the-money or at-the-money, it has an intrinsic value of zero. Time value reflects the range of possible values for the option between the valuation date and expiration. Time value is based on the volatility of the underlying asset and the time to maturity. The value of an option can be written as

$$V_t = \text{Intrinsic Value} + \text{Time Value}$$

Example: Consider an INTC April 2004 call option with a strike price of 30.0 from Exhibit 8.2. Since the price of INTC is $34.00, the option is in-the-money and has an intrinsic value of $4.00. The market value of the options is $4.80. Therefore the market assessment of time value is $0.80.

For most options, time value can be observed in the market. A difficult task in option valuation is estimating the time value for options that do not trade in the market. To do this we must make assumptions about the expected value of the asset price over the term of the option. This requires an examination of the distribution and the volatility of the underlying asset. In the sections that follow, we discuss option pricing models. We begin by establishing lower and upper bound values for an option.

LOWER AND UPPER BOUND VALUES FOR AMERICAN OPTIONS

The value of an option is equal to intrinsic value plus time value. As an option approaches its maturity, its time value approaches zero. Recall that the intrinsic value of a call option is $MAX[S_t - X, 0]$. A call option will always be worth at least its intrinsic value. This is the lower bound limit of a call option.

We define the upper bound in terms of the value of the underlying asset. A call option increases in value as the asset price increases. As an option becomes deep in-the-money, its value approaches intrinsic value. Price changes of a deep-in-the-money call option are similar to those of the underlying stock. If the price of a call option exceeds the price of the underlying asset, an arbitrage opportunity exists. Specifically, an investor can earn riskless profit by selling the option and buying the asset. In this case, the investor receives an up-front payment equal to the call price minus the asset price. If the option is exercised, the investor delivers the asset and receives the strike price. If the option is not exercised, the investor sells the asset. In either case, the investor earns the up-front payment plus the proceeds from selling the asset. Therefore, the upper-bound limit for the value of the call option is the value of the underlying asset S_t. Exhibit 8.14 shows the upper and lower bound limits for the value of a call option. The option value must lie on or between the two lines and cannot be in the shaded regions.

The lower bound value for a put option can be developed with the same reasoning we used to develop the lower bound for a call option. The time value is equal to zero at maturity. A put option will always be worth at least its intrinsic value, $MAX[X - S_t, 0]$. This is the lower bound limit of a put option.

The upper bound for a put option is its strike price. A put is worth its maximum value if the asset price is zero. Since the asset value is bounded on the downside by zero, the most a put can be worth is its strike price. Exhibit 8.15 shows the upper and lower bound limits for the value of a put option. The option value must lie on or between the two lines and cannot be in the shaded regions.

BINOMIAL OPTION PRICING

Merton (1973) and Cox, Ross, and Rubinstein (CRR, 1979) developed models for pricing American options with the use of a binomial lattice. A

EXHIBIT 8.14

Lower and Upper Bound Values for a Call Option

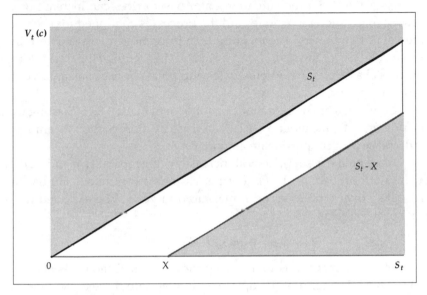

EXHIBIT 8.15

Lower and Upper Bound Values for a Put Option

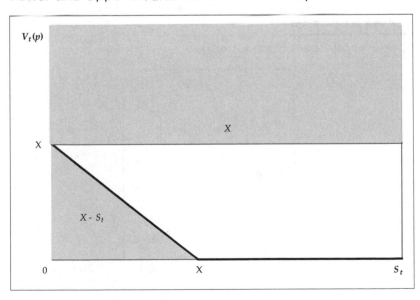

lattice represents possible paths for the underlying asset's price over the life of the option. Prices are mapped over a number of time intervals or nodes, starting from the valuation date. Asset prices can increase or decrease at each successive node, and the process is continued for each time interval until maturity. The magnitude of price movements is determined by the volatility of the underlying asset and the length of the time interval. The model assumes that interest rates and volatility are constant over the life of an option.

Consider a one-period model, as shown in Exhibit 8.16. Starting from the pricing date, the asset price can increase by a proportionate amount u or decrease by a proportionate amount d.

Assume the asset price will increase with probability p and will decrease with probability $1 - p$. Further assume a continuous annual risk-free rate r over a time period n measured in years. The expected future price of the asset is

$$S_0 e^{rn} = puS_0 + (1 - p)dS_0$$

We can expand this to a three-period binomial model as shown in Exhibit 8.17. The term of the option is divided into three equal intervals, and the asset price is mapped over each interval. In each successive period, the asset price can increase or decrease by u and d, respectively.

EXHIBIT 8.16

One-Period Asset Price Changes

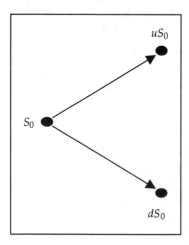

EXHIBIT 8.17

Asset Price Changes from a Three-Period Binomial Lattice

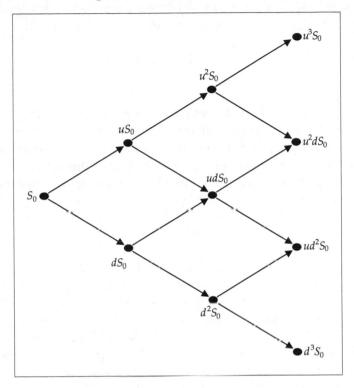

The magnitude of price movement at each node is based on the volatility of the underlying asset. It is common to use a continuous time specification of changes in the asset price in the discrete pricing model. There are many different specifications for the expected price movement. Generally it is assumed that $u = 1/d$. With this assumption, the lattice has recurring values, and it is said to recombine. CRR (1979) specify the asset price movements in continuous time as

$$u = e^{\sigma\sqrt{n/m}}$$

and

$$d = \tfrac{1}{u} = e^{-\sigma\sqrt{n/m}}$$

where σ is the annual standard deviation of the asset price, m is the number of intervals in the model, and n is the maturity of the option in years. Based on the expected future value of the asset price above, we can solve for the probability of an increase in the stock price p as follows:

$$p = \frac{e^{r(n/m)} - d}{u - d}$$

To value an option, the asset prices generated at each node are compared with the strike price to determine the value at each node. The intrinsic values at the terminal nodes represent the possible option values at maturity. If the option is out-of-the-money at the terminal node, it has a value of zero. The values are discounted to arrive at an expected value for the option.

Example: Consider the valuation of an INTC April 2004 call option with a strike price of $35.00 as of January 9, 2004. Assume the volatility of INTC stock is 20.00% per year, the risk-free rate of interest is 2.00%, and the current stock price is $34.00. Assuming the option is European, we use a three-period binomial model to compute the value of the option. There are 99 days to expiration of the option (0.275 years). The discount factor for each node is $e^{-(0.02)(0.275/3)}$ or 0.9982. The values for u, d, and p are 1.0624, 0.9412, and 0.5000, respectively, as shown below

$$u = e^{0.20\sqrt{0.275/3}} = 1.0624$$

$$d = \frac{1}{1.0624} = 0.9412$$

$$p = \left(\frac{1.0018 - 0.9412}{1.0624 - 0.9412}\right) = 0.5000$$

Exhibit 8.18 shows the expected prices for INTC and the option values (in parentheses) at the terminal nodes. For a European option, the option is in-the-money in the top two terminal nodes when the asset values are $40.77 and $36.12. The probability that the price of INTC is $40.77 is p^3, and the probability that the price is $36.12 is $p^2(1 - p)$. The terminal cash flows are discounted at the appropriate discount factor for the terminal

EXHIBIT 8.18

Expected Asset and European Option Prices
(option prices in parentheses)

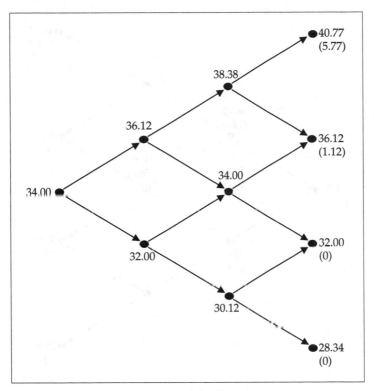

node, which is equal to $e^{-(0.02)(0.275)}$ or 0.9945. Therefore, the value of the option is equal to

$$\frac{(0.5000)^3(40.77 - 35.00) + (0.5000)^2(0.5000)(36.12 - 35.00)}{(1.0055)} = \$0.8565$$

For an American call option, exercise can take place on any date prior to maturity. Therefore, the value of the option must be analyzed at each node. This is calculated by starting at the terminal nodes and working backward to establish a value for the option at each node. Exhibit 8.19 shows

EXHIBIT 8.19

Expected Asset and American Option Values for INTC
(option prices in parentheses)

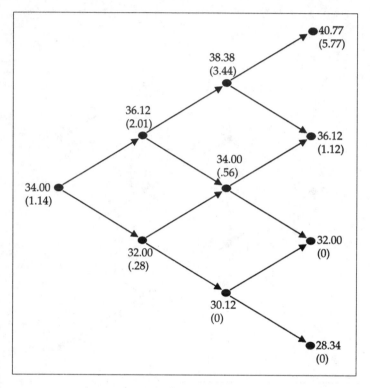

the expected asset and option values for the INTC example above. The
option values at the terminal nodes are established in the same manner as
the example above. Each option value is equal to the discounted value of
the expected cash flows from the following period. For example, the up-
permost option value at the end of the second interval is $3.44 and is cal-
culated as

$$\frac{(0.5000)5.77 + (0.5000)1.12}{e^{0.00183}} = 3.44$$

At each node, the decision must be made based on the expected value
whether to exercise or hold the option. If the intrinsic value exceeds the
expected value at any node, the option will be exercised. In the example

below, the option is held at every node. This process, called backward induction, is repeated at each node. The resulting option value is $1.14.

In application, several hundred intervals are used when an option price is calculated with this model. Increasing the number of intervals increases the accuracy of the model. Computer models make the calculations instantaneous. If we apply 50 intervals to the option in the example, the value is $1.07. While we do not replicate the 50-period model here, the procedure is the same as that outlined above.

MEASURING OPTION VOLATILITY
WITH A BINOMIAL MODEL

In Chapter 4, we discussed the volatility of a bond in terms of its modified duration. For options, we measure the sensitivity of the option price to a change in the price of the underlying asset. This is referred to as an *option delta*, Δ, or hedge ratio, which is a measure of the percentage change in the value of an option for a change in the price of the underlying asset. With the binomial model, this change can be estimated directly from the binomial lattice. Consider the end of the first interval. If the asset value goes up, we represent the value of the asset as uS_0 and the value of the call as $V_u(c)$. If the asset value goes down, we represent the value of the asset as dS_0 and the value of the call as $V_d(c)$. Therefore, delta can be estimated as

$$\Delta = \frac{\Delta V(c)}{\Delta S} = \frac{V_u(c) - V_d(c)}{uS_0 - dS_0}$$

Example: From the example above and the binomial lattice in Exhibit 8.19, the delta at the end of the first interval is 0.4199:

$$\Delta = \frac{2.01 - 0.28}{36.12 - 32.00} = 0.4199$$

The price of the call option is expected to increase by $0.4199 for a $1.00 change in the stock price. As a hedge ratio, this implies that 2.38 options (1/0.4199) are required to hedge each share of stock.

We can estimate volatility by using the observed price of the option and solving for σ. The volatility that results in an option value equal to the market price is referred to as the *implied volatility*. The implied volatility is the market's assessment of the risk of the underlying asset.

Example: In the 50-period binomial option pricing example mentioned above, the value of the INTC April 35 call option is calculated as $1.07. However, from Exhibit 8.2, the market value is $1.65. Therefore the volatility estimate of 20.00% is too low. Using the 50-period binomial model and solving iteratively for the volatility that makes the option price equal to $1.65 results in an implied volatility of 28.11%.

BLACK-SCHOLES OPTION PRICING MODEL

Black and Scholes (1973) developed the most popular continuous-time option pricing model. For large numbers of observations, the binomial distribution approaches the normal distribution. If we increase the number of intervals in the binomial option pricing model, the model approaches a continuous-time model based on a lognormal distribution of asset prices.

Consider the following notation: S_0 equals the price of the underlying asset, X_c equals the exercise price on a call option, $N(d_1)$ and $N(d_2)$ represent the cumulative normal probability density for the values of d_1 and d_2, σ equals the annual volatility of the underlying asset, r is the annual risk-free rate of interest for the term of the option, and n is the term of the option in years. With this notation, the value of a call option can be calculated as

$$V_t(c) = S_0 N(d_1) - X_c e^{-rn} N(d_2)$$

where

$$d_1 = \frac{\ln\left(\dfrac{S_0}{X_c}\right) + \left(r + \dfrac{\sigma^2}{2}\right)n}{\sigma\sqrt{n}}$$

and

$$d_2 = d_1 - \sigma\sqrt{n}$$

Example: We again consider the valuation of the INTC April 2004 call option with a strike price of $35.00 as of January 9, 2004. The valuation parameters are $S_0 = \$34.00$, $X_c = \$35.00$, $r = 2.00\%$, $n = 99/360 = 0.275$, and $\sigma = 20.00\%$. We begin with d_1 and d_2:

$$d_1 = \frac{\ln(34/35) + (0.02 + 0.02)(0.275)}{0.20\sqrt{0.275}} = -0.1715$$

$$d_2 = -0.1715 - 0.20\sqrt{0.275} = -0.2764$$

The values for $N(-0.1715) = 0.4319$ and $N(-0.2764) = 0.3911$. Therefore, the value of the option is

$$V_t(c) = 34.00(0.4319) - 35.00e^{-(0.02)(0.275)}0.3911 = 1.07$$

The value for a 50-period binomial model is $1.07. This shows the convergence of the two models. Using the value of the call from above and put-call parity, we can calculate the value of the put.[1] Restating put-call parity to represent the value of a put,

$$V_t(p) = V_t(c) - S_0 + Xe^{-rn}$$

Example: Using the example above, we value the INTC April 2004 put option with a strike price of $35.00 as of January 9, 2004. The following variables are required: $S_0 = \$34.00$, $X_p = \$35.00$, $r = 2.00\%$, and $n = 99/360 = 0.275$. The theoretical value of the put is $1.88, as shown below:

$$V_t(p) = 1.07 - 34.00 + 35.00e^{-(0.02)(0.275)} = 1.88$$

MEASURING OPTION VOLATILITY WITH BLACK-SCHOLES

Recall from our discussion of binomial option pricing that we can measure the implied volatility of the underlying asset by solving for volatility, given the current market price of the option. The option in the example

---

1. The value of a put can also be calculated as $V_t(p) = X_c e^{-rn} N(-d_2) - S_0 N(-d_1)$. Since $N(x) + N(-x) = 1.00$, it is easy to show that the value of a call minus a put is equal to $S_0 - Xe^{-rn}$ as stated by put-call parity.

above has a current market price of $1.65 (from Exhibit 8.2). Since the option value obtained with Black-Scholes is $1.07, the volatility estimate of 20.00% is low. Using the implied volatility of 28.11% results in an option value of $1.65.

Delta is easily measured with Black-Scholes. Delta is the partial derivative of the option price with respect to the underlying asset. In the example above, the delta for the call option, $N(d_1)$, is equal to 0.4319. Therefore, the price of the call option is expected to increase by $0.43 for a $1.00 change in the stock price. The delta for a put option, $N(d_1) - 1$, with the same strike price and maturity is -0.5681. The price of the put option is expected to decrease by approximately $0.57 for a $1.00 increase in the stock price.

Gamma is the second derivative of the option price with respect to the underlying asset. It is a measure of the change in delta for a change in the price of the underlying asset. Like convexity in the fixed-income market, gamma measures how sensitive a hedge ratio is to changes in the value of the underlying asset. Deep-in-the-money options move very closely with changes in the underlying asset. Therefore, as options become more in-the-money, delta approaches 1 and gamma approaches 0. A call and a put with the same strike price and maturity have the same gamma. Gamma is calculated as

$$\Gamma(c) = \Gamma(p) = \frac{e^{-0.5(d_1)^2}}{S_0 \sigma \sqrt{2(\pi)(n)}}$$

From the example above, gamma for a call option, $\Gamma(c)$, and gamma for a put option, $\Gamma(p)$, are 0.1102 as shown below. This implies that the delta of the option is expected to increase by 0.1102 for a $1.00 increase in the price of the underlying asset

$$\Gamma(c) = \frac{e^{-0.5(-0.1715)^2}}{(34.00)(0.20)\sqrt{2(3.1419)(0.275)}} = 0.1102$$

Exhibit 8.20 shows the directional changes in the value of an option and delta for a change in the value of the underlying asset. Expected changes in the value of an option are measured by delta, and expected changes in deltas are measured by gamma. As an asset price increases, deltas for a long call and long put increase. As an asset price increases, deltas of a short call and short put decrease.

E X H I B I T   8.20

Effect of Change in Asset Price on Option Price and Delta

| | Effect of Increase in Asset Price | | | | |
Variable	Long Call	Short Call	Long Put	Short Put	Sensitivity Measure
$V(c)$, $V(p)$	+	−	−	+	Delta
Δ	+	−	+	−	Gamma

Other factors influence the value of an option, such as time to maturity, changes in volatility, and changes in the risk-free rate of interest. The sensitivity measures of these factors are beyond the scope of this book. Delta and gamma are the most important measures for an option hedge.

INTEREST RATE OPTIONS

Interest rate options are common in the fixed-income market. The valuation of interest rate options has been studied extensively, and many widely accepted models exist. In this section we discuss the characteristics and pricing of embedded bond options, interest rate caps and floors, swaptions, and currency options.

BOND OPTIONS

A callable bond allows an issuer to purchase a bond from investors at a predetermined price or call price. Bond options are typically European to the first call date and Bermudan thereafter. Bond options are valuable to the issuer since they provide the ability to refinance bonds in low-interest-rate markets. Callable bonds subject an investor to reinvestment risk. Some corporate bonds contain a put option, which allows an investor to sell the bond to the issuer at a strike price on or after a specific date. Put options are valuable to bond investors because they protect them against loss in value from rising interest rates or credit downgrades.

BOND OPTION VALUATION

The application of conventional valuation models, such as Black-Scholes, to bond options poses many problems. First, bond options are typically long-dated, often having maturities of 10 years or more. Second, their value is determined by the level of interest rates, which in turn determines the value of the underlying asset. Third, unlike equity options, bond options typically cannot be separated from the underlying asset. This makes it impossible to directly observe market values or implied volatilities. Fourth, the underlying asset is expected to have decreasing volatility over time. Finally, they are often Bermudan options.

Many extensions to conventional option pricing models have been proposed to address these problems. Generally, two types of models are considered: stochastic models of interest rate movements and binomial models of short-tem interest rate and price movements. The stochastic interest rate model was proposed by Vasicek (1977). Under this model, interest rates are assumed to revert to a long-term mean, a process known as *mean reversion*. The parameters that define the interest rate process are the long-term mean μ, the speed of adjustment to the mean a, the short-term rate of interest r, and the volatility of the short-term rate σ. The model for estimating a change in the short rate dr for a given change in time dt is specified as

$$dr = a(\mu - r)dt + \sigma\,dz$$

where dz is an increment to a Brownian motion process and $\sigma\,dz$ represents a normally distributed random variable with expected value equal to zero.

Many variations of the Vasicek model have been proposed to improve upon the assumptions of the original model. The mean reversion process is often replaced with a process that fits the current term structure of interest rates. Models based on short-term rates include Cox-Ingersoll-Ross (1985), Ho-Lee (1985), Black-Karasinski (1990), Black-Derman-Toy (1991), Heath-Jarrow-Morton (1991), and Hull-White (1994). Models have been adopted by market participants for various applications, as outlined in Exhibit 8.21.

INTEREST RATE CAPS AND FLOORS

An *interest rate cap* is a contract that makes periodic payments to the buyer when interest rates on a floating-rate index exceed a benchmark rate,

EXHIBIT 8.21

Interest Rate Option Pricing Models
and Common Applications

Model	Common Application
Vasicek (1977)	European bond options
Cox-Ross-Rubinstein (1979)	American equity and futures options
Cox-Ingersoll-Ross (1985)	European bond options
Ho-Lee (1986)	American bond options
Heath-Jarrow-Morton (1991)	European bond options
Hull-White (1994)	American bond options, swaptions
Black (1976)	Interest rates caps/floors, futures options
Black-Karasinski (1991)	American bond options, swaptions, caps/floors
Black-Dorman Toy (1990)	American bond options
Black-Scholes (1973), Merton (1973)	European equity options

similar to a strike price. Like interest rate swaps, payments are based on a notional principal amount. The payoff profile for an interest rate cap is similar to that of a call option. Unlike a call option, interest rate caps do not have to be exercised for the buyer to receive payment. If the cap is in-the-money, on average, during the cap period, the cap buyer will receive a payment. Interest rate caps are used as a hedge against increases in interest rates. For example, an issuer of floating-rate bonds may use an interest rate cap to prevent excessive debt payments in high-interest-rate markets. The payment on an interest rate cap based on a notional principal amount F, assuming a periodic reset of 0.25 years, an index level of S_I, and a strike price of X_c, is

$$\text{Payment (cap)} = 0.25\ (F)\ \text{MAX}(S_I - X_c, 0)$$

An *interest rate floor* is a contract that makes periodic payments to the buyer when interest rates on a floating-rate index fall below a benchmark rate. Payments are also based on a notional principal amount. The payoff profile for an interest rate floor is similar to that of a put option. If the floor is in-the-money, on average, during the floor period, the floor buyer will receive a payment. Interest rate floors are used as a hedge

EXHIBIT 8.22

Example Cap and Floor Levels

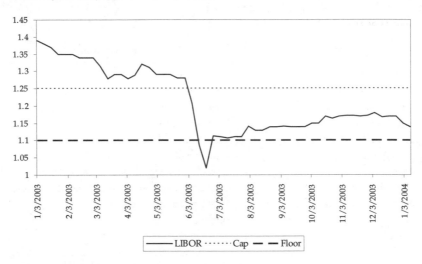

against a decrease in interest rates. For example, a portfolio manager invested in floating-rate bonds may use an interest rate floor to protect the yield on the bonds in low-interest-rate markets. The payment on an interest rate floor based on a notional principal amount F, assuming a periodic reset of 0.25 years, an index level of S_I, and a strike price of X_f, is

$$\text{Payment (floor)} = 0.25\,(F)\,\text{MAX}(X_f - S_I, 0)$$

Exhibit 8.22 shows weekly three-month LIBOR yields from January 3, 2003 to January 3, 2004. Also shown are hypothetical cap and floor levels of 1.25% and 1.10%, respectively. In the example, when LIBOR is above the cap line or below the floor line, a payment is due to the respective parties.

CAP AND FLOOR VALUATION

A simple and commonly used approach to valuing interest rate caps and floors was developed by Black (1976). Like other models, it assumes constant volatility. This is not much of a problem for interest rate options, because they are valued over small time intervals of one to six months. To apply this model, the option must be viewed as a series of smaller options, called *caplets* or *floorlets*. Each caplet or floorlet represents the interest rate option between interest rate reset periods. For example, if the interest rate option makes periodic payments every three months, the caplets and floorlets are valued at three-month intervals. The value of the interest rate option is the sum of these individual values. The expected index rate in each period is estimated from the implied forward rate, $_{t-1}f_t$. The value of an interest rate cap $V_0(\text{cap})$ for Black's model is specified as

$$V_0(\text{cap}) = \sum_{t=1}^{mn} \frac{\tau}{1 + (\tau)(_{t-1}f_t)} Fe^{-n(t)(\tau)}\{_{t-1}f_t N(d_1) - X_c N(d_2)\}$$

where

$$d_1 = \frac{\ln(_{t-1}f_t/X_c) + \dfrac{\sigma^2(t)(\tau)}{2}}{\sigma\sqrt{(t)(\tau)}}$$

and

$$d_2 = d_1 - \sigma\sqrt{(t)(\tau)}$$

In the equations above, F equals the notional principal amount, r_t equals the implied zero-coupon rate at time t, τ equals the individual cap period, n equals the number of cap periods of length τ per year, m equals the periods per year and is calculated as $1/\tau$, and σ equals the annual standard deviation of the implied forward rate.

Example: Consider an interest rate cap with semiannual settlement dates ($\tau = 0.5$). The cap rate is 2.00% and the cap matures in one year. The cap has a $10 million notional principal amount and is based on three-month LIBOR. Our calculations use the following one-year semiannual yield curve:

Period	r_t	$_{t-1}f_t$
1	2.000%	2.000%
2	2.500%	3.002%

Assuming a volatility estimate of 0.10, the value of the cap is calculated as follows. This interest rate cap consists of two caplets. We begin with d_1 and d_2 for the first caplet:

$$d_1 = \frac{\ln(0.02 / 0.02) + \dfrac{(0.10)^2(1)(0.5)}{2}}{0.10\sqrt{(1)(0.5)}} = 0.0354$$

and

$$d_2 = 0.0354 - 0.10\sqrt{(1)(0.5)} = 0.0353$$

The value for $N(0.0354) = 0.5141$ and $N(-0.0353) = 0.4859$. Therefore, the value of the first caplet is

$$V_0(\text{cap}_1) = \frac{0.5}{1 + (0.5)(0.02)}\$10{,}000{,}000e^{-(0.02)(1)(0.5)}$$

$$\{(0.02)(0.5141) - (0.02)(0.4859)\} = \$2{,}764.30$$

The second caplet is valued in a similar way. Calculating d_1 and d_2 for the second caplet, we get

$$d_1 = \frac{\ln(0.03/0.02) + \dfrac{(0.10)^2(2)(0.5)}{2}}{0.10\sqrt{(2)(0.5)}} = 4.1047$$

and

$$d_2 = 4.1047 - 0.10\sqrt{(2)(0.5)} = 4.0047$$

The value for $N(4.1047) = 0.9999$ and $N(4.0047) = 0.9999$. Therefore, the value of the second caplet is

$$V_0(\text{cap}_2) = \frac{0.5}{1 + (0.5)(0.03)}\$10{,}000{,}000e^{-(0.025)(2)(0.5)}$$

$$\{(0.03)(0.9999) - (0.02)(0.9999)\} = \$48{,}040.02$$

The value of the two-period cap is the sum of the two caplets:

$$V_0(\text{cap}) = \$2{,}764.30 + \$48{,}040.02 = 50{,}804.32$$

An interest rate floor can be valued as a series of floorlets according to the formula

$$V_0(\text{floor}) = \sum_{t=1}^{mn} \frac{\tau}{1 + (\tau)(_{t-1}f_t)} Fe^{-h(t)(\tau)}\{X_f N(-d_2) - {}_{t-1}f_t N(-d_1)\}$$

SWAPTIONS

A *swaption* is the right to enter into an interest rate swap at a future date. The terms of the swap are established when the swaption is executed. The exercise provisions can be American, European, or Bermudan. The right to pay fixed and receive the floating rate is a *call or payer swaption*. The right to pay the floating rate and receive the fixed rate is a *put or receiver swaption*.

Swaptions are used as a hedge against changes in interest rates. Institutions with delayed financing needs can use a swaption as a way to lock in a financing cost. For example, consider a corporation with a callable bond issue. Under current market conditions, it would be profitable to issue new bonds and call the outstanding bonds. However, the call provisions prevent the corporation from calling the bonds for nine months. The corporation can lock in an option on a fixed-rate swap by buying a call swaption. If interest rates increase over the next nine months, the corporation will exercise its call option and enter into a swap under which it pays the fixed rate and receives the floating rate. Simultaneously, the corporation will issue floating-rate bonds and use the proceeds to call the outstanding bonds. The net result is a synthetic fixed-rate bond at a cost savings to the outstanding bonds. If interest rates stay the same or fall over the nine-month period, the issuer can let the option expire and issue fixed-rate bonds. A swaption is more valuable than a forward-delivery swap because of the ability to decide the course of action in the future.

VALUATION

The value of a swaption at expiration is determined by the strike price relative to the at-market swap rate. A call swaption will be exercised at maturity if the at-market swap rate c exceeds the strike price X. The spread between the two can be locked in by entering into the opposite swap at maturity. Therefore, assuming a notional principal amount of F, the gross payoff at maturity to a call swaption $V_n(c)$ is equal to

$$V_n(c) = (F) \sum_{t=1}^{mn} \frac{\text{Max}(0, c - X)\left(\frac{\text{days}}{360}\right)}{\left(1 + \dfrac{r}{m}\right)^t}$$

and the value of a put swaption is equal to

$$V_n(p) = (F) \sum_{t=1}^{mn} \frac{\text{Max}(0, X - c)\left(\frac{\text{days}}{360}\right)}{\left(1 + \dfrac{r}{m}\right)^t}$$

Pricing the option prior to maturity requires the use of a model of the term structure of interest rates to generate expected swap values over the life of the option. The models typically follow the form of those discussed above. The most popular models for valuing swaptions are Black-Karasinski (1991) and Hull-White (1994).

FUTURES OPTIONS

A *futures option* is the right to buy or sell a futures contract at the strike price. A *futures call option* gives the buyer the right to purchase the underlying futures contract at the strike price. A *futures put option* gives the buyer the right to sell the underlying futures contract at the strike price. Futures options are written on frequently traded futures contracts in the interest rate, equity, agricultural, currency, and metals markets. Exhibit 8.23 lists popular futures options, the underlying contract sizes, and the exchanges where they trade.

Futures options act to complete markets when the underlying asset does not have an active exchange-traded option market. While the U.S.

EXHIBIT 8.23

Example Futures Options Contracts

Option Contract	Exchange	Underlying Contract Size
Agricultural		
Corn	CBOT	5,000 bushels
Wheat	CBOT	5,000 bushels
Interest Rate		
10-year U.S. Treasury note	CBOT	$100,000
90-day eurodollar	CME	$1,000,000
Currency		
Yen	CME	¥12,500,000
Euro	CME	€125,000
Metals		
Gold	COMEX	100 troy ounces
Silver	COMEX	5,000 troy ounces
Equity		
S&P 500	CME	250 times index

Treasury cash market is liquid, options on specific bonds are not exchange-traded. As in the futures market, the many different maturities make it difficult to establish a generic bond on which to base an option contract. The U.S. Treasury futures exchanges have addressed this problem by establishing the cheapest-to-deliver on which to base a generic contract. Therefore, the use of U.S. Treasury futures as a proxy for the bond market is an efficient way to trade options. The same is true for other futures options contracts. Exhibit 8.24 shows prices of active options on the 10-year U.S. Treasury note as of the market close on January 26, 2004.

VALUATION

A common approach to valuing futures options is a European option pricing model developed by Black (1976). The model is an extension of the of the Black-Scholes (1973) option pricing model. Recall from Chapter 6

E X H I B I T   8.24

Options on the 10-year U.S. Treasury Note Futures Contract

Strike Price	Open	Change (ticks)	High	Low	Close
		Call Options			
112	2'20	−22	2'20	2'00	2'00
113	1'32	−18	1'32	1'21	1'21
114	1'00	−12	1'00	0'49	0'51
115	0'32	−8	0'35	0'26	0'27
116	0'15	−4	0'17	0'12	0'13
117	0'06	−2	0'07	0'05	0'05
118	0'02	−1	0'03	0'02	0'02
		Put Options			
110	0'08	3	0'10	0'07	0'10
111	0'14	4	0'18	0'13	0'17
112	0'24	8	0'31	0'22	0'30
113	0'40	12	0'51	0'38	0'51
114	1'01	18	1'17	1'00	1'17
115	1'39	22	1'57	1'36	1'57
116	2'21	26	2'43	2'19	2'43

Source: www.CBOT.com. Underlying contract price: 113–17 as of January 26, 2004. Price quotations are in points and 64ths.

that the futures contract price F_0 is related to the spot price of an asset S_0 as follows

$$F_0 = S_0 e^{gn}$$

where g is the carrying costs on the underlying asset relative to the spot price and n is the time to maturity in years. Under the assumption that carrying costs can be treated as a continuous cost equal to the risk-free rate r the value of the underlying asset is

$$S_0 = F_0 e^{-rn}$$

Replacing the spot asset price with the value derived above, and given the strike price on the option X and the volatility of the underlying futures contract σ, the value of a futures call option $V_t(c)$ is specified as

$$V_t(c) = e^{-rn} \{F_0 N(d_1) - X_c N(d_2)\}$$

where

$$d_1 = \frac{\ln\left(\dfrac{F_0}{X_c}\right) + \left(\dfrac{\sigma^2 n}{2}\right)}{\sigma \sqrt{n}}$$

and

$$d_2 = d_1 - \sigma \sqrt{n}$$

Example: Consider a futures call option with a strike price X_c of 113 from Exhibit 8.24. The options closed at a price of 1 21/64 on January 26, 2004. The underlying asset price F_0 was 113 17/32 and the 30-day historical volatility of the futures contract σ was 7.92% as of the pricing date. Assume a risk-free rate r of 0.90%. The maturity date of the option is February 20, 2004, or 25 days from the pricing date. Therefore the time to maturity n is $25/360 = 0.0694$ years. As we did earlier, we begin by calculating d_1 and d_2

$$d_1 = \frac{\ln\left(\dfrac{113.53125}{113.0}\right) + \left(\dfrac{(0.0792)^2 (0.0694)}{2}\right)}{0.0792 \sqrt{0.0694}} = 0.2364$$

and

$$d_2 = 0.2364 - 0.792 \sqrt{0.0694} = 0.2156$$

The values for $N(0.2364) = 0.5935$ and $N(0.2156) = 0.5854$. Therefore, the value of the call option is 1.23 or 1 15/64:

$$V_t(c) = e^{-(0.0090)(0.0694)} \{(113.53125)(0.5935)$$
$$- (113.00)(0.5854)\} = 1.23$$

The theoretical option value is less than the market value as of the pricing date. Therefore the implied volatility is higher than the estimate based on historic volatility. In the example, the implied volatility is close to 9.00%.

The model relies on several important assumptions. In particular, volatility is assumed to be constant, and cost-of-carry g is only a function of time to maturity n. In practice, this model is appropriate for valuing options on commodity, currency, and equity futures. However, the assumptions of this model do not generally hold in interest rate futures markets. For options on interest rate futures a binomial model, such as CRR (1979), is more appropriate.

SUMMARY

Options are an important risk management tool. Unlike forwards, futures, and swaps, they do not obligate the hedger to perform in the future. For this reason they are more valuable and allow for more flexibility for hedging. Equity and futures options are primarily exchange traded, whereas interest rate options trade over-the-counter. Options can be efficiently traded on most liquid assets.

A basic understanding of the pricing process and the accepted models is important to a hedger. This understanding consists of a basic knowledge of binomial option pricing, the Black-Scholes options pricing model and extensions, and the various interest rate models summarized in the chapter. Knowing the assumptions of the models and which model to apply is important for the hedger.

REFERENCES

Black, F. "The Pricing of Commodity Contracts." *Journal of Financial Economics* 3 (March 1976), 167–79.

Black, F., E. Derman, and W. Toy. "A One-Factor Model of Interest Rates and Its Application to Treasury Bond Options." *Financial Analysts Journal* 46 (January–February 1990), 33–39.

Black, F., and P. Karasinski. "Bond Option Pricing When Short Rates Are Lognormal." *Financial Analysts Journal* (July–August 1991), 52–59.

Black, F., and M. Scholes. "The Pricing of Options and Corporate Liabilities." *Journal of Politcal Economy* 81 (May–June 1973), 637–59.

Cox, J. C., S. A. Ross, and M. Rubinstein. "Option Pricing: A Simplified Approach." *Journal of Financial Economics* 7 (September 1979), 229–64.

Cox, J. C., J. E. Ingersoll, and S. A. Ross. "A Theory of the Term Structure of Interest Rates." *Econometrica* 53 (March 1985), 385–407.

Cox, J. C., and Mark Rubinstein. *Option Markets*. Englewood Cliffs, NJ: Prentice Hall, 1985.

Heath, D., R. Jarrow, and A. Morton. "Contingent Claim Valuation with Random Evolution of Interest Rates." *Review of Futures Markets* 9.1 (1991), 55–76.

——. "Bond Pricing and the Term Structure of Interest Rates: A New Methodology for Contingent Claim Valuation." *Econometrica* 60 (January 1992), 77–106.

Ho, Thomas S. Y., and Sang-Bin Lee. "Term Structure Movements and Pricing Interest Rate Contingent Claims." *Journal of Finance* 41 (December 1986), 1011–29.

Hull, J. *Introduction to Futures and Options Markets*. Englewood Cliffs, NJ: Prentice Hall, 1991.

Hull, John, and Alan White. "Numerical Procedures for Implementing Term Structure Models I: Single-Factor Models." *Journal of Derivatives* 2 (Fall 1994), 7–16.

——. "Numerical Procedures for Implementing Term Structure Models II: Two-Factor Models." *Journal of Derivatives* 2 (Winter 1994), 37–48.

Merton, Robert C. "Theory of Rational Option Pricing." *Bell Journal of Economics and Management* 4 (Spring 1973), 141–83.

Vasicek, O. A. "An Equilibrium Characterization of the Term Structure." *Journal of Financial Economics* 5 (November 1977), 177–88.

CHAPTER 9

Commodities

A *commodity* is a physical substance, such as food, grain, or metal, that is interchangeable with another product of the same type. Modern commodity markets have their origins in the trading of agricultural products. In the United States, there were established central markets for grains in cities like Chicago by the 1840s. Spot market transactions between farmers and dealers eventually led to the development of forward and futures contracts as these market participants committed to future exchanges of grain.

Companies routinely commit to future purchases or sales of commodity goods. Fluctuations in the prices of these goods expose the company to the risk of increased future costs or reduced future revenues. For example, oil producers face the risk of lower revenues associated with a decrease in the price of oil. Companies with significant production inputs, such as energy and metals, face the risk of increased costs associated with an increase in the cost of these inputs.

In this chapter, we examine hedging techniques for companies facing exposure to commodity price fluctuations. We discuss alternative methods of hedging that use commodity futures contracts, commodity swaps, and commodity options. Finally, we compare hedges constructed with various instruments.

THE COMMODITY DERIVATIVES MARKET

Most commodity trading occurs in the commodity futures market. A commodity traded in the spot market is known as a *cash commodity*, which is the actual physical commodity on which a futures contract is written. Futures contracts have standardized terms, which specify the terms under which the commodity is to be delivered. The terms include the contract size, delivery date(s), and delivery point, as well as the quality of the cash commodity.

Commodity futures and options contracts trade on 20 different exchanges in the United States. As of September 30, 2003, there were 452 commodity futures and options contracts authorized for trading by the Commodity Futures Trading Commission (CFTC).[1] Exhibit 9.1 presents descriptive statistics on U.S. commodity futures contracts for the period 1994–2003. Contracts trade on grains, oilseed products, livestock products, other agriculturals, energy/wood products, and metals. Energy/wood products are the most actively traded, followed by oilseed products, grains, and metals. The overall number of contracts traded has increased by 53% since 1994, with the largest increase coming from energy/wood products.

In most cases, buyers and sellers do not deliver on the cash commodity underlying the futures contract, opting instead to liquidate their positions before the contract expires. Exhibit 9.2 shows the percentage of futures contracts settled through delivery. During the period 1994–2003, less than 1% of all contracts were settled through delivery.

There is an active market for options on commodities in the United States. Most exchange-traded commodity options contracts are futures options; the exercise of futures options results in the establishment of a position in the underlying futures contract. Exhibit 9.3 presents descriptive statistics on commodity options in the United States. In terms of the number of traded options contracts, energy/wood products are the most actively traded and fastest growing segment of the market. The overall number of contracts traded has increased by 96% during the period 1994–2003.

HISTORIC COMMODITY DATA

For the examples presented in this chapter, we use daily spot prices for jet fuel, crude oil, gold, aluminum, and copper. Many different spot prices

---

1. Excluding financial and currency contracts.

EXHIBIT 9.1

Commodity Futures Average Month-End Open Interest
and Number of Contracts Traded by Major Groups,
1994–2003

Fiscal Year	Total	Grain	Oilseed Products	Livestock Products	Other Agriculturals	Energy/ Wood Products	Metals
Average Month-End Open Interest (thousands of contracts)							
1994	2,370	422	323	126	328	807	363
1995	2,385	503	332	119	357	696	378
1996	2,560	594	383	149	357	708	369
1997	2,569	485	378	159	400	793	355
1998	2,882	561	410	156	425	969	351
1999	3,077	582	420	179	395	1,140	361
2000	3,083	684	424	200	441	1,015	319
2001	3,112	687	435	186	429	1,089	286
2002	3,298	681	472	145	460	1,224	317
2003	4,033	625	528	174	508	1,801	398
Number of Contracts Traded (thousands of contracts)							
1994	128,106	19,970	20,988	6,137	12,319	50,461	18,231
1995	126,103	21,094	20,688	6,239	12,745	47,944	17,393
1996	138,707	30,217	25,592	7,049	12,019	46,892	16,939
1997	141,987	25,507	27,132	7,551	13,191	51,512	17,093
1998	153,169	26,140	26,854	7,386	14,040	61,705	17,045
1999	163,914	26,860	25,625	7,439	13,754	72,942	17,294
2000	160,711	27,415	24,663	6,840	13,807	74,066	13,920
2001	156,665	27,486	24,695	7,000	12,560	72,476	12,448
2002	178,524	29,173	27,881	6,698	13,658	86,831	14,282
2003	195,824	28,917	30,918	7,191	15,560	94,636	18,602

Source: Commodity Futures Trading Commission, *Annual Report*, 2000–2003.

are available based on quality and delivery points. We chose spot prices corresponding to the most liquid commodities. For jet fuel spot prices, we use the New York Harbor 54 Grade Jet Fuel Spot Price. The crude oil price is the light sweet crude oil index price. For metals, we use the Metal

EXHIBIT 9.2

Percentage of Futures Contracts Settled by Delivery/Cash
Settlement by Major Groups, 1994–2003

Fiscal Year	Total	Grain	Oilseed Products	Livestock Products	Other Agriculturals	Energy/ Wood Products	Metals
1994	0.4%	0.4%	0.4%	0.1%	0.4%	0.2%	1.0%
1995	0.4%	0.3%	0.8%	0.2%	0.5%	0.2%	0.9%
1996	0.3%	0.1%	0.7%	0.2%	0.3%	0.2%	0.8%
1997	0.4%	0.1%	0.5%	0.4%	0.3%	0.2%	0.8%
1998	0.4%	0.5%	0.4%	0.6%	0.2%	0.2%	1.0%
1999	0.3%	0.4%	0.4%	0.6%	0.2%	0.2%	0.7%
2000	0.4%	0.5%	0.6%	0.6%	0.5%	0.1%	1.1%
2001	0.4%	0.6%	0.5%	0.6%	0.5%	0.1%	1.4%
2002	0.3%	0.4%	0.3%	0.5%	0.5%	0.1%	1.5%
2003	0.7%	0.3%	0.2%	0.5%	0.6%	0.9%	1.1%

Source: Commodity Futures Trading Commission, *Annual Report*, 2000–2003.

Bulletin copper high grade cathode spot price, the spot price of gold, and the Metal Bulletin high-grade aluminum ingot mid-west spot price.

We use several different hedging instruments for the above commodities. Heating oil futures are typically used to hedge diesel fuel and jet fuel. For our jet fuel examples, we use the NYMEX New York Harbor heating oil futures contract. Our crude oil hedges are constructed with the NYMEX light sweet crude oil futures contract and futures option contract. The COMEX 100-oz. gold futures contract is used for our gold hedging examples. Copper hedges are constructed with the COMEX copper futures contract and the LME three-month forward contract.

The choice of hedging instrument is affected by a number of factors. In many cases, the asset underlying the hedging instrument may not be identical to the asset being hedged. The hedger may also wish to have flexibility regarding the expiration of the hedge because of an uncertain sale or purchase date of an asset. This is of particular concern if hedgers prefer to settle their positions in cash instead of taking delivery of the underlying commodity. For traded hedging instruments, such as futures

EXHIBIT 9.3

Commodity Options Average Month-End Open Interest and Number of Contracts Traded by Major Groups, 1994–2003

Fiscal Year	Total	Grain	Oilseed Products	Livestock Products	Other Agriculturals	Energy/ Wood Products	Metals
Average Month-End Open Interest (thousands of contracts)							
1994	1,604	241	226	61	250	576	251
1995	1,724	348	186	73	376	429	312
1996	2,195	537	290	82	303	588	394
1997	2,436	490	298	90	343	771	445
1998	2,756	476	339	85	441	895	521
1999	2,979	461	391	102	420	1,011	594
2000	3,289	631	281	110	450	1,238	578
2001	3,018	570	270	121	401	1,303	354
2002	3,824	581	262	82	457	2,151	291
2003	3,865	570	292	92	465	2,013	433
Number of Contracts Traded (thousands of contracts)							
1994	22,084	3,340	3,493	719	3,266	8,076	3,191
1995	22,207	4,311	3,140	768	4,224	6,461	3,303
1996	29,861	8,574	5,758	896	3,446	7,817	3,370
1997	30,344	6,963	6,249	960	3,837	9,575	2,758
1998	33,164	6,251	5,663	1,001	4,937	12,133	3,178
1999	34,295	5,915	6,587	993	4,881	12,759	3,158
2000	36,472	6,994	5,190	883	5,046	14,905	3,455
2001	33,700	6,921	4,958	1,102	3,839	14,463	2,416
2002	43,350	7,472	5,254	827	4,178	23,109	2,511
2003	43,179	6,772	5,285	897	5,288	20,682	4,254

Source: Commodity Futures Trading Commission, *Annual Report*, 2000–2003.

contracts, prices tend to be erratic during the delivery month. It is preferable to choose a hedging instrument with an expiration that is as near to, but later than, the expiration of the hedge. The liquidity of alternative hedging instruments is also a consideration.

The above situations give rise to *basis risk*. Basis risk refers to changes in the value of the hedging instrument that do not correspond with changes in the value of the asset being hedged. The relationship between changes in spot prices and changes in hedging instrument prices can be examined by calculation of correlation coefficients and hedge ratios. A high correlation is generally associated with low basis risk. Hedge ratios provide information about the relative movements of a target portfolio and the hedging instrument. We calculate hedge ratios for selected hedge instruments based on the following equation:

$$\Delta S_t = \beta_0 + \beta_1 \Delta F_t + \varepsilon_t$$

where
ΔS_t = change in the spot price at time t
β_0 = intercept coefficient
β_1 = hedge ratio beta
ΔF_t = change in futures or forward price at time t
ε_t = error term, $E(\varepsilon) = 0$

Sample hedge ratios $\hat{\beta}_1$ and sample correlation coefficients r are presented in Exhibit 9.4.[2] As shown by the correlations, the strongest relationship between changes in spot and futures prices is found in the crude oil and gold markets. Jet fuel is hedged with a related commodity, and the resulting relationship is weaker, as shown by the correlation coefficient of 0.6277. The correlations and hedge ratios for the copper market are lower because of differences in grades between the spot commodity and the underlying asset of the futures/forward markets.

TECHNIQUES FOR HEDGING COMMODITY RISK

Companies faced with exposure to fluctuating commodity prices can choose from among several hedging methods. The appropriate method is determined by the cash flows associated with each method, the size of the position, the expiration of the hedge, and the goals of the hedger. We discuss four methods of hedging commodity risk: futures hedge, forward hedge, swap hedge, and commodity option hedge.

---

2. All calculations use prices expressed in identical units.

E X H I B I T   9.4

Summary of Historic Commodity Market
and Hedge Data Daily Price Changes,
2000–2004

Hedge	$\hat{\beta}_1$	r	Obs.
Jet Fuel			
Heating Oil Futures	1.2893	0.6277	338
Crude Oil			
Futures	0.8973	0.8580	121
Gold			
Futures	0.9722	0.9608	477
Copper			
Futures	0.3729	0.3205	472
Forward	0.5678	0.5108	651
Aluminum			
Futures	0.3916	0.3100	1,008
Forward	0.6614	0.4437	1,008

COMMODITY FUTURES HEDGE

Commodity futures can hedge commodity price exposure by providing hedgers with a cash flow stream that offsets losses in their spot position. The resulting net cash flows from the combined positions in the commodity and the commodity futures contract effectively establish a fixed price. If the underlying asset on the futures contract is identical to the spot asset and the hedger intends to hold the contract until delivery, it may be sufficient to establish a hedge position equal in value to the spot position. However, if the spot position is highly sensitive to changes in the futures price, a larger number of futures contracts will be required to generate sufficient cash flows to establish an effective hedge. Spot positions may be sensitive because of a high hedge ratio, a high market value, or both. The number of contracts required for a minimum variance hedge is calculated as

$$N^* = \frac{V_S}{V_H} h^*$$

where

N^* = units (contracts) of the futures contract,
h^* = *ex ante* hedge ratio, equal to the expected change in the spot price per change in the futures price.
V_S = market value of the spot position,
V_H = market value per contract of the hedging instrument.

Example: A mining company expects to have 25,000 ounces of gold available for sale in June 2004. On January 5, 2004, gold is trading at $423.65, its highest price in more than two years. The company considers the current price to be favorable, given current production costs. The company decides to lock in a profit by taking a short position in gold futures contracts. Since the hedge expires in the expiration month for the July 2004 contract, the company decides to hedge by using the August contract. On January 5, 2004, the COMEX August 2004 gold futures price is $427.80. The company closes its position on June 10, 2004, when the spot price is $386.05 and the futures price is $386.60.

To estimate the hedge ratio, we regress changes in spot market prices against the futures price prior to January 5, 2004. Using a 60-day period, we find a hedge ratio of 0.9726 for the observation period. The adjusted R^2 is 0.9574, indicating a very strong positive correlation between spot and futures prices over the time period. Since each gold futures contract is for the delivery of 100 ounces, the number of contracts required to hedge the sale is equal to

$$N^* = \frac{(\$423.65)(25,000)(0.9726)}{(\$427.80)(1,000)} \approx 24$$

Exhibit 9.5 summarizes the transactions and the company's gains and losses on each position.

The gain on the short futures position is an offset to the reduced price of selling gold on the expiration date at a price at the spot price S_n. The unhedged value of gold has decreased by $37.60/ounce (423.65 − 386.05), or $940,000, while the futures position increased by $988,800. Exhibit 9.6 shows the daily net value of the hedged and unhedged positions during the period.

EXHIBIT 9.5

Cumulative Payoff on Short Futures Hedge on Gold

Date	Position	Futures Price	Cumulative Payoff
1/5/04	Sell 24 Futures Contracts	$423.65	$427.80 - S_n$
6/10/04	Buy 24 Futures Contracts	$386.60	$S_n - 386.60$
Cumulative Payoff at Maturity		$24,000(\$427.80 - 386.60) = \$988,800$	

CARRYING COSTS WITH COMMODITY FUTURES CONTRACTS

In the above example, the initial futures price exceeded the spot price of gold, a market condition called *contango*. Precious metals markets are almost always in contango. The lower spot price reflects the storage costs

EXHIBIT 9.6

Dollar Value of Hedged and Unhedged Sale of 25,000 Ounces of Gold, January 5, 2004 to June 10, 2004

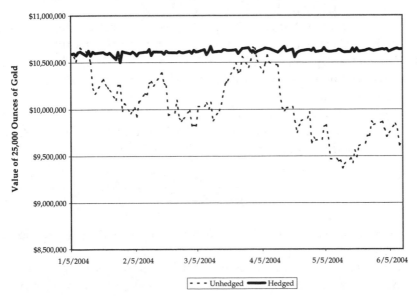

associated with a spot position in the commodity. The net value of the hedged position on day t is given by

$$V_t = S_t + F_0 - F_t = F_0 + b_t$$

where

S_t = the spot price at time t
F_t = the futures price at time t
F_0 = the futures price at time 0 (1/05/2004)
$b_t = S_t - F_t$, the basis on the commodity futures contract at time t

The Law of One Price requires that spot and futures prices be equal when the futures contract matures. As the spot and futures prices converge toward the maturity of the futures contract at time n, the basis will approach zero, $b_n = S_n - F_n = 0$. In contango markets, the negative initial basis implies that short hedges will tend to increase in value and long hedges will tend to decrease in value. More generally, short hedges increase in value and long hedges will tend to decrease in value (increase in cost) whenever the basis increases during the hedging period. In the above example, the short hedge increased in value by $48,800 over the time period.

Example: A refiner expects to purchase 50,000 barrels of crude oil in June 2004. The spot price on April 1, 2004 is $33.19. The company decides to hedge its risk by buying the August NYMEX light sweet crude oil futures contract. Trading on the August 2004 contract expires on July 20, 2004, and each contract is for the delivery of 1,000 barrels. The futures price quotation on the August contract is $32.85 on April 1, 2004. The company closes its position on June 10, 2004, when the spot price is $36.94 and the futures price is $38.65.

Using the 60-day period prior to April 1, 2004, we find a hedge ratio of 0.7769 for the 60-day observation period. The adjusted R^2 is 0.6743. The number of contracts required to hedge the purchase is equal to

$$N^* = \frac{(\$33.19)(50,000)(0.7769)}{(\$32.85)(1,000)} \approx 39$$

Exhibit 9.7 summarizes the transactions and the refiner's gains and losses on each position.

The gain on the futures position is an offset to the increased price of purchasing crude oil in the spot market. The unhedged cost of purchasing

EXHIBIT 9.7

Cumulative Payoff on Long Futures Hedge on Crude Oil

Date	Position	Futures Price	Cumulative Payoff
4/1/04	Buy 39 Futures Contracts	$32.85	$S_n - \$32.85$
6/1/04	Sell 39 Futures Contracts	$38.65	$38.65 - S_n$
Cumulative Payoff at Maturity		$39,000(\$38.65 - \$32.85) = \$226,200$	

crude oil has increased by $3.75/barrel (36.94 − 33.19), or $187,500, while the futures position increased by $226,200. Exhibit 9.8 shows the daily net value of the hedged and unhedged positions during the period.

In the above example, the initial hedge is established when the spot price exceeds the futures price, a market condition known as *backwardation*. In a backwardated market, the positive initial basis is expected to decrease as the futures contract approaches maturity, thereby decreasing the net cost of purchasing crude oil with a long hedge. When the hedge expires, the spot price falls below the futures price in our example. The net cost of purchasing crude oil with a long hedge decreased by $38,700 over the time period.

CROSS-MARKET COMMODITY HEDGING WITH FUTURES

When the asset underlying the hedging instrument is not identical to the asset being hedged, there is increased basis risk associated with hedging. This situation is often faced by hedgers when the spot commodity is not traded in the futures market or when there is a difference in grades between the two commodities. Using different commodities can have a pronounced effect on both the hedge ratio and the correlation between spot and futures price changes. If the hedger can choose from many different instruments, a good rule of thumb is to choose the futures contract with price changes that have the highest correlation with the price changes of the underlying asset.

E X H I B I T   9.8

Dollar Cost of Hedged and Unhedged Purchase of 50,000
Barrels of Crude Oil Long Hedge with Futures Contracts,
April 1, 2004 to June 10, 2004

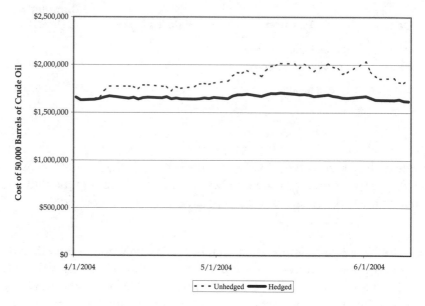

Example: An airline expects to purchase 1,000,000 barrels (42 million
gallons) of jet fuel in three months. The spot price on April 1, 2004 is
$0.9087/gallon. The company is concerned that the price of jet fuel will
rise and decides to hedge with NYMEX New York Harbor heating oil futures contracts. Trading on the August 2004 contract is halted on July 20,
2004; each contract is for the delivery of 1,000 barrels (42,000 gallons). The
futures price quotation on the August contract is $0.8356/gallon on April 1,
2004. The company closes its position on June 1, 2004, when the spot price
is $1.1054 and the futures price is $1.0688.

The company has estimated the hedge ratio to be 1.13 for the time
period. The number of contracts required to hedge the purchase is equal to

$$N^* = \frac{(\$0.9087)(42{,}000{,}000)(1.13)}{(\$0.8356)(42{,}000)} \approx 1{,}229$$

EXHIBIT 9.9

Cumulative Payoff on Long Futures Hedge on Crude Oil

Date	Position	Futures Price	Cumulative Payoff
4/1/04	Buy 1,229 Futures Contracts	$0.8356	$S_n - \$0.8356$
6/1/04	Sell 1,229 Futures Contracts	$1.0688	$1.0688 - S_n$
Cumulative Payoff at Maturity		(1,229)(42,000)($1.0688 − $0.8356) = $12,037,318	

Exhibit 9.9 summarizes the transactions and the refiner's gains and losses on each position.

The gain on the futures position is an offset to the increased price of purchasing jet fuel in the spot market. The unhedged cost of purchasing jet fuel has increased by $0.1967/gallon (1.1054 − 0.9087), or $8,261,400, while the hedged position increased by $12,037,318. The net cost of purchasing jet fuel has decreased by $3,775,918. Exhibit 9.10 shows the daily net value of the hedged and unhedged positions during the period.

STABILITY OF FUTURES HEDGE RATIOS

Effective hedging requires the hedger to make an accurate estimate of the hedge ratio. Hedge ratios can be unstable and may require the hedger to adjust the size of the futures position, especially for long-term hedges. Exhibit 9.11 shows empirical hedge ratios for gold, crude oil, and jet fuel. The hedge ratios were estimated from a regression of spot market price changes on futures price changes for a lagging 60-day period. The hedge ratio for jet fuel decreases from 1.51 to 1.10 for the three-month period. The crude oil hedge ratio is slightly more stable, increasing from 0.77 to 1.00 during the hedging period. The hedge ratio of gold is the most stable of the three, fluctuating between 0.88 and 0.96.

For the jet fuel example, we estimated an *ex ante* hedge ratio of 1.13 with the use of a ordinary least-squares regression model for 30 days prior to the establishment of the hedge. The *ex post* hedge ratio for the time period was 1.06. More sophisticated methods may be used that account for the time-varying nature of commodity hedge ratios.[3]

EXHIBIT 9.10

Dollar Cost of Hedged and Unhedged Purchase of 1,000,000 Barrels of Jet Fuel Long Hedge with Heating Oil Futures Contracts, April 1, 2004 to June 1, 2004

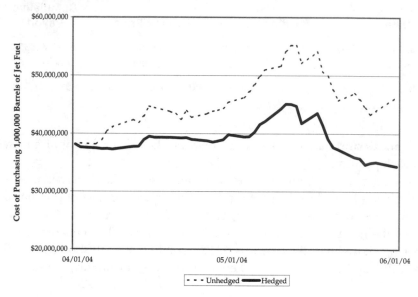

COMMODITY HEDGING WITH SWAPS

There are many situations where firms have a series of future transactions in a commodity. Recurrent purchases or sales can be hedged with a commodity swap. In a fixed-for-floating commodity price swap, the buyer agrees to pay a fixed price to the seller for a specific quantity of an underlying asset on a series of future dates. The seller agrees to make periodic payments to the buyer based on a floating price for the same quantity of the underlying asset. The floating price is typically based on a well-known reference price for the underlying asset, and a net payment is made at each payment date based on the difference between the floating and fixed prices.

---

3. For example, see Garcia, Roh, and Leuthold (1995), Myers (1991), and Myers and Thompson (1989).

EXHIBIT 9.11

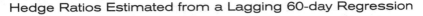

Hedge Ratios Estimated from a Lagging 60-day Regression

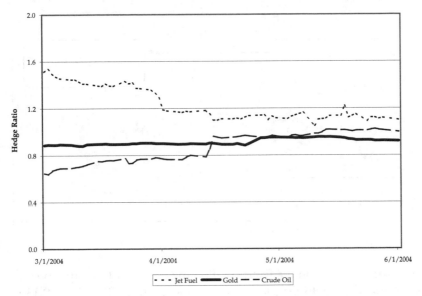

Example: On January 4, 2000, an aluminum producer plans to produce and sell on the spot market 30,000,000 pounds of aluminum over the next three years. The sales will occur every six months and will be sold at the high-grade aluminum ingot mid-west spot price. The company is concerned that the price of aluminum will drop, thereby leading to losses in future revenues.

To hedge this risk, the company enters into a three-year fixed-for-floating commodity price swap. Every six months, the swap requires the company to pay the swap dealer the average daily aluminum spot price over the previous six months. The swap dealer will pay the company $0.75/lb for 7,500,000 lbs of aluminum. Through the use of this swap, the company has effectively locked in an aluminum price of $0.75/lb. Exhibit 9.12 shows the cash flows associated with the swap.

The company will generate sales revenues by selling aluminum in the spot market. If the price of aluminum falls, sales revenues will decrease. In this situation, the decrease in sales revenues will be offset by the

EXHIBIT 9.12

Cash Flows on a Commodity Swap Hedge

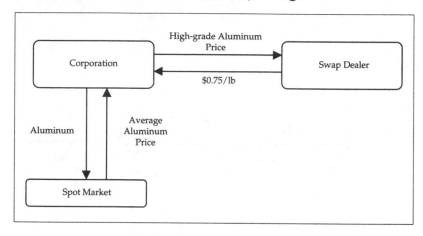

decreased payment on the fixed-for-floating commodity swap. The net effect of the swap is to lock in sales revenue at $0.75/lb. Exhibit 9.13 presents sales revenues along with the cash flows from the swap.

COMMODITY HEDGING WITH OPTIONS

In the examples in this chapter, we have seen how investors can lock in a price by hedging with futures or swaps. Consider a company that establishes a short hedge to lock in the price at which it will sell crude oil. In addition to the transactions costs and carrying costs associated with this hedge, there is also an implicit opportunity cost associated with foregone profits. If crude oil were to rise in price, the company would be better off in an unhedged position. In this situation, the implicit cost of hedging to eliminate unfavorable price movements is the elimination of favorable price movements as well.

An alternative method of hedging is to use commodity options. Commodity options permit the hedger to eliminate unfavorable price movements while benefiting from favorable price movements. Hedgers using options incur an explicit up-front cost in the form of an option premium.

E X H I B I T   9.13

Payments from a Fixed-for-Floating Commodity Swap

		Commodity Swap			Revenues	
Period	Average Aluminum Price	Floating Payment	Fixed Payment Received	Net Payment	Spot Market Sales Revenue	Net Sales Revenue
1	0.7663	5,747,053	5,625,000	122,053	5,747,053	5,625,000
2	0.7463	5,596,925	5,625,000	−28,075	5,596,925	5,625,000
3	0.7346	5,509,147	5,625,000	−115,853	5,509,147	5,625,000
4	0.6523	4,892,496	5,625,000	−732,504	4,892,496	5,625,000
5	0.6622	4,966,613	5,625,000	−658,387	4,966,613	5,625,000
6	0.6480	4,860,037	5,625,000	−764,963	4,860,037	5,625,000

Example: Consider our previous example, where a refiner expects to purchase 50,000 barrels of crude oil in June 2004. The company is concerned that the price of crude oil will rise above $36 per barrel. The company decides to hedge its risk by buying the August NYMEX light sweet crude oil futures call option contract with a strike price of $36. August 2004 futures call options on crude oil are traded at a premium of $0.80. The call option is an American option that gives the holder the right to enter into a long position in the August NYMEX light sweet crude oil futures contract with a delivery price of $36 per barrel. The option expires on July 15, 2004, three business days prior to the expiration of the underlying futures contract. On April 1, 2004, the spot price is $33.19 and the premium on the option is $0.80 per barrel.

The company pays the option premium to ensure that it pays no more than $36/barrel. If the spot price remains below $36/barrel, the company will pay the market price for crude oil but will have incurred the cost of purchasing the option. Exhibit 9.14 summarizes the company's transactions.

The optimal number of contracts depends on the goals of the hedger. If the objective is to minimize the intraday volatility of the hedged

EXHIBIT 9.14

Spot and Futures Option Prices on Crude Oil

Date	Crude Oil Spot Price	Crude Oil Futures Call Option Premium
4/1/2004	$33.19	$0.80
6/1/2004	$40.73	$6.56

position prior to the hedge expiration, as was the case in our previous example, then the hedger should calculate the optimal number of contracts based on the futures hedge ratio and the market value of the underlying spot and futures positions. However, if the objective is to place a cap on the price paid for crude oil upon expiration of the hedge, then a one-to-one hedge is appropriate. The company purchases 50 August call options at a cost of $40,000. The company plans to sell the option contracts on June 1, 2004 instead of holding them to expiration.

On June 1, 2004, the company purchases crude oil in the spot market and sells the call option. The hedged cost of purchasing crude oil on this date is $1,708,500, which is equal to the spot market cost of $2,036,500 less the $328,000 premium received from selling the call. The net hedged cost is equal to $1,748,500, which is the hedged cost plus the $40,000 premium paid for the call. Exhibit 9.15 shows the daily net value of the hedged and unhedged positions.

In the above example, the hedged cost of purchasing crude oil would be higher than the unhedged cost when the price is relatively low. As the price of crude oil rises, the higher premium at which the company can sell the option will offset the company's losses in the spot market. The call option ensures that the hedged cost of purchasing crude oil never exceeds $1,800,000 ($36/barrel), excluding the call premium. In this case, the hedger incurs a slightly lower net cost ($34.97/ barrel).

SUMMARY

Companies with significant purchases or sales of commodity goods are faced with price exposure related to fluctuations in commodity prices. In

EXHIBIT 9.15

Net Hedged and Unhedged Costs of Purchasing
50,000 Barrels of Crude Oil Long Hedge with Call Options,
April 1, 2004 to June 1, 2004

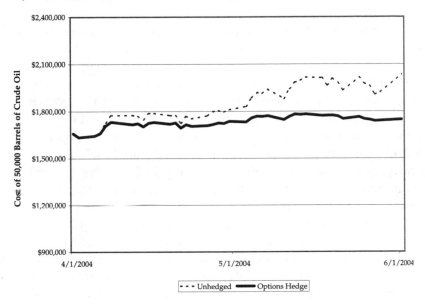

COMPARISON OF HEDGING ALTERNATIVES

Hedge	Pros	Cons
Commodity Futures	Liquid	Standardized terms
	Low transaction costs	Daily mark-to-market
		May require rolling hedge
		Basis risk
		No benefit from favorable price movements
Commodity Forwards	Customized terms	Illiquid
	No basis risk	High transaction costs
	No intermediate cash flows	No benefit from favorable price movements
Commodity Swaps	Customized terms	Expensive
	Useful for recurrent cash flows	No benefit from favorable price movements
Commodity Options	Benefit from favorable price movements	Expensive

this chapter, we focused on hedging techniques to manage commodity price risk. Commodity price risk is the risk that the value of future transactions in a commodity will fluctuate as commodity prices fluctuate. Commodity price exposure can be hedged with commodity futures, swaps, or options.

Commodity futures contracts may be used effectively for short-term hedges. Futures provide hedgers with a cash-flow stream that offsets losses in their spot commodity position, effectively establishing a fixed price. The correlation between price changes in spot and futures markets is not perfect, which subjects hedgers to a certain amount of basis risk. The size of the futures position is determined by the value of the target position relative to each futures contract and the sensitivity of the target position to changes in futures prices. Depending on the initial basis, there may be a carrying cost associated with commodity futures. This carrying cost implies that the value of a position hedged with futures may increase or decrease in value over time.

A commodity swap is an agreement to exchange cash flows on a series of future dates. Commodity swaps may be used to hedge recurrent purchases or sales of a commodity. Through the use of a commodity swap, a hedger can effectively lock in a price for future transactions. We provided an example of a fixed-for-floating commodity swap to hedge a stream of future revenues subject to fluctuating aluminum prices.

Commodity options permit hedgers to eliminate unfavorable price movements while still benefiting from favorable price movements. Hedging with options is more expensive than hedging with futures or swaps because it requires the payment of the option premium when the hedge is established. We examine the use of call options to establish a maximum price a hedger will pay for crude oil.

REFERENCES

Commodity Futures Trading Commission. *2003 Annual Report*. Washington, D.C.

Garcia, P., J. S. Roh, and R. M. Leuthold. "Simultaneously Determined, Time-Varying Hedge Ratios in the Soybean Complex." *Applied Economics* 27(1995), 1127–1134.

Myers, R. J. "Estimating Time-Varying Optimal Hedge Ratios on Futures Markets." *Journal of Futures Markets* 11(1991), 39–53.

Myers, R. J., and S. T. Thompson. "Generalized Optimal Hedge Ratio Estimation."
     American Journal of Agricultural Economics 71(1989), 858–68.
New York Mercantile Exchange. *A Guide to Energy Hedging.* New York, 2002.
New York Mercantile Exchange. *A Guide to Metals Hedging.* New York, 2001.

CHAPTER 10

Currencies

As business becomes more global, corporations conduct an increasing number of their transactions in foreign currencies. Many domestic companies export finished products for sales overseas or import supplies from foreign manufacturers. Multinational corporations (MNCs) operating in foreign markets may have sales and production inputs paid for in local currencies and debt denominated in foreign currencies.

As an example, consider McDonalds Corporation. McDonalds operates more than 30,000 restaurants with worldwide sales of more than $40 billion. In 2001, more than one-half of the company's restaurants operated outside of the United States, accounting for 48% of revenues and approximately 40% of operating profit. In addition, 57% of the company's debt was denominated in foreign currencies.[1]

Companies transacting in foreign markets are exposed to exchange rate risk. *Exchange rate risk* is defined as the risk that a company's financial performance will be affected by exchange rate fluctuations. *Transaction exposure* refers to the risk that the domestic currency value of future cash flows denominated in foreign currencies will fluctuate as exchange rates fluctuate. For example, consider a U.S. exporter selling products in Europe that are invoiced in euros. If the euro depreciates by 5% against the U.S. dollar and euro-denominated prices are constant, the dollar value of a given amount of foreign currency revenues received by the exporter will decline by 5%.

---

1. McDonalds 2001 10-K Report, March 25, 2002.

The effect of exchange rate fluctuations may be more complex than simply the conversion of foreign currency to domestic currency. *Economic exposure* refers to changes in the *value* of a firm's cash flows associated with an unanticipated change in exchange rates. For example, consider a U.S. manufacturing company selling goods in Europe. If exchange rate changes are passed on to European customers in the form of changes in euro-denominated prices, then the company faces no transaction exposure. In this case, depreciation in the value of the euro is equal to the price increase. For a given sales volume, a depreciation of the euro against the dollar will not affect the company's revenues. However, if the price increase results in a reduction in sales, revenues will decrease, even in the absence of transaction exposure.[2]

In this chapter, we examine hedging techniques for companies facing transaction exposure to exchange rate risk. Initially, we examine changes in spot exchange rates over a four-year period beginning in January 2000. We discuss alternative methods of hedging with currency forward contracts, currency futures contracts, currency swaps, and currency options.

THE FOREIGN EXCHANGE MARKET

The foreign exchange market is the largest and most liquid market in the world. In 2001, the Bank for International Settlements (BIS) estimated the average daily turnover in traditional foreign exchange markets at around $1.21 trillion. Exhibit 10.1 shows global foreign exchange turnover by instrument. The market has grown dramatically since 1989, with total turnover increasing by 105% during this period. More than 90% of the increase is attributable to growth in the market for currency forward and swap contracts. Spot market transactions comprised approximately 32% of total turnover in 2001. U.S. dollar transactions represented more than 90% of total turnover in 2001.

Most foreign currency derivatives are traded in the over-the-counter market. Exhibit 10.2 presents statistics on notional amounts outstanding for over-the-counter and exchange-traded derivative contracts. Over-the-counter derivatives account for more than 99% of all foreign exchange derivative contracts outstanding.

---

2. A third type of exchange rate exposure, *translation exposure,* is related to the risk that exchange rate fluctuations affect a company's consolidated financial statements when subsidiary financial statements are translated into the reporting currency of the parent company.

EXHIBIT 10.1

Global Foreign Exchange Market Turnover:
Daily Averages (billions of U.S. dollars), April 2001

Instrument	1989	1992	1995	1998	2001
Spot transactions	317	394	494	568	387
Forwards	27	58	97	128	131
Foreign exchange swaps	190	324	546	734	656
Estimated gaps in reporting	56	44	53	60	36
Total turnover	**590**	**820**	**1,190**	**1,490**	**1,210**

Source: Bank for International Settlements.

HISTORIC CURRENCY DATA

For the examples presented in this chapter, we use daily exchange rates between the U.S. dollar (USD) and the British pound (£), Canadian dollar (CAD), Japanese yen (¥), and euro (€) for the period January 2000 to December 2003. Exhibit 10.3 presents quarterly spot exchange rates for each currency. Exchange rates for the British pound, Canadian dollar, and euro are shown as *direct quotations*, or the number of dollars per unit of foreign

EXHIBIT 10.2

Amounts Outstanding in Foreign Exchange Derivative
Instruments (billions of U.S. dollars), December 2002

Instrument	Notional Amount	Percentage of Total
Over-the-Counter Contracts		
Forwards and foreign exchange swaps	10,719.0	57.6
Currency swaps	4,503.0	24.2
Currency options	3,328.0	17.9
Exchange-Traded Contracts		
Exchange-traded futures	47.0	0.3
Exchange-traded currency options	27.4	0.1
Total	**18,624**	**100.0**

Source: Bank for International Settlements.

EXHIBIT 10.3

Quarterly Exchange Rates for Selected Currencies

Date	British Pound (USD/£)	Canadian Dollar (USD/CAD)	Japanese Yen (¥/USD)	Euro (USD/€)
Jan-00	1.636	0.691	101.450	1.024
Apr-00	1.596	0.689	104.900	0.955
Jul-00	1.514	0.675	105.690	0.950
Oct-00	1.466	0.662	108.830	0.877
Jan-01	1.503	0.670	114.360	0.952
Apr-01	1.419	0.633	126.800	0.879
Jul-01	1.418	0.661	124.120	0.848
Oct-01	1.479	0.636	120.220	0.917
Jan-02	1.447	0.626	132.130	0.903
Apr-02	1.441	0.625	133.480	0.881
Jul-02	1.533	0.660	119.730	0.992
Oct-02	1.566	0.632	122.630	0.983
Jan-03	1.594	0.638	120.080	1.036
Apr-03	1.578	0.679	117.920	1.092
Jul-03	1.663	0.739	119.430	1.156
Oct-03	1.669	0.742	110.670	1.172
Jan-04	1.786	0.771	107.220	1.260

Source: Bloomberg

currency. Exchange rates for the Japanese yen are indirect quotations, which is the number of yen per dollar. The indirect quotation is the reciprocal of the direct quotation.

Currencies were volatile during this period and exhibit similar exchange rate movements relative to the dollar. Exhibit 10.4 shows the dollar value of $100 exchanged for each currency in January 2000.[3] Each currency depreciated relative to the USD for the first two years of the period and showed strong appreciation during the last two years. With the exception

---

3. The figures used in Exhibit 10.2 show the dollar value of $100 exchanged into each currency on January 3, 2000 and exchanged back into dollars at the exchange rate that prevails on the first business day of each quarter.

EXHIBIT 10.4

Dollar Value of $100 Exchanged in January 2000

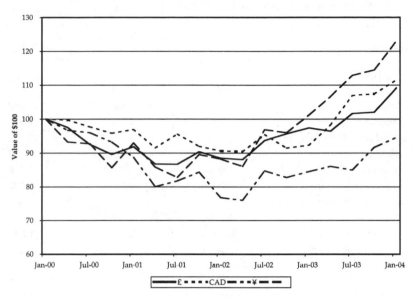

of the Japanese yen, each currency appreciated relative to the dollar over the full four-year period.[4]

The relationship between price changes in spot exchange rates and hedging instruments can be examined by calculating correlation coefficients and hedge ratios. Hedge ratios provide information about the relative movements of a target portfolio and the hedging instrument. We calculate hedge ratios for selected hedge instruments based on the following equation:

$$\Delta S_t = \beta_0 + \beta_1 \Delta F_t + \varepsilon_t$$

where

ΔS_t = change in the spot exchange rate at time t

β_0 = intercept coefficient

β_1 = ex post hedge ratio

---

4. The depreciation of the Japanese yen relative to the dollar can be explained by interest rate parity. Japan experienced deflation during the period 2000–2004, with consumer prices falling by approximately 3.4% during the period 2000–2003. Nominal interest rates on Japanese government bonds were near zero during this period.

EXHIBIT 10.5

Summary of Historic Currency Market and Hedge Data:
Daily Exchange Rates, 2000–2003

Hedge	$\hat{\beta}_1$	r	Obs.
British pound (£)			
Futures	0.9523	0.9361	1,006
3-Month Forward	1.0010	0.9967	1,040
12-Month Forward	1.0152	0.9933	1,040
Canadian dollar (CAD)			
Futures	0.9201	0.9272	1,005
3-Month Forward	1.0002	0.9955	1,028
12-Month Forward	1.0078	0.9924	1,028
Japanese yen (¥)			
Futures	0.9036	0.9497	1,006
3-Month Forward	0.9873	0.9996	1,042
12-Month Forward	0.9601	0.9958	1,042
Euro (€)			
Futures	0.9599	0.9400	1,006
3-Month Forward	0.9966	0.9965	1,040
12-Month Forward	0.9924	0.9945	1,040

ΔF_t = change in futures or forward exchange at time t
ε_t = error term, $E(\varepsilon) = 0$.

Sample hedge ratios $\hat{\beta}_1$ and sample correlation coefficients r are presented in Exhibit 10.5. The calculations are based on direct quotations of each currency. The sample hedge ratios are all close to one and range from 0.9036 for the yen futures contract to 1.0152 for the 12-month British pound forward contract. The correlations indicate a strong relationship between changes in exchange rates in the spot market and hedging instruments.

TECHNIQUES FOR HEDGING TRANSACTION EXPOSURE

Companies faced with transaction exposure can choose from among several hedging methods. The appropriate method is determined by the cash flows associated with each method, the size of the position to be hedged, and the goals of the hedger. We discuss four methods of hedging currency risk: futures hedge, forward hedge, swap market hedge, and currency option hedge. In general, these methods are very effective in reducing transaction exposure due to the high correlation between changes in spot and hedging instrument exchange rates.

CURRENCY FUTURES HEDGE

Currency futures can hedge transaction exposure by providing hedgers with a cash-flow stream that offsets losses in their spot currency position. The resulting net cash flows from the combined positions in the currency and the currency futures contract effectively establish a fixed exchange rate. Currency futures prices are closely related to spot market exchange rates.

Example: On January 2, 2002, a company realizes it will have €10,000,000 to convert into dollars in 60 days (on March 1, 2002). The current spot price is $0.903/€. The company decides to hedge its risk by selling March futures contracts on euros. The March futures contract expires on March 18, 2002. Since each contract is for the delivery of 125,000 euros, the company shorts 80 contracts. The futures price quotation on the March contract is $0.901/€ on January 2, 2002. On March 1, 2002, the spot exchange rate is $0.866/€ and the futures price is $0.865/€. Exhibit 10.6

EXHIBIT 10.6

Cumulative Payoff on Short Futures Hedge on Euros

Date	Position	Futures Price (USD/€)	Cumulative Payoff
1/2/02	Short 80 Euro Futures Contracts	$0.901	$0.901 − S_n
3/1/02	Buy 80 Euro Futures Contracts	$0.865	S_n − $0.865
Cumulative Payoff at Maturity		10,000,000($0.901 − $0.865) = $360,000	

EXHIBIT 10.7

Dollar Value of Hedged and Unhedged Positions
in 10,000,000 Euros, January 2, 2002 to March 1, 2002

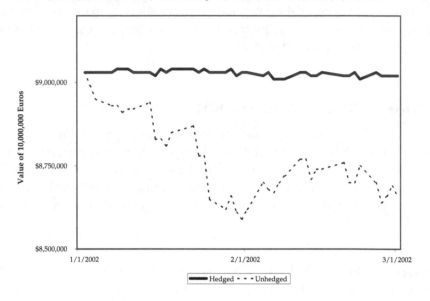

summarizes the transactions and the company's gains and losses on each position.

The gain of $360,000 on the futures position is an offset to the drop in value of the company's position in euros associated with the change in spot exchange rates.

In the absence of hedging, the value of the company's position decreased by $0.037/€ ($0.903 – $0.966), or $370,000, while the hedged position decreased by $10,000. Exhibit 10.7 shows the daily net value of the hedged and unhedged positions during the period.

CARRYING COSTS WITH CURRENCY FUTURES CONTRACTS

In the above example, there were minimal carrying costs associated with the hedged position in euros because the original basis was close to zero. In circumstances where the basis is nonzero when the hedge is established, the carrying cost may impose additional costs on the hedger. The net value of the hedged position on day t is given by

$$V_t = S_t + F_0 - F_t = F_0 + b_t$$

where
  S_t = the spot exchange rate at time t
  F_t = the futures price at time t
  F_0 = the futures price at time 0 (1/02/2002)
  $b_t = S_t - F_t$, the basis on the currency futures contract

The Law of One Price requires that spot and futures prices be equal when the futures contract matures. As the spot and futures prices converge toward the maturity of the futures contract at time n, the basis will approach zero, $b_n = S_n - F_n = 0$. This imposes a carrying cost on short hedges with positive initial basis and long hedges with negative initial basis. Short hedge positions with negative initial basis and long hedge positions with positive initial basis will increase in value over the hedging period.

Example: A company will need ¥200,000,000 on December 1, 2003 to pay for Japanese imports. The spot price on October 1, 2003 is 110.67 ¥/USD. The company hedges its risk by buying December futures contracts on yen, which expire on December 15, 2003. Since each contract is for the delivery of 12,500,000 yen, the company buys 16 contracts. The futures price quotation on the December contract is 110.3631 ¥/USD on October 1, 2003. On December 1, 2003, the spot exchange rate is 109.41 ¥/USD and the futures price is 109.4811 ¥/USD. Exhibit 10.8 summarizes the transactions and the company's gains and losses on each position.

    Given the relative appreciation in the yen during this period, the cost of purchasing yen has increased. If the company purchases yen in the spot market on December 1, 2003, it will do so at a cost of $1,827,986 (200,000,000 ¥/109.41). The gain on the futures contract reduces the net cost of purchasing yen. The net cost of purchasing yen is $1,827,986 − $14,600 = $1,813,386. The negative initial basis implies that the gain of $14,600 on the futures contract only partially offsets the increased cost of purchasing yen. On October 1, 2003, the value of the position is $1,807,174 (¥200,000,000/110.67). Hence, the hedged cost of buying yen

E X H I B I T   10.8

Cumulative Payoff to Long Futures Hedge on Yen

Date	Position	Futures Price (¥/USD)	Futures Price (USD/¥)	Cumulative Payoff (USD/¥)
10/1/03	Buy 16 Yen Futures Contracts	¥110.3631	$0.009061	$S_n - \$0.009061$
12/1/03	Sell 16 Yen Futures Contracts	¥109.4811	$0.009134	$\$0.009134 - S_n$
Cumulative Payoff on Futures		200,000,000 ($0.009134 − $0.009061) = $14,600		

has increased by $6,212.[5] Exhibit 10.9 shows the daily net value of the hedged and unhedged positions during the period.

ROLLING THE HEDGE FORWARD

In the above examples, the expiration date of the hedge occurs before the delivery date of the futures contract. A hedge that expires after the expiration of the futures contract requires the hedger to close out one futures contract and open another. This method of constructing a hedge from multiple contracts is known as *rolling the hedge forward*.

Example: A company plans to buy 10,000,000 Canadian dollars on June 2, 2003. The spot exchange rate on November 1, 2002 is $0.6414/CAD. The company decides to hedge its risk by buying CME futures contracts on Canadian dollars. Although the June 2003 contract is traded, the company does not believe the contract has sufficient liquidity. Therefore, the

---

5. The increased cost of $6,212 can be thought of as an annualized financing cost of 2.06%. Under cash-and-carry arbitrage, the company could have purchased yen in the spot market on October 1, 2003 at a cost of $1,807,174 and held it for delivery in 60 days. The 2.06% is approximately equal to the annualized 60-day interest rate differential between the two currencies.

E X H I B I T   10.9

Dollar Cost of Purchasing 200,000,000 Yen, October 1, 2003
to December 1, 2003

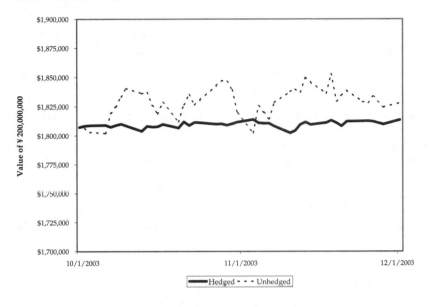

company buys the March 2003 contract. Since each contract is for the delivery of CAD 100,000, the company buys 100 contracts. The futures price quotation on the March contract is $0.6392/CAD on November 1, 2002. The company rolls the hedge forward into the June contract on March 3, 2003, time t. On this date, the March futures price is $0.6732/CAD and the June futures price is $0.6703/CAD. When the company closes its position on June 2, 2003, time n, the spot exchange rate, is $0.7305/CAD and the June futures price is $0.7295/CAD. Exhibit 10.10 summarizes the transactions and the company's gains and losses for each position.

The cost of purchasing Canadian dollars in the spot market has increased because of the appreciation of the currency relative to the U.S. dollar. If the company purchases Canadian dollars in the spot market on June 2, 2003, the cost is $7,305,000. The gain on the futures contract reduces the net cost of purchasing Canadian dollars by $932,000. The net cost to the company is $6,373,000 ($7,305,000 − $932,000). The positive initial basis implies that the gain of $932,000 on the futures contract more than offsets the increased cost of purchasing Canadian dollars. On November 1, 2002, the value of the hedged position is $6,414,000. Hence, the

EXHIBIT 10.10

Cumulative Payoff to Long Rolling Futures Hedge
on Canadian Dollars

Date	Position	Futures Price (USD/CAD)	Cumulative Payoff
11/1/02	Buy 100 March CAD Futures	$0.6392	$S_t - \$0.6392$
3/3/03	Sell 100 March CAD Futures	$0.6732	$\$0.6732 - S_t$
3/3/03	Cumulative Payoff on Initial Long Hedge	$10,000,000(0.6732 - 0.6392) =$ **$340,000**	
3/3/03	Buy 100 June CAD Futures	$0.6703	$S_n - \$0.6703$
6/2/03	Sell 100 June CAD Futures	$0.7295	$\$0.7295 - S_n$
6/2/03	Cumulative Payoff on Rolled Long Hedge	$10,000,000(0.7295 - 0.6703) =$ **$592,000**	
Total Cumulative Payoff on Long Hedge		$340,000 + 592,000 =$ **$932,000**	

hedged cost of buying Canadian dollars has decreased by $41,000. Exhibit 10.11 shows the daily net value of the hedged and unhedged positions during the period.

CURRENCY FORWARD HEDGE

The simplest and most direct way to hedge transaction exposure is by with currency forward contracts. A *currency forward contract* is an obligation to buy (long position) or sell (short position) some amount of a currency at a specified future exchange rate on a specified future date. A currency hedger taking a short position in a currency forward contract locks in the future exchange rate at which the currency will be sold. This is known as a *short forward currency hedge*. A *long forward currency hedge* is a long position in a currency forward that locks in the exchange rate at which the currency will be bought in the future.

Currency forward contracts are over-the-counter products provided by commercial banks and are typically used for large transactions. Unlike currency futures, currency forwards do not have standardized contract specifications. Hedgers negotiate the units of currency, the exchange rate,

EXHIBIT 10.11

Dollar Cost of Purchasing 10,000,000 Canadian Dollars, November 1, 2002 to June 2, 2003

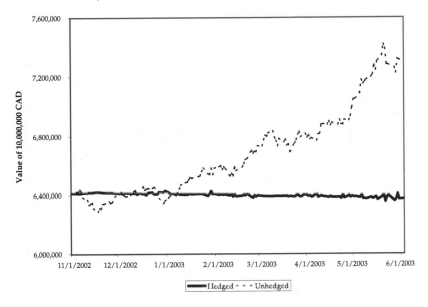

and the date of the forward transaction. The flexibility in designing the terms of forward contracts makes them relatively more attractive for long-term hedge positions. There is no daily mark to market associated with a forward contract. The purchase or sale of the currency occurs on the expiration date of the contract.

Example: A company will have 50,000,000 British pounds to convert into dollars one year from today. On January 3, 2000, the company sells 50,000,000 British pounds for forward delivery in one year. The current spot exchange rate is $1.636/£ and the 12-month forward exchange rate is $1.634/£. When the company makes delivery on the currency on January 3, 2001, it receives $81,700,000 = (£50,000,000)(1.634). The company receives $100,000 less on the forward delivery than the spot value on January 3, 2000 of $81,800,000. Exhibit 10.12 shows the daily net value of the hedged and unhedged positions on this transaction.

EXHIBIT 10.12

Dollar Value of Hedged and Unhedged
Sales of £50,000,000, January 3, 2000 to January 3, 2001

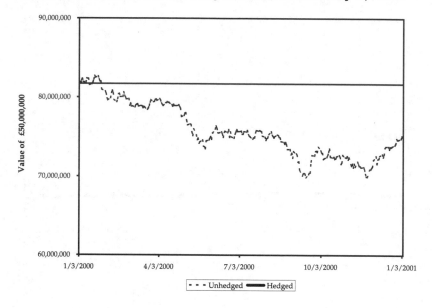

CARRYING COSTS WITH CURRENCY FORWARD CONTRACTS

In the above example, the fixed forward exchange rate implies that there is no basis risk associated with forward contracts. However, there is a cost of carry imposed on the hedger. As discussed in Chapter 6, the relationship between spot and forward rates reflects the relative interest rate differential between the two currencies. For direct exchange rate quotations, the forward rate will be at a discount to the spot rate if domestic interest rates are less than foreign interest rates for the forward period. Hence, there is a carrying cost on short hedges when there is a forward discount and on long hedges when there is a forward premium.

Example: A Japanese corporation will need to convert $10,000,000 from its U.S. subsidiary into yen on December 4, 2001. The spot price on

EXHIBIT 10.13

Yen Value of Hedged and Unhedged Positions in $10,000,000, December 4, 2000 to December 4, 2001

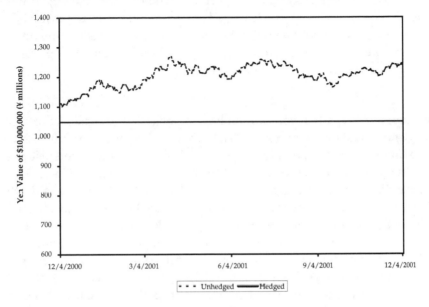

December 4, 2000 is 111.12 ¥/USD, and the 12-month forward rate is 104.84 ¥/USD. The company hedges its risk by selling dollars forward for one year. When the company makes delivery on the currency on December 4, 2001, it receives ¥1.0484 billion. This is ¥62.8 million less than the spot exchange on December 4, 2000. Exhibit 10.13 shows the daily net value of the hedged and unhedged positions on this transaction.

In the above example, the company agrees to sell dollars in one year for less than the spot price on December 4, 2000. The discount of 5.65% in the forward price, the *forward discount*, reflects the one-year interest rate differential between the two currencies.[6] Even in the situation where exchange rates remain at their December 4, 2000 level, the reduced price received for dollars is a carrying cost paid by the hedger.

6. On December 4, 2004, the one-year Japanese yen deposit rate was 0.52%, and the one-year U.S. dollar deposit rate was 6.45%. From interest rate parity, the implied forward discount from these rates was 5.57%.

HEDGING TRANSACTION EXPOSURE WITH SWAPS

There are many situations in which firms have a series of payables or receivables in a foreign currency. Recurrent cash flows can be hedged with a foreign currency swap. As discussed in Chapter 7, a currency swap is an agreement to exchange one currency for another at a predetermined exchange rate, known as the *swap rate*, on several future dates. Swaps can be thought of as multiperiod forward contracts.

Example: A Canadian corporation has an obligation to make six remaining semiannual payments on a $20,000,000 note beginning on July 1, 2000. The interest rate on the note is 6.00%, and the semi-annual interest payments will be made in U.S. dollars ($600,000). The company will use Canadian dollar (CAD) cash flows converted to U.S. dollars (USDs) to make the payments. The company is concerned that the USD will strengthen against the CAD, thereby leading to foreign currency losses in the required interest payments and in the principal payoff. To hedge this risk, on January 1, 2000 the corporation enters into a three-year fixed-for-fixed currency swap under which it pays fixed at CAD 5.928% and receives fixed at USD 6.000%. The notional principal on the swap is $20,000,000, and the exchange rate is CAD 1.447 (CAD/USD). The fixed receive rate is chosen such that the payment received in dollars equals the company's semiannual interest payments. Initially, the corporation will pay $20,000,000 and receive CAD 28,940,000. At tenor, these initial principal amounts will be re-exchanged. Semiannually, starting six months after settlement, the corporation will pay CAD 857,853 and receive $600,000. The payment in each currency is equal to the fixed interest rate times the notional principal divided by 2. Through the use of this swap, the corporation has effectively swapped its CAD cash flows for USD cash flows that can be used to pay its debt service. The cash flows for this swap are shown in Exhibit 10.14.

Fixed-for-fixed currency swaps are priced based on the prevailing yield curves in each currency. The fixed pay rate is calculated as the swap rate that makes the present value of the payments equal to the present value of the receipts. Exhibit 10.15 presents the valuation of the six-period swap based on semiannual zero-coupon short-term rates for each currency.[7]

---

7. For this example, we use U.S. Treasury rates and the Canadian Sovereign rate as of 12/31/99.

EXHIBIT 10.14

Cash Flows on a Currency Swap Hedge

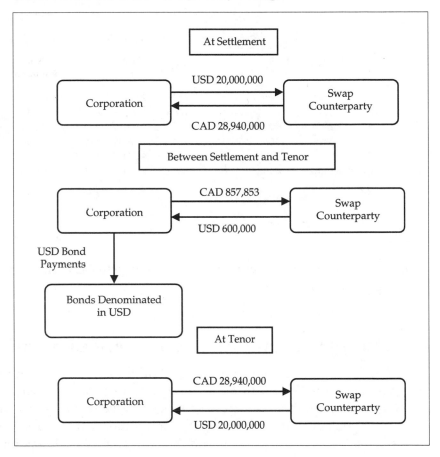

The company will make its semiannual USD interest payments by converting CAD cash flows to USD cash flows at the prevailing spot exchange rate at each six-month interval. If the USD strengthens against the CAD, the amount of CADs required to make the interest payments will increase. In this situation, the cost will be offset by the fixed-for-fixed currency swap because the company would be receiving the appreciating currency and paying the depreciating currency. The net effect of the swap is to convert dollar-denominated interest payments into CAD-denominated interest payments at an exchange rate of CAD 1.4298/USD in each of the six periods. Exhibit 10.16 presents the CAD interest payment obligations

EXHIBIT 10.15

Calculation of a Fixed-for-Fixed Currency Swap Rate

Year	t	$\frac{r_t}{2}$ (USD)	Swap Rate	PV$_{\text{fixed}}$	$\frac{r_t}{2}$ (CAD)	Swap Rate	PV$_{\text{fixed}}$	Net Payment
		Receives USD			**Pays CAD**			
0.5	1	3.066%	3.000%	2.911%	2.576%	2.964%	2.890%	−0.021%
1.0	2	3.214%	3.000%	2.816%	2.766%	2.964%	2.807%	−0.009%
1.5	3	3.292%	3.000%	2.722%	2.884%	2.964%	2.722%	0.000%
2.0	4	3.372%	3.000%	2.627%	3.003%	2.964%	2.633%	0.006%
2.5	5	3.380%	3.000%	2.541%	3.046%	2.964%	2.551%	0.011%
3.0	6	3.390%	3.000%	2.456%	3.089%	2.964%	2.470%	0.014%
	Total			16.073%			16.073%	0.000%

along with the CAD cash flows from the swap and actual exchange rates for the subsequent three years.

HEDGING TRANSACTION EXPOSURE WITH OPTIONS

In the examples in this chapter, we have seen how investors can lock in an exchange rate by hedging with futures, forwards, or swaps. Consider a company that establishes a short hedge to lock in the exchange rate at which it will exchange euros for U.S. dollars. In addition to the transaction costs and carrying costs associated with this hedge, there is also an implicit opportunity cost associated with forgone profits. If the euro appreciates against the dollar, the company will be better off in an unhedged position. In this situation, the implicit cost of hedging to eliminate unfavorable exchange rate movements is the elimination of favorable exchange rate movements as well.

An alternative method of hedging is to use currency options to eliminate transaction exposure. Currency options permit the hedger to eliminate unfavorable exchange rate movements while still benefiting from favorable exchange rate movements. While enjoying the benefit of favorable exchange rate movements, hedgers using options incur an explicit up-front cost in the form of an option premium.

EXHIBIT 10.16

Net Interest Payments from Hedging with a Fixed-for-Fixed Swap

		Swap				Bond	
t	Exchange Rate (CAD/USD)	Fixed Payment (CAD)	Payment Received (USD)	Equivalent Payment Received (CAD)	Net Payment (CAD)	Interest Payment (CAD)	Net Interest Payment (CAD)
1	1.481	857,853	600,000	888,600	(30,747)	888,600	857,853
2	1.493	857,853	600,000	895,800	(37,947)	895,800	857,853
3	1.514	857,853	600,000	908,400	(50,547)	908,400	857,853
4	1.597	857,853	600,000	958,200	(100,347)	958,200	857,853
5	1.516	857,853	600,000	909,600	(51,747)	909,600	857,853
6	1.567	857,853	600,000	940,200	(82,347)	940,200	857,853

Example: A U.S. company will need to purchase €10,000,000 in three months. The spot exchange rate is $1.15/€. The company is concerned that the dollar will depreciate against the euro during the next three months and does not wish to pay more than $1.20/€. Call options on euros are traded at a premium of $0.02/€. Each option gives the holder the right to buy 10,000,000 euros for $1.20/€ in three months.

The company pays the option premium of $200,000 to ensure that it pays no more than $1.20/€. If the euro remains below $1.20/€, the company will benefit from the exchange rate movement but will have incurred the cost of purchasing the option. Exhibit 10.17 shows several scenarios of exchange rates at the maturity of the option.

If the exchange rate rises to $1.30/€, the payoff on the call option offsets the cost of purchasing euros in the spot market. The net cost to the company of purchasing euros is $12,200,000. In this situation, the company saves $800,000, which is equal to the call option payoff less the premium. If the exchange rate falls to $1.00/€, the net cost to the company of purchasing euros is $10,200,000. Although the company benefits from the favorable exchange rate movement, it still pays the premium on the call option. In this situation, the unhedged cost of purchasing yen would have been lower than the hedged cost by the amount of the premium.

EXHIBIT 10.17

Net Hedged Cost of Purchasing Euros
Using Call Options

Exchange Rate Scenario	Spot Cost of Purchasing Euros	Call Option Payoff	Hedged Cost of Purchase	Net Hedged Cost of Purchase
$1.50/€	$15,000,000	$3,000,000	$12,000,000	$12,200,000
$1.40/€	$14,000,000	$2,000,000	$12,000,000	$12,200,000
$1.30/€	$13,000,000	$1,000,000	$12,000,000	$12,200,000
$1.20/€	$12,000,000	$0	$12,000,000	$12,200,000
$1.10/€	$11,000,000	$0	$11,000,000	$11,200,000
$1.00/€	$10,000,000	$0	$10,000,000	$10,200,000

Example: A U.S. company will need to purchase €10,000,000 on February 4, 2004. The spot exchange rate on August 4, 2003 is $1.136/€. The company is concerned that the dollar will depreciate against the euro during the next six months and does not wish to pay more than $1.20/€. March 2004 call options on euro futures are traded at a premium of $0.016/€. Each option gives the holder the right to buy one June 2004 euro futures contract at a delivery price of $1.20/€. Exhibit 10.18 summarizes prices in the spot market and futures option market.

Since each euro futures contract is for the delivery of 125,000 euros, the company purchases 80 March call options at a total cost of $160,000. The company plans to sell the option contracts on February 4, 2004 instead of holding them to expiration. On February 4, 2004, the company purchases euros in the spot market and sells the call option. The hedged cost of purchasing euros on this date is $11,930,000, which is equal to the spot market cost of $12,540,000 less the $610,000 premium received from selling the call. The net hedged cost is equal to $12,090,000, which is the hedged cost plus the $160,000 premium paid for the call. Exhibit 10.19 shows the daily net values of the hedged and unhedged positions.

In the above example, the hedged cost of buying yen is higher than the unhedged cost when the exchange rate is relatively low. As the euro appreciates against the dollar, the higher option premium offsets the company's losses in the spot market. The call option ensures that the hedged cost of purchasing euros in February 2004 never exceeds $12,000,000 ($1.20/€), excluding the call premium. In this case, the hedger incurs a slightly higher net cost due to the initial option premium.

EXHIBIT 10.18

Spot, Futures, and Futures Option Prices on Euros Direct Quotations ($/€)

Date	Euro Spot Exchange Rate	Euro Futures Call Option Premium
8/4/2003	$1.136	$0.016
2/4/2004	$1.254	$0.061

EXHIBIT 10.19

Net Hedged and Unhedged Costs of Purchasing
€10,000,000 Long Hedge Using Call Options, August 4, 2003
to February 4, 2004

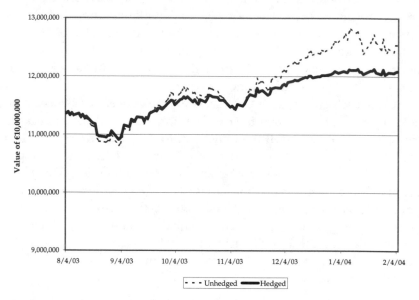

COMPARISON OF HEDGING ALTERNATIVES

Hedge	Pros	Cons
Currency Futures	Liquid Low transaction costs	Standardized terms Daily mark-to-market May require rolling hedge Basis risk No benefit from favorable exchange rate movements

Currency Forwards	Customized terms
	No basis risk
	No intermediate
	    cash flows
		Illiquid
		High transaction costs
		No benefit from favorable
		    exchange rate movements

Currency Swaps	Customized terms
	Useful for recurrent
	    cash flows
		Expensive
		No benefit from favorable
		    exchange rate movements

Currency Options	Benefit from favorable exchange rate fluctuations	Expensive

SUMMARY

The foreign exchange market is by far the largest and most liquid market in the world. In this chapter we examined hedging strategies in the foreign exchange market. Our primary focus was on managing transaction exposure. Transaction exposure is the risk that the domestic currency value of future cash flows denominated in foreign currencies will fluctuate as exchange rates fluctuate. Transaction exposure can be hedged with currency futures, forward contracts, swaps, or options. In general, there is a strong relationship between price movements in the spot market and in the derivative market, and the resulting hedges are very effective at reducing transaction exposure.

Futures are the most liquid hedges in the currency market and may be used effectively for short-term hedges. Futures provide hedgers with a cash-flow stream that offsets losses in their spot currency position. The resulting net cash flows from the combined positions in the currency and the currency futures contract effectively establish a fixed exchange rate. Although currency futures prices are closely related to spot market exchange rates, the correlation between price changes in the two markets is not perfect, which subjects hedgers to a certain amount of basis risk. Futures have standard expiration dates, which require the use of sequential contracts for long-term hedges. We described how futures can be used for longer-term hedges by rolling the hedge forward. Futures may also require the payment of intermediate cash flows due to the daily mark-to-market feature. Depending on the initial basis, there may be a carrying cost associated with currency futures. This carrying cost implies that the value of a position hedged with futures may increase or decrease in value over time.

Forward contracts and swaps are the most popular currency derivative products and are traded in the over-the-counter market. A currency forward contract is an obligation to buy or sell some amount of a currency at a specified future exchange rate on a specified future date. A currency swap is similar to a currency forward, allowing for transactions on multiple future dates. Both types of contracts can be customized to a particular contract size and expiration. Currency forwards and swaps have no basis risk, but are less liquid than futures contracts because of their customization. We examined the use of currency forwards to hedge against exchange rate movements for companies with a single future transaction. We also provided an example of a fixed-for-fixed currency swap to hedge a stream of future interest payments denominated in a foreign currency. Like futures, there is a cost of carry associated with currency forwards or swaps. The carrying cost implies that the hedger will lock in a higher or lower forward exchange rate than the current rate.

Currency options permit hedgers to eliminate unfavorable exchange rate fluctuations while still benefiting from favorable exchange rate fluctuations. Hedging with options is more expensive than hedging with futures, forwards, or swaps because it requires the payment of an option premium when the hedge is established. We examined the use of call options to establish a maximum exchange rate a hedger will pay for a foreign currency. The cost of carry on options is much higher than that of futures, forwards, or swaps.

REFERENCES

Bank for International Settlements. *Quarterly Review* (March–June 2004).

Cross, Sam Y. *The Foreign Exchange Market in the United States*. New York: Federal Reserve Bank of New York, 1998.

Eun, Cheol S., and Bruce G. Resnick. *International Financial Management*, 3rd Ed. New York: McGraw-Hill/Irwin, 2004.

Lewent, Judy C., and A. John Kearney. "Identifying, Measuring, and Hedging Currency Risk at Merck," in *The International Finance Reader*, edited by Robert W. Kolb, pp. 434–43. Miami: Kolb Publishing Company, 1993.

Madura, Jeff. *International Financial Management*, 7th Ed. Cincinnati: Southwestern Publishing, 2003.

McDonald's Corporation, 10K report. Oakbrook, IL, 2001.

CHAPTER 11

Equities

The equity market is one of the largest markets for individual and institutional investors. Equity mutual funds are the largest fund class in the United States. As of the end of 2003, pure equity funds had net assets of $3.7 trillion. This accounted for approximately 50% of the net assets of all U.S. mutual funds.[1]

The equity market has been volatile in recent years. In the two-year period from June 1998 to June 2000, the S&P 500 increased by more than 32%. Over the following two-year period ending June 2002, the S&P 500 decreased by almost 30%. With increased volatility, investors have an increased need for hedging.

Equities can be hedged with equity index futures, equity swaps, and index options. A hedger must consider several factors when choosing a hedging instrument. The primary issue is how well a particular hedge tracks the value of a portfolio. The flexibility, liquidity, and costs of the various hedges are also important.

In this chapter we concentrate on portfolio risk management. We begin by discussing the types of risk faced by an equity manager. We explain hedging strategies that use equity futures, swaps, and options. We begin with a discussion of the risks faced by an equity investor.

---

1. Source: Investment Company Institute, www.ici.org.

STOCK MARKET RISKS

Equity investors face two types of risk: *systematic risk* and *unsystematic risk*. Systematic risk represents the risk of the stock market. Changes in stock prices are caused by changes in the economy, taxes, and other market factors. When these factors change, it affects the entire stock market. Although systematic changes in the market affect each stock to a different degree, all stocks are affected.

Unsystematic risk is specific to a company. Unsystematic risk is often referred to as *diversifiable risk* and is affected by the decisions made by a corporation. Unsystematic risk can be hedged by holding several stocks. Holding many stocks in different industries for the purpose of reducing unsystematic risk is referred to as *diversification*.

Exhibit 11.1 summarizes the results of a study that examines the marginal amount of diversification achieved by adding additional stocks to a portfolio. The volatility of individual stocks is measured by standard deviation. The average standard deviation for an individual stock in the study was found to be 49.24%. According to the findings, it takes about 10 randomly selected stocks to remove about 51% of the volatility of a portfolio and reduce the volatility to 23.93%. The volatility of a 10-stock portfolio was not significantly less than the volatility of a 1000-stock port-

E X H I B I T   11.1

Portfolio Standard Deviations

Number of Stocks in Portfolio	Average Standard Deviation of Annual Portfolio Returns	Ratio of Portfolio Standard Deviation of a Single Stock
1	49.24%	100%
2	37.36%	76%
6	26.64%	54%
10	23.93%	49%
50	20.20%	41%
100	19.69%	40%
300	19.34%	39%
500	19.27%	39%
1000	19.21%	39%

Source: Statman (1987).

folio. The remaining volatility of a 1000-stock portfolio represents systematic risk.

In addition to the number of stocks held, diversification is affected by the relationship among the returns of the stocks in a portfolio. More effective diversification will result from the selection of stocks from different types of industries. Stocks selected from different industries have returns that tend to offset one another, thereby reducing portfolio volatility.

MARKET RISK

Given that diversification effectively removes unsystematic risk from a portfolio, the only remaining risk for a portfolio manager is systematic or market risk. All firms have different levels of market risk. Beta is a measure of the systematic risk for a stock or portfolio. The market has a beta of 1.0, as does a stock or portfolio with the same percentage price movement as the market. A stock that generally moves more than the market has a beta greater than 1.0. A stock or portfolio that moves less than the market has a beta less than 1.0.

Beta can be estimated based on historic returns of a stock or portfolio relative to the market. Specifically, the beta of stock i, β_i, is equal to

$$\beta_i = \frac{COV(r_s, r_m)}{\sigma_m^2}$$

where r_s and r_m represent the returns on a stock and the market, respectively. The beta of a portfolio is the weighted average of the betas of the individual stocks in the portfolio.

Example: Consider the portfolio of stocks in Exhibit 11.2. Assume $1 million is invested in each stock for a total portfolio value of $10 million. The portfolio consists of 10 stocks and is equally weighted. The portfolio statistics are based on daily returns from January 2, 1998 to December 31, 2003. Betas are calculated from daily returns on the S&P 500 over the same time period. The betas of the stocks range from 0.419 to 1.426, and standard deviations range from 0.0170 to 0.0347. The portfolio beta, β_p, is the weighted average of the individual stock betas and is calculated as follows:

$$\beta_p = \sum_{i=1}^{10} w_i \beta_i$$

EXHIBIT 11.2

Sample Equally Weighted 10-Stock Portfolio

Company	Symbol	β_i	σ	w_i	$w_i\beta_i$
Kellogg's	K	0.419	0.0200	0.10	0.042
Home Depot	HD	1.233	0.0276	0.10	0.123
Microsoft	MSFT	1.331	0.0266	0.10	0.133
Ford	F	0.995	0.0267	0.10	0.100
Citigroup	C	1.426	0.0258	0.10	0.143
Pfizer	PFE	0.795	0.0222	0.10	0.079
Yum! Brands	YUM	0.616	0.0249	0.10	0.062
Staples	SPLS	1.270	0.0347	0.10	0.127
Exxon-Mobil	XOM	0.533	0.0170	0.10	0.053
Kroger	KR	0.605	0.0249	0.10	0.060
Portfolio		0.922	0.0149		

Source: Data from January 2, 1998 to December 31, 2003.

where w_i is the proportion invested in the ith stock. We can also estimate beta by using the regression analysis techniques described in Chapter 3. The regression equation takes the form

$$r_p = \beta_0 + \beta_p r_m + \varepsilon$$

where r_p and r_m are the returns on the portfolio and the market, respectively. The beta of the portfolio measured over the entire time period is calculated as 0.922. Exhibit 11.2 shows the individual stock betas and the weighted betas used to calculate the portfolio beta.

We can measure the total volatility of the portfolio with the use of the portfolio standard deviation. The portfolio standard deviation, σ_p, is calculated as

$$\sigma_p = \sqrt{\sum_{i=1}^{10}\sum_{j=1}^{10} w_i w_j \sigma_i \sigma_j \rho_{ij}}$$

The standard deviation of the portfolio returns is 0.0149, which is lower than the lowest standard deviation of the individual stocks. Diversification leads to a reduction in volatility due to the removal of unsystematic risk.

EXHIBIT 11.3

Annual Beta for Sample Portfolio

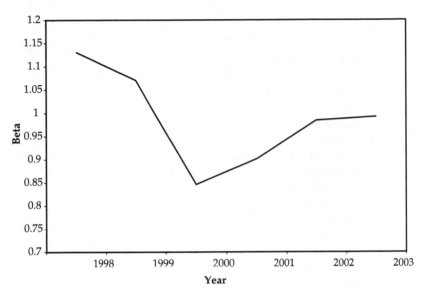

Effective hedging requires an estimate of portfolio beta; however, the calculated beta may not be stationary. Exhibit 11.3 shows betas of the sample portfolio calculated from one year of daily returns. Portfolio beta ranges from 0.0846 to 1.131 over the six-year time period. Because of the volatility of beta, a hedger must monitor it closely over time.

HEDGING WITH EQUITY INDEX FUTURES

Market risk can be managed with equity index futures, equity swaps, or index options. Equity index futures are traded on all major indices. Exhibit 11.4 lists the popular index futures contracts and the exchanges on which they trade.

The sample portfolio closely tracks the S&P 500; therefore, we use the S&P 500 futures contract in our example. The S&P 500 futures contract trades on the CME and has a contract size of 250 times the index. Exhibit 11.5 shows the relationship between the level of the S&P 500 and the price of the portfolio over the six-year time period.

E X H I B I T   11.4

Popular Equity Futures Contracts

Underlying Index	Exchange
Dow Jones Industrial Average	CBOT
Dow Jones Transportation Average	CBOT
Dow Jones Utility Average	CBOT
Dow Jones Composite Average	CBOT
S&P 500	CME
NASDAQ-100	CME
E-mini NASDAQ Composite	CME
S&P MidCap 400	CME
S&P SmallCap 600	CME
Russell 2000	CME
E-mini S&P 500	CME
E-mini NASDAQ-100	CME
Nikkei 225	CME
E-mini S&P MidCap 400	CME
Russell 1000	CME
E-mini Russell 2000	CME
FTSE 250 Index	LIFFE
FTSE Eurotop	LIFFE

Example: Assume a portfolio manager owns the 10-stock portfolio listed in Exhibit 11.2. The portfolio was formed on January 5, 1998 with a beginning value of $10 million split evenly into $1,000,000 increments among the 10 stocks. By January 3, 2000, the portfolio value has grown to $17,124,131, which affects the relative weighting of the individual stocks in the portfolio. The portfolio manager wants to hedge the market risk for a one-month period beginning January 3, 1999 with S&P 500 index futures. Since beta may change over time, it is typical to use a short time period just prior to the hedging period to calculate beta. We begin by estimating the portfolio beta for the 60-day period prior to January 3, 2000. Using regression analysis, we find that the portfolio beta is 0.8807 for the 60-day observation period. The adjusted R^2 is 0.568, indicating a strong relationship between the portfolio and the market over the time period. The regression results are summarized in Exhibit 11.6.

EXHIBIT 11.5

S&P 500 and Sample Portfolio Prices, January 2, 1998 to December 31, 2003

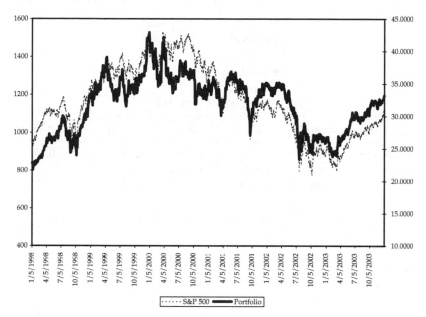

The calculated portfolio beta is 0.8807, which indicates that the portfolio is less volatile than the market over the 60-day time period. In our example, we assume that the historic beta is a predictor of future beta. Therefore, the *ex ante* hedge ratio h^* is estimated to be

$$h^* = \beta_p = 0.8807$$

To calculate the number of contracts needed to hedge this position, we must consider the hedge ratio, the level of the index, and the contract specification. As of January 3, 2000, the S&P 500 index was 1455.22 and the value of the S&P 500 futures contract was 1466.80. Therefore, the value of one S&P 500 contract was equal to ($250)(1466.80) or $366,700. The number of contracts required to hedge the portfolio N^* is

$$N^* = \frac{(\$17,124,131)(0.8807)}{(\$366,700)} \approx 41.00$$

EXHIBIT 11.6

Portfolio Beta Summary Regression Statistics

	R^2	0.5754
	Adjusted R^2	0.5681
	Standard Error	0.0080
	Observations	60

Analysis of Variance

	df	SS	MS	F	p value
Regression	1	0.0051	0.0051	78.6072	0.0000
Residual	58	0.0038	0.0001		
Total	59	0.0088			

Regression Equation

	β_I	Standard Error	t-statistic	p value
Intercept	0.0004	0.0011	0.3351	0.7388
S&P 500	0.8807	0.0993	8.8661	0.0000

FUTURES HEDGE PERFORMANCE

We examine the daily performance of the portfolio and the hedge over a one-month time period. The two positions have a strong negative correlation. The correlation between the change in the portfolio value and the change in the hedge value is –0.835. Exhibit 11.7 shows values for the hedged portfolio and the unhedged portfolio over the one-month time period.

The daily portfolio values, hedge values, and net values are shown in Exhibit 11.8. We find that the unhedged portfolio results in a loss of $974,982 and the hedged portfolio results in a net loss of $300,532. Therefore, the gain on the hedge is $674,450. There are two factors that may explain why the portfolio and the futures contracts do not perfectly track. First, the actual beta over the hedge period is higher than the estimated beta. The beta over the hedging period is 0.9817. Second, tracking risk exists

EXHIBIT 11.7

Hedged and Unhedged Portfolio Values

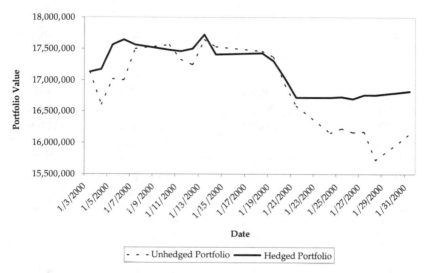

between the value of the futures contract and the value of the portfolio. Although we expect the portfolio and the hedge to move together, outliers may affect the net value of the portfolio.

TAILING THE HEDGE

In our discussions of futures contracts and cost-of-carry, we treat futures contracts much like forward contracts. Unlike forward contracts, however, futures contracts require daily adjustments to margin account balances because of the mark-to-market feature of futures contracts. An adjustment can be made to the hedge ratio to account for the impacts of mark-to-market. This adjustment is referred to as *tailing the hedge*.

Tailing the hedge involves using more or fewer futures contracts based on the time value of money implications of paying or receiving daily cash flows. For example, if borrowing costs exceed the dividend yield on an equity index, the futures price is expected to exceed the spot price. A short position in futures will result in a net gain over time, other things

EXHIBIT 11.8

Hedge Portfolio Results

Date	Portfolio Value	Hedge Value	Net Change
01/03/00	17,124,131	(15,034,700)	
01/04/00	16,607,830	(14,470,950)	47,448
01/05/00	17,016,662	(14,488,375)	391,407
01/06/00	16,999,690	(14,391,000)	80,403
01/07/00	17,496,911	(14,970,125)	(81,904)
01/10/00	17,560,529	(15,118,750)	(85,007)
01/11/00	17,324,840	(14,906,575)	(23,514)
01/12/00	17,241,816	(14,780,500)	43,050
01/13/00	17,639,730	(14,949,625)	228,790
01/14/00	17,525,524	(15,149,500)	(314,082)
01/18/00	17,453,910	(15,062,375)	15,512
01/19/00	17,362,561	(15,093,125)	(122,099)
01/20/00	16,923,111	(14,934,250)	(280,575)
01/21/00	16,582,759	(14,900,425)	(306,528)
01/24/00	16,156,748	(14,470,950)	3,464
01/25/00	16,231,860	(14,540,650)	5,412
01/26/00	16,171,045	(14,507,850)	(28,014)
01/27/00	16,176,110	(14,450,450)	62,465
01/28/00	15,729,074	(14,006,625)	(3,211)
01/31/00	16,149,149	(14,360,250)	66,450
Total Change	**(974,982)**	**674,450**	**(300,532)**

being equal. Net positive daily cash flows are expected on the futures position as the contract converges. Therefore, to adjust for the time value of the positive daily cash flows, a smaller hedge ratio is used.

In practice, the effects of daily mark-to-market are small, and most hedgers ignore the effects. Tailing the hedge is difficult to maintain because as interest rates change, a constant adjustment must be made to the tail. In addition, derivatives markets are becoming more generic over time. The daily mark-to-market feature was historically unique to the futures market; however, the over-the-counter derivatives markets are increasingly adopting similar collateral requirements.

EQUITY FUTURES COST-OF-CARRY

Recall from Chapter 6 that the value of an equity futures contract based on cost-of-carry is calculated as

$$F_0 = S_0{}^{(r-d)n}$$

where r is the short-term continuous time borrowing rate and d is the continuous dividend yield. This pricing equation is based on the cash-and-carry argument that a hedged position will earn the borrowing cost over time. When the borrowing rate exceeds the dividend yield, futures contracts have a positive cost-of-carry and the index futures price exceeds the spot index price. This is referred to as *contango*. In this case, a long futures position will lose value and a short futures position will gain value over time if the index remains unchanged.

To estimate the cost of carry, we compare a long position in the S&P 500 with the value of a short position in the S&P 500 equity index futures contract from January 1998 to December 2003. The long position in the S&P 500 can be established in several ways, such as buying S&P Depository Receipts (SPY) or iShares S&P Index trust (IVV), which are closed-end mutual funds traded on the American Stock Exchange. For simplicity, we use the actual performance of the index to represent movements in the market. We assume an initial $25 million long position starting on January 2, 1998. The S&P 500 on the starting date was 975.04. The short position consists of selling 102 futures contracts and rolling the futures position each quarter into the nearest contract at expiration.

The dividend yield on equity indices is generally not as volatile as the short-term interest rate. For example, over the six-year period, the dividend yield on the S&P 500 ranged from 1.05% to 2.02%. Over the same time period, three-month LIBOR ranged from 1.00% to 6.87%. The cost-of-carry on equity index futures changes considerably over time, primarily because of the fluctuation in short-term interest rates.

As an example of the cost-of-carry relationship, consider the futures prices at the beginning of the second quarter of 1998. On March 23, 1998, the closing values of the S&P 500 Index and the futures contract were 1095.55 and 1108.30, respectively. There were 87 days or 0.238 years to the maturity of the futures contract. Given these prices, we can solve for the implied cost-of-carry based on the following equation:

$$1108.30 = 1095.55e^{(r-d)0.238}$$

Solving this equation for the difference between the three-month LIBOR rate and the dividend yield $(r - d)$, we get

$$(r - d) = \ln\left(\frac{1108.30}{1095.55}\right)\left(\frac{1}{0.238}\right) = 4.86\%$$

where ln is the natural logarithm. As of March 23, 1998, three-month LIBOR was 5.69% and the dividend yield on the S&P 500 was 1.37% for a net annualized expected cost-of-carry of 4.32%. In this example, the difference between the implied cost and the actual cost is 0.54%. This difference may be explained by two factors. First, the interest rate from a cash-and-carry analysis should represent the funding rate available to market participants, which is likely to be higher than the three-month LIBOR rate. Second, the dividend yield on the S&P 500 is not precise. Since dividends are not continuous and occur at different intervals, the expected dividend yield may be higher or lower than the quoted dividend yield used as an estimate.

We monitor the performance of the hedged position by calculating the change in the S&P 500 minus the change in the short futures position in each quarter. The hedged portfolio over the time period results in a gain of $5,942,548. Since the contracts are held to maturity, there is no tracking risk; therefore the total gain or loss is from cost-of-carry.

Exhibit 11.9 summarizes the cost-of-carry findings quarterly from 1998 to 2003. Two estimates are presented: (1) expected COC represents three-month LIBOR on the first day of the futures contract and (2) actual COC represents the gain on the hedged portfolio plus the dividend yield. The two costs track each other closely, with the differences coming from the factors described above.

EQUITY SWAPS

As we discussed in Chapter 7, equity swaps can be structured in many ways. A typical equity swap requires one counterparty to pay the change in value of an underlying stock, portfolio, or stock index. In exchange for the equity-based payment, the other counterparty pays a fixed or floating rate. Equity swaps can have monthly, quarterly, semiannual, or annual payment frequencies and customized maturity dates. They can be struc-

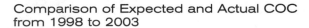

EXHIBIT 11.9

Comparison of Expected and Actual COC
from 1998 to 2003

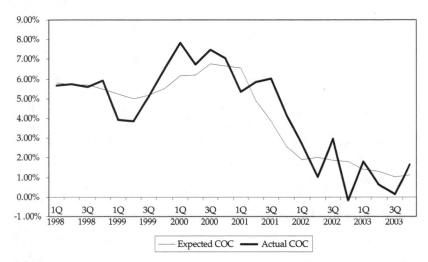

tured to reflect changes in the value of an individual stock, index, or portfolio. An equity swap is an effective way for a portfolio manager to protect the value of an individual stock or portfolio.

Example: A portfolio manager owns the 10-stock portfolio in Exhibit 11.2. The manager wants to protect the position from a downturn in the market over the next nine months. To do so, the manager can enter into an equity swap with the cash flows shown in Exhibit 11.10. An initial value of the portfolio is established when the swap is settled. At the end of the swap (or on periodic payment dates) the portfolio manager receives the decrease in the value of the portfolio, if applicable, and a spread adjusted floating rate. The portfolio manager must pay the increase in the value of the portfolio (if applicable) and any dividends as they are received. Similar to a short equity futures hedge, the net cost of carry on the hedge in the example is the portfolio funding rate r.

EXHIBIT 11.10

Cash Flows on an Example Equity Swap

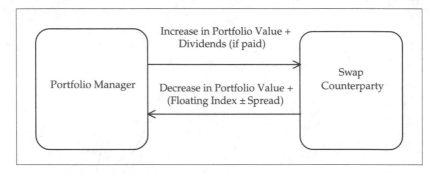

HEDGING WITH EQUITY INDEX OPTIONS

In this section we examine the use of equity index options to protect the value of a rising portfolio. As discussed in Chapter 8, protective puts are an effective way to protect the value of a portfolio. Options require the payment of an up-front premium. As an example of this strategy, we examine the Philadelphia Semiconductor (SOX) Index from December 18, 1998 to December 22, 2000. This was a very volatile time period for stocks, particularly in the semiconductor industry. Over this time period eight option positions were used to lower the volatility of the index value.

The SOX Index is a price-weighted index comprising companies involved with the design, distribution, manufacturing, and sale of semiconductors. It consists of 16 major semiconductor stocks, including Intel (INTC; NASDAQ), Applied Materials (AMAT; NASDAQ), and Micron (MU; NYSE). The index was started on December 1, 1993 with a base value of 100 and experienced a period of extreme volatility beginning in the third quarter of 1999 and continuing through the end of 2000. Between December 14, 1999 and March 27, 2000, the SOX index more than doubled, increasing from 587.99 to 1305.96. By December 22, 2000, the index had fallen back to 587.14.

Options on the SOX index are traded on the Philadelphia Stock Exchange and are available in 10-point increments. Each option represents 100 notional shares of the index. One way to decrease the volatility of the index over this time period without eliminating upside gains is through the use of protective puts. Consider a portfolio manager with

EXHIBIT 11.11

SOX Index and Put Option Exercise Prices

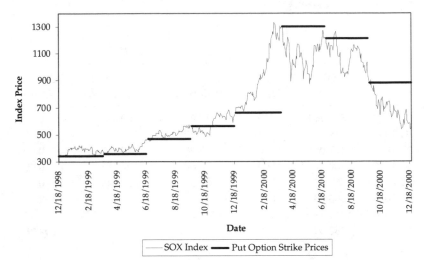

investments that closely match the value of the SOX Index. The manager can buy the put options quarterly and continually roll to the next option contract. Unlike hedging with futures, the portfolio is fully protected if the index falls and has unlimited gains reduced by the amount of the put premium.

Exhibit 11.11 shows the levels of the SOX Index over the sample time period and the put strike prices over the term of each put option. While the index is rising, the put options have little value. In fact, the first five options expire worthless. When the market falls in the last three quarters, however, the puts have significant value at expiration.

Exhibit 11.12 shows the costs and benefits of the protective put strategy for the SOX Index. Beginning December 18, 1998, three-month put contracts are purchased with a strike price nearest to and below the spot index level. In our example, each contract is purchased and held to maturity to protect against the value of the index.[2] In contrast, under a delta-

---

2. Since one option represents 100 shares of the index, the actual trade would consist of buying one put to protect against 100 times the index. To simplify the analysis, we assume that the option represents the value of the index. The percentage hedging costs are the same.

EXHIBIT 11.12

SOX Index Protective Put Strategy:
Costs and Benefits

Quarter	SOX Index	Put Strike Price	Put Premium	Put Premium as % of Index (annualized)	Terminal Value
1Q 1999	349.25	340	17.89	20.49%	0.00
2Q 1999	369.83	360	18.57	20.09%	0.00
3Q 1999	477.05	470	23.68	19.85%	0.00
4Q 1999	560.27	560	33.84	24.16%	0.00
1Q 2000	667.30	660	37.55	22.51%	0.00
2Q 2000	1305.46	1300	76.35	23.39%	82.72
3Q 2000	1216.57	1210	64.83	21.31%	283.47
4Q 2000	880.36	880	47.30	21.49%	292.86
Total			320.01		659.05

neutral hedging strategy, the number of options would be selected, so the change in the value of the options would closely offset the change in the value of the underlying portfolio. The values of the options are estimated over the time period based on historic volatility and the Black-Scholes option pricing model. The premiums on the puts are significant, ranging from 17.89 to 76.35. As an annualized percentage of the index, the put premiums range from 19.85% to 24.16%. The terminal value of the option represents the intrinsic value at expiration. For the first five options, the terminal values are zero. The puts in the last three quarters have significant value.

The value of the strategy can be compared with the index value over time. We calculate the net value of the put options by subtracting the cumulative costs of the put options and adding the cumulative option values when the puts expire in-the-money. To calculate the net hedged index value, we add the net value of the put options to the spot SOX Index price and add the value of the current put option. The net hedged index value relative to the SOX Index is shown in Exhibit 11.13. The strategy has a significant cost over the first five quarters and lowers the return on the index

EXHIBIT 11.13

Comparison of the SOX Index with the Net
Hedged Index Value

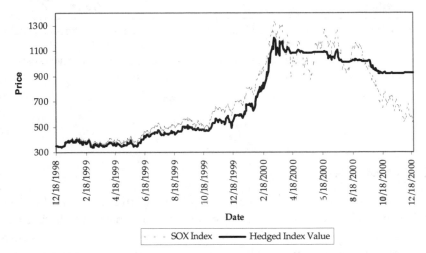

by that amount. However, the strategy provides significant protection in
the final three quarters.

ADJUSTING DELTA

In Chapter 8, we discussed the concepts of delta and gamma. Delta represents the change in the price of the option for a given change in the value
of the underlying asset. The concept of being delta neutral is similar to the
concept of being duration hedged.

A long stock position has a delta of 1.0. A long call option that is at the
money has a delta that is close to 0.5. This means that each dollar increase in
the price of the underlying asset causes an approximately $0.50 increase in
the price of the option. As a long call option becomes more valuable, delta
approaches 1.0. Long put options have negative deltas. An increase in value
of the underlying asset decreases the value of a put option.

Options can be used to adjust the delta of a portfolio. For example, a
portfolio manager who wants to increase the delta of a portfolio can do so
by buying call options. This is an efficient way to adjust the delta in the
short term.

COMPARISON OF HEDGING ALTERNATIVES

Hedge	Pros	Cons
Index Futures	Liquid, low transaction costs	Standard terms, tracking risk, daily mark-to-market
Equity Swaps	Customized terms, no tracking risk	Illiquid, high transaction costs
Index Options	Unlimited profit	Expensive

SUMMARY

In this chapter we examined hedging strategies in the equity market. The risk of an equity position consists of systematic and unsystematic risk. Unsystematic or firm-specific risk can be removed by diversification of a portfolio. Systematic or market risk can be hedged with equity index futures, index options, or equity swaps.

Futures are the most liquid hedges in the equity market. They have standard expiration dates and contract terms but may not track the value of a portfolio well. We examine the use of futures contracts to hedge the value of a sample portfolio. The portfolio hedge ratio is determined by beta, a measure of systematic risk. Beta changes over time, however, and must be monitored closely. Over long periods of time, hedges must be adjusted to account for changes in beta.

Swaps can be customized, and track portfolio values well, but they are less liquid than futures. Unlike futures, equity swaps have no tracking risk. We examined the use of equity swaps to hedge the value of a portfolio against a market downturn. The cost-of-carry on an equity swap is essentially the same as a futures contract.

Options are generally standardized, may be customized in some cases, offer the best payoff profiles, but have the highest cost of capital. We examined the use of a protective put strategy to protect against market downturns. Unlike futures or swaps, options do not remove gains; they simply lower them by the option premium. Options are an effective way to provide short-term protection against market changes while maintaining exposure to the market. The cost-of-carry on options, however, is much higher than that of futures or swaps.

REFERENCES

Gray, G., P. Cusatis, and J. R. Woolridge. *The Streetsmart Guide to Valuing a Stock.* New York: McGraw-Hill, 2004.

Statman, Meir. "How Many Stocks Make a Diversified Portfolio?" *Journal of Financial and Quantitative Analysis* 22 (September 1987), 353–64.

CHAPTER 12

Municipal Bonds

The municipal market comprises thousands of bond issuers with varying credit ratings and sources of revenues. According to the Bond Market Association, there were approximately $1.9 trillion in municipal bonds outstanding as of the end of the third quarter of 2003. Interest on municipal bonds is generally exempt from federal and state taxes. Because of the tax exemption, the municipal market behaves differently from taxable fixed-income markets. Unlike U.S. Treasuries, municipal bonds are not fungible. Bonds trade differently, based on the state of issuance, revenue source for payment, and underlying credit of the issuer. For these reasons, traditional fixed-income hedges, such as U.S. Treasury futures, have proved to be a poor hedge for municipal bonds.

Historically, an issue for hedgers in the municipal bond market has been the lack of a consistent hedge instrument. Although the taxable and tax-exempt markets are correlated over time, they generally do not move together over short time periods. The most liquid hedges are based on taxable interest rates, such as LIBOR swaps, and U.S. Treasury futures. Municipal swaps correlate highly with the LIBOR swap market. As we discussed in Chapter 6, the CBOT recently introduced a municipal contract based on an underlying portfolio of approximately 200 municipal bonds. The new contract is meant to follow movements in the municipal market.

In this chapter we examine hedging techniques for municipal bonds. We begin by examining perfect capital markets. We then relax this assumption and examine the effects of basis shifts on hedge ratios in a hypothetical market. We discuss the impact of changes in the relationship between taxable and tax-exempt yields for cross-market hedging and develop an *ex ante* hedge ratio based on this relationship. Next we examine market changes over an 11-year period beginning January 1993, with the use of market indices as a measure of the market. We compare cost-of-carry on various hedges over a sample time period. We also examine the historic performance of an individual noncallable bond over a seven-year period. Finally, we examine issues related to hedging callable municipal bonds and discuss hedging techniques for municipal issuers.

MUNICIPAL BASIS

A concern of hedgers in all markets is the relationship between the hedge instrument and the target portfolio. This is an important issue in the municipal market because of the tax exemption of municipal bonds and the unique characteristics of the market. The hedger in the municipal market must be concerned with municipal *basis*. Basis, in this sense, refers to the ratio of municipal bond yields to taxable yields. Small changes in this relationship will increase the volatility of a hedged municipal portfolio. As a measure of the municipal market, we use two indices. The Bond Buyer 40 Index (BB-40) is a long-term municipal bond index that was initially created for the municipal bond futures contract in 1985. The BB-40 is composed of 40 long-term general obligation and revenue bonds.[1] The Municipal Market Data AAA General Obligation Index (MMD) is a daily generic index published by Thomson Financial. Thompson began publishing the AAA curve in 1981. The yields reflect the offer side of the market determined from trading activity. Exhibit 12.1 shows the historic basis relationship of the MMD and BB-40 with the 30-year LIBOR swap yield. The upper line represents the basis calculated from the yield-to-maturity on the BB-40, and the lower line represents the basis calculated from the yield on the MMD. The MMD basis is consistently lower because the index is a high-grade scale. Over the time period, BB-40 basis averaged 0.8552 and MMD basis averaged 0.8178. The basis statistics for both indices are summarized in Exhibit 12.2.

In the sections that follow, we outline the importance of basis changes on a hedged portfolio. We develop an *ex ante* hedge ratio based on an

---

1. Eligible bonds have a minimum term size of $50 million; an A rating or better by Moody's and an A rating or better by Standard and Poor's; a remaining maturity of at least 19 years; at least seven years to first call date, if callable; an original issue price of between 85 and 105; and a fixed, semiannual coupon payment.

E X H I B I T   12.1

Historic Municipal to LIBOR Swap Basis

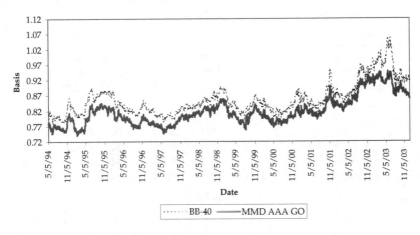

expected basis relationship. We begin by considering perfect capital markets and then examine markets with changing basis.

HEDGING MUNICIPAL MARKET RISK: PERFECT CAPITAL MARKETS

As a starting point, consider the example of perfect capital markets. Under the assumptions of perfect capital markets, municipal bonds would trade at a static basis. Under perfect capital markets basis is a constant function of the marginal tax rate and risk of the municipal bonds. Exhibit 12.3

E X H I B I T   12.2

Descriptive Statistics on Basis Municipal Yields versus 30-Year LIBOR Swap Yields, 1993–2003

	BB-40	MMD
Mean	0.8552	0.8178
Median	0.8416	0.8085
Standard Deviation	0.5160	0.4550
Maximum	1.0578	0.9479
Minimum	0.7793	0.7396

EXHIBIT 12.3

Perfect Capital Markets Hedge Ratios

n	0	1	2	3	4	5	6
Pricing Date	1/1/04	1/1/05	1/1/06	1/1/07	1/1/08	1/1/09	1/1/10
Basis	0.855	0.855	0.855	0.855	0.855	0.855	0.855
Change in Rates		+0.50%	+0.50%	+0.50%	−0.50%	−0.50%	−0.50%
Municipal Bond							
Yield	4.49%	4.92%	5.35%	5.77%	4.06%	3.63%	3.21%
Price	100.000	93.430	87.653	82.558	106.826	113.968	121.358
Modified Duration	16.394	15.659	14.972	14.329	15.635	15.643	15.578
PV01(bond)	0.164	0.146	0.131	0.118	0.167	0.178	0.189
LIBOR Swap							
Yield	5.25%	5.75%	6.25%	6.75%	4.75%	4.25%	3.75%
Price	100.000	92.984	86.856	81.479	107.420	115.307	123.601
Modified Duration	15.024	14.287	13.605	12.973	14.536	14.653	14.696
PV01(swap)	0.150	0.133	0.118	0.106	0.156	0.169	0.182
Hedge Ratios							
h^*		0.933	0.942	0.950	0.957	0.915	0.902
h		0.937	0.943	0.948	0.936	0.906	0.891

outlines a perfect capital markets scenario under which a 30-year non-callable municipal bond is hedged with a 30-year LIBOR swap. Basis is assumed to stay constant at 0.855, the approximate historic average, for a given change in swap yields. Annual fluctuations in 50-basis-point increments are assumed for a maximum fluctuation of 150 basis points in either direction. Swap prices are calculated under the assumption of a parallel shift in implied forward rates, which allows the swap to be priced as a bond with a coupon equal to the established fixed rate. For both the bond and the swap, modified duration is calculated for each time period. The present value of a one-basis-point change, PV01, is calculated for the swap and the bond by multiplication of the appropriate modified duration by the price of the bond or swap. For example, for the swap, the present value of a one-basis-point change in yields is calculated as follows:

$$PV01(\text{swap}) = D_m(\text{swap})P_t(\text{swap})$$

Given the constant basis assumptions, an *ex ante* hedge ratio h^* is estimated as follows:

$$h^* = \frac{0.8552\,\text{PV01(bond)}}{\text{PV01(swap)}}$$

An *ex post* hedge ratio h is calculated based on the ratio of the actual change in the municipal bond price to the change in the swap price:

$$h = \frac{P_t(\text{bond}) - P_{t-1}(\text{bond})}{P_t(\text{swap}) - P_{t-1}(\text{swap})}$$

where $P_t(\text{swap})$ and $P_t(\text{bond})$ are the prices of the swap and bond at time t, respectively. The resulting hedge ratios result in a net zero price change for a hedged portfolio over the time period.

The values of h^* and h are shown in Exhibit 12.3. Because of the static basis assumption, the hedge ratios are close in value. The breakeven hedge ratios range from 0.891 to 0.937, which is higher than the basis assumption of 0.855. This is due to the higher relative duration of municipal bonds. This result implies that the yield basis will tend to underestimate the optimal hedge ratio under the assumption of perfect capital markets.

The resulting hedge ratios are much higher than those typically employed by portfolio managers. Historic data suggest that the use of a hedge ratio with a magnitude of 0.930 will result in extreme portfolio volatility. This is due to basis shifts that accompany changes in market rates. The next section relaxes the assumption of static basis. Estimates of the expected movements in basis are calculated from historic data, given the direction of the swap market.

HEDGING MUNICIPAL MARKET RISK: SHIFTS IN BASIS

Municipal basis is partially determined by the absolute level of interest rates. Historically, the municipal market on average has outperformed taxable markets when interest rates have risen and underperformed when interest rates have fallen. This is due, in part, to the increased value placed on tax benefits in high-interest-rate markets. Since basis changes over time, a static basis assumption leads to price volatility in a hedged portfolio. In the sections that follow, we relax the assumption of perfect capital markets to examine the effects of shifts in basis on hedge ratios.

LEVEL CHANGE IN BASIS

To measure the impact of a change in basis, we initially assume a constant change in basis for a given increase or decrease in swap yields. It is assumed that basis decreases by 0.0004 for a one-basis-point increase in swap yields. This corresponds to a decrease in basis of 0.020 for a 50-basis-point increase in swap yields. It is also assumed that the opposite relationship holds—basis *increases* by 0.020 for a 50-basis-point *decrease* in swap yields.

As shown in Exhibit 12.4, basis shifts have a dramatic impact on the optimal *ex post* hedge ratio. The hedge ratios range from 0.645 to 0.694 when basis is altered as discussed above. These hedge ratios are more consistent with those typically employed in the market.

HISTORIC CHANGE IN BASIS

To further examine the basis relationship, regression analysis is performed to estimate the historic change in municipal market to LIBOR swap basis

EXHIBIT 12.4

Level Change in Basis of 2.00%

n	0	1	2	3	4	5	6
Pricing Date	1/1/04	1/1/05	1/1/06	1/1/07	1/1/08	1/1/09	1/1/10
Basis	0.855	0.835	0.815	0.795	0.815	0.835	0.855
Change in Rates		+0.50%	+0.50%	+0.50%	−0.50%	−0.50%	−0.50%
Municipal Bond							
Yield	4.49%	4.80%	5.10%	5.37%	5.10%	4.80%	4.49%
Price	100.000	95.135	91.025	87.559	91.333	95.478	100.000
Modified Duration	16.394	15.785	15.227	14.714	14.709	14.672	14.600
PV01(bond)	0.164	0.150	0.139	0.129	0.134	0.140	0.146
LIBOR Swap							
Yield	5.25%	5.75%	6.25%	6.75%	6.25%	5.75%	5.25%
Price	100.000	92.984	86.856	81.479	87.230	93.412	100.000
Modified Duration	15.024	14.287	13.605	12.973	13.231	13.427	13.556
PV01(swap)	0.150	0.133	0.118	0.106	0.115	0.125	0.136
Hedge Ratios							
h^*		0.933	0.944	0.956	0.969	0.949	0.933
h		0.694	0.670	0.645	0.656	0.671	0.686

EXHIBIT 12.5

Historic Change in Basis—Regression Statistics, May 5, 1994
to December 31, 2003 ($n = 2418$)

	Coefficients	Standard Error	t-statistic	p value
Intercept	−0.000000	0.000001	−0.7552	0.4502
Δy(swap)	−0.000905	0.000012	−76.6016	0.0000

for a given change in the yield on 30-year LIBOR swaps. The regression
equation takes the form

$$\Delta b = \beta_0 + \beta_1 \Delta y(\text{swap}) + \varepsilon$$

where

Δb	= change in basis
β_0	= intercept coefficient
β_1	= change in basis attributable to change in swap yield
$\Delta y(\text{swap})$	= change in swap yield
ε	= error term, $E(\varepsilon) = 0$

The relationship is examined daily from May 5, 1994 to December 31, 2003.
As a measure of the municipal market, we use the yield on the BB-40. The
regression statistics based on the BB-40 are summarized in Exhibit 12.5.
The regression analysis results in an estimate of β_1 equal to −0.000905.
The coefficient is significant at the 0.01 level.[2] This suggests that on average, a one-basis-point increase (decrease) in swap yields leads to a decrease (increase) in basis of 0.000905. Applying this to the prior analysis, a
50-basis-point increase (decrease) in swap yields corresponds to a decrease (increase) in basis of 0.04525.

Historic data suggest that the magnitude of basis changes for a given
change in the market varies based on the direction of the market movement. Specifically, an increase in rates causes a larger basis change than a
decrease in rates. To examine the impact of market direction on basis

---

2. The regression has an adjusted R^2 of 0.71. Regression analysis based on the Municipal
   Market Data (MMD) AAA General Obligation Index as a measure of municipal
   yields results in a coefficient of −0.000692. This coefficient is significant at the 0.01
   level, and the regression has an adjusted R^2 of 0.56.

changes, the data set is split between observations in which swap yields increase and observations in which swap yields decrease. Observations in which swap yields are unchanged are eliminated. The regression above is performed on each subset of data.

In instances where swap yields decrease (n = 1208) , the sample regression coefficient, $\hat{\beta}_1$, has a value of -0.000980, suggesting that a 50-basis-point decrease in swap yields results in an increase in basis of 0.000490. In instances where swap yields increase (n = 1088), $\hat{\beta}_1$ has a value of -0.0832, suggesting that a 50-basis-point increase in swap yields results in a decrease in basis of 0.0416. These coefficients vary with the time period over which they are calculated and with the index used to represent the municipal market.[3] Given the effect of changes in basis on hedge ratios, these results indicate that an optimal hedge ratio, allowing for shifts in basis, is at or below the levels indicated in Exhibit 12.4.

Basis ranges from 0.7793 to 1.0578 over the 11-year period. The changes in basis make a static hedge ratio inefficient over the time period. Consider an example where basis begins at the average level of 0.855, increases to the maximum basis of 1.058 over three years, and then decreases to the minimum basis of 0.779. Exhibit 12.6 displays the hypothetical market and hedge ratios for these assumptions. The large shifts in basis require adjustments to hedge ratios. The optimal hedge ratios in this example range from 0.143 to 0.456.

Basis appears to increase more when interest rates are falling than it decreases when interest rates are rising. This result creates a dilemma for the hedger. If the hedge ratio is set based on historic basis shifts when rates are falling, the resulting hedge will provide expected hedge losses when rates increase. If the hedge ratio is set based on the change in basis when rates are rising, the resulting hedge ratio will provide expected hedge losses when rates decrease. Therefore, one of two approaches can be taken. A ratio can be set in the middle of the expected basis shifts (approximately 0.40–0.60), which will result in expected net losses. A second approach is to set hedge ratios based on expected future basis levels. We discuss this approach in the next section.

---

3. The results presented here are based on BB-40 basis. The same analysis based on MMD basis results in coefficients of -0.000740 and -0.000626 when swap yields decrease and increase respectively.

EXHIBIT 12.6

Hedge Ratios Assuming Random Change in Municipal Basis

n	0	1	2	3	4	5	6
Pricing Date	1/1/04	1/1/05	1/1/06	1/1/07	1/1/08	1/1/09	1/1/10
Basis	0.855	0.923	0.990	1.058	0.965	0.872	0.779
Change in Rates		+0.50%	+0.50%	+0.50%	−0.75%	−0.75%	−0.75%
Municipal Bond							
Yield	4.49%	4.38%	4.21%	3.97%	4.34%	4.58%	4.68%
Price	100.000	101.744	104.600	108.621	102.285	98.685	97.334
Modified Duration	16.394	16.244	16.138	16.060	15.384	14.859	14.456
PV01(bond)	0.164	0.165	0.169	0.174	0.157	0.147	0.141
LIBOR Swap							
Yield	5.25%	4.75%	4.25%	3.75%	4.50%	5.25%	6.00%
Price	100.000	107.828	116.281	125.331	111.426	100.000	90.525
Modified Duration	15.024	15.340	15.587	15.762	14.756	13.833	12.990
PV01(swap)	0.150	0.165	0.181	0.198	0.164	0.138	0.118
Hedge Ratios							
h^*		0.933	0.922	0.922	0.934	0.923	0.924
h		0.223	0.338	0.444	0.456	0.315	0.143

EX ANTE OPTIMAL HEDGE RATIO

The hedger must make a decision whether to trust historic basis levels or to form expectations on future basis levels. If basis changes were independent of movements in the market, hedge ratios based on average basis changes would provide a reliable hedge. However, since basis changes tend to be larger when rates decrease, an efficient static hedge ratio is difficult to determine. Consider an *ex ante* hedge ratio based on expected changes in basis. A solution for the *ex ante* estimate of the hedge ratio h^*, given an expected shift in basis for a one-basis-point increase in swap yields, is

$$h^* = \frac{[(b_0 + \Delta b_t)(y_0(\text{swap}) + 0.01) - y_0(\text{bond})](100)\text{PV01(bond)}}{\text{PV01(swap)}}$$

where

b_0 = basis at time 0
Δb_t = expected change in basis from time 0 to time t
y_0(swap) = swap yield at time 0
y_0(bond) = bond yield at time 0

Example: Consider the estimate of the hedge ratio for a one-basis-point increase in swap yields. Assume a basis shift of -0.000832 indicated by the basis regression analysis above for increasing swap yields. With average BB-40 basis as the starting basis, the hedge ratio is calculated as follows:

$$h^* = \frac{[(0.8552 - 0.000832)(5.26) - 4.4898](100)(0.164)}{0.150} = 0.4565$$

The *ex ante* approach requires an estimate of expected basis. Historically, basis is a function of the supply and demand of municipal bonds and the absolute level of interest rates. The supply and demand of municipal bonds tends to be seasonal and is somewhat predictable. The absolute level of interest rates, however, tends to be the more important determinant of basis and is the most difficult to forecast. Shifts in basis make it difficult to establish a consistent hedge strategy. In the next section we examine the historic relationship between the municipal market and the hedge markets. We measure *ex post* hedge ratios in each of the markets.

HISTORIC MUNICIPAL BOND AND HEDGE DATA

As a measure of municipal market performance we use the BB-40 index. Because of the unique characteristics of municipal bonds, the use of an index as a proxy for market movements is not a true measure of portfolio performance; however, it is a good measure of the accuracy of hedge choices for general market movements. We collected prices on the BB-40 from January 2, 2000 to January 31, 2003.

To examine historic hedge efficiency in the municipal market, we constructed a database of relevant hedging vehicles. We assembled prices for the swap and futures market. In the swap market, we collected daily

EXHIBIT 12.7

Summary of Historic Municipal Market and Hedge Data

	Exchange	Mean	Median	Standard Deviation	Obs.
BB-40 Index	—	104.28	104.91	5.63	999
Swaps					
20-year BMA	OTC	113.47	113.75	7.36	999
20-year LIBOR	OTC	116.69	116.06	10.46	999
Futures					
Municipal note	CBOT	102.43	102.09	2.21	257
U.S. Treasury bond	CBOT	104.82	104.09	6.44	999
10-year swap	CBOT	108.62	109.73	5.26	544

prices in the BMA and LIBOR interest rate swap markets.[4] The prices are derived from fixed swap rates on quarterly reset interest rates swaps versus BMA and three-month LIBOR with 20-year tenors. In the futures market, we collected daily prices for the municipal note, U.S. Treasury note, U.S. Treasury bond, and 10-year swap futures contracts. The data are limited by the change in the contract specification on the U.S. Treasury futures contracts at the end of 1999, so we begin the data series on January 2, 2000. The municipal note and swap futures contracts are relatively new, and all available data are collected on the contracts. Exhibit 12.7 lists descriptive statistics on the hedge data.

The hedge alternatives in the municipal market come primarily from the taxable market. The only exchange-traded municipal hedge is the Municipal note contract, which began trading at the end of 2002. BMA swaps are over-the-counter contracts and are not pure municipal market hedges. The yields on BMA swaps correlate highly with the yields on LIBOR swaps.

The relationship between the hedge data and the market index can be examined by calculating minimum variance hedge ratios and adjusted R^2 measures with the use of regression analysis. We also computed correlation

---

4. The daily BMA swap rates were provided by Wachovia Capital Markets.

coefficients, ρ, between the hedge data and the market index. We calculated minimum variance hedge ratios for selected hedge instruments based on the following equation:

$$\Delta P(\text{index}) = \beta_0 + \beta_1 \Delta P(\text{hedge}) + \varepsilon$$

where

$\Delta P(\text{index})$ = change in BB-40 index price
β_0 = intercept coefficient
β_1 = minimum variance hedge ratio
$\Delta P(\text{hedge})$ = change in price of the hedge instrument
ε = error term, $E(\varepsilon) = 0$

We performed the analysis outlined above for the time period from January 3, 2000 to December 31, 2003. Since the municipal note and 10-year swap futures contracts are relatively new, the analysis is performed over a shorter time period for those contracts. Sample hedge ratios $\hat{\beta}_1$ adjusted R^2 values, and correlation coefficients r are presented in Exhibit 12.8. The hedge ratios range from 0.2274 for the 20-year LIBOR swap to 0.5700 for the municipal note futures. Although all of the hedge ratios are significant, the adjusted R^2 values are low and range from 0.3409 for the 20-year BMA swap to 0.5135 for the 10-year swap futures. The highest correlation of price changes is between the BB-40 index and the 10-year swap futures contract.

The resulting hedge ratios are lower than *ex post* measures, such as duration, would suggest. This is due to the fact that the minimum vari-

EXHIBIT 12.8

Sample Corporate Bond Market Relationships

Hedge	$\hat{\beta}_1$	Adj. R^2	r	Obs.
20-year BMA swap	0.2703*	0.3409	0.5839	998
20-year LIBOR swap	0.2274*	0.3752	0.6125	998
Municipal note futures	0.5700*	0.4522	0.6725	256
U.S. Treasury bond futures	0.2998*	0.4458	0.6677	998
10-year swap futures	0.4364*	0.5135	0.7166	543

*Significant at the 0.01 level.

ance hedge ratios are affected by changes in basis over time. These results are consistent with the low hedge ratios predicted for random changes in basis (Exhibit 12.6).

HISTORIC HEDGE EFFICIENCY

To test the efficiency of hedges historically, we select a noncallable New York City Water Finance Authority (NYCWFA) bond dated October 29, 1996 and due June 15, 2021. The bond has a 6.00% coupon and was issued with an original issue premium of 104.958 to yield 5.625%. The bond is insured by the FSA and is rated AAA/Aaa by Standard & Poor's and Moody's, respectively. The total maturity size of the bond is $25 million. The bond is described in Exhibit 12.9.

We collected daily prices and yields on the NYCWFA bonds from January 2, 1997 to December 21, 2003. We begin by examining the yield basis relative to a 20-year LIBOR swap over the time period. Exhibit 12.10 shows the relationship between yields and basis over the seven-year time period. Basis ranges from 74.14% to 102.89% and has a standard deviation of 5.99%. The yields and basis have a strong negative correlation of −0.895.

To hedge the NYCWFA bond selected for this example, a hedger must make a decision about the various hedge instruments and the hedging methodology. The optimum hedge instrument is that with the highest

EXHIBIT 12.9

Description of NYCWFA Bond

Dated Date	October 29, 1996
Maturity	June 15, 2021
Coupon	6.00%
Call Date	Non-callable
Ratings	AAA/Aaa
Yield-to-Maturity*	5.733
Price	103.489
Duration	12.908

*Pricing statistics as of January 2, 1997.

EXHIBIT 12.10

Historic Basis and Yields on NYCWFA Bonds

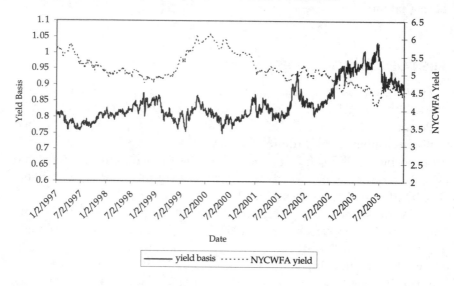

correlation with the underlying bond and the lowest costs of carry. The appropriate hedging methodology will attempt to address the issues of basis shifts over time. We begin by examining the historic efficiency of the hedges, realizing that shifts in basis make traditional hedging approaches inappropriate.

We selected hedges with similar durations when possible and collected all available daily data for each hedging instrument. The hedges consist of a 20-year quarterly reset BMA swap, a 20-year quarterly reset LIBOR swap, the municipal futures contract, the U.S. Treasury bond futures contract, and the 10-year swap futures contract. The BMA and LIBOR swaps are seasoned over the time period and are priced based on seasoned yields. The swap prices include net interest accrual over the time period.

We begin by calculating a static hedge ratio based on the initial ratio of the expected change in the bond relative to the expected change in the swaps, adjusted for current basis. This approach is appropriate if the basis relationship is static.[5] Assuming D_m(bond) and D_m(hedge) are the initial

---

5. An alternative methodology is to calculate a yield beta based on historic data. The yield beta is based on a simple linear regression between the market and the hedge yields and is used in place of current basis. Since basis changes occur regularly, either methodology will result in high volatility.

modified durations of the bond and hedge, respectively, we find the hedge ratio h^* as follows:

$$h^* = \frac{P_0(\text{bond})D_m(\text{bond})}{P_0(\text{hedge})D_m(\text{hedge})}b = \frac{\text{PV01(bond)}}{\text{PV01(hedge)}}b$$

Exhibit 12.11 displays the hedging results based on a static hedge ratio. Part A of the table presents results for the time period over which a comparable data set exists for all of the hedges, and Part B presents results for the entire data set. Based on initial duration, U.S. Treasury bond futures provide the lowest absolute mark to market (MTM) of -0.2368 per $100. This corresponds to a loss of $59,200 for a hedged position of $25 million. The lowest MTM volatility is achieved with the municipal futures contract.

Regardless of changes in the market, the durations of the bond and the hedge will change over time and periodic adjustments are required. The efficiency of the hedges can be improved by relaxing the assumption that the hedge ratio is static over the hedging period. Adjustments to hedge ratios when one is hedging with futures can be made easily since

EXHIBIT 12.11

Historic MTM Based on Initial PV01 Ratio

Hedge	h^*	Obs.	Net MTM per $100	MTM Volatility
A: Hedging Results for a Comparable Time Period				
20-yr BMA swap	1.061	256	3.9725	0.5741
20-yr LIBOR swap	1.023	256	−1.6135	0.6255
Municipal futures	1.473	256	−4.7762	0.5055
U.S. T-bond futures	1.038	256	−0.2368	0.6657
10-yr swap futures	1.426	256	−2.2204	0.7169
B: Hedging Results for the Entire Time Period				
20-yr BMA swap	1.061	998	−1.5916	0.5844
20-yr LIBOR swap	1.023	1749	−4.2333	0.5701
Municipal futures	1.473	256	−4.7762	0.5055
U.S. T-bond futures	1.038	998	−14.5275	0.5949
10-yr swap futures	1.426	543	−12.2160	0.7214

the contracts are very liquid and trade in relatively low denominations. Adjusting the size of swap contracts can be costly. Futures can be layered on a swap hedge to efficiently adjust hedge ratios over time.

An alternative approach is to estimate a minimum variance hedge ratio based on historic data.[6] While historic basis is not an unbiased predictor of future basis, it can provide an estimate of an appropriate hedge ratio. We calculate hedge ratios for each of the hedges based on the following regression equation:

$$\Delta P(\text{bond}) = \beta_0 + \beta_1 \Delta P(\text{hedge}) + \varepsilon$$

where

$\Delta P(\text{bond})$ = daily change in price of the NYCWFA bond
β_0 = intercept coefficient
β_1 = minimum variance hedge ratio h
$\Delta P(\text{hedge})$ = daily change in hedge price
ε = error term, $E(\varepsilon) = 0$

Exhibit 12.12 summarizes the results of the regression analysis, MTM, average basis, and volatility of basis for two sets of data. Part A contains the data for the time period over which a comparable data set exists for all of the hedges. The data are limited by the municipal note contract, which has 256 observations. The hedge ratios range from 0.3144 to 0.5508. The hedge ratios based on minimum variance are about one-fifth the level of the initial duration hedge ratios calculated above. Minimum variance hedge ratios are lower because they are influenced by basis shifts. Hedge ratios based on historic data may not be appropriate for all market conditions because they are not predictive of expected basis relationships. The minimum variance hedge ratios in Exhibit 12.12 are biased downward because interest rates fall and basis rises over the time period examined.

MTM values represent the cumulative marks-to-market over the hedging time periods. For a perfect hedge, the expected MTM is zero. The absolute MTM values are generally high, ranging from −2.2204 to 3.4304 per $100. The municipal note contract has the lowest MTM of 0.1991. For a $25 million bond position, this equates to a net gain over the time period of $49,775.

---

6. This approach was first introduced by Ederington (1979).

EXHIBIT 12.12

Historic Hedge Ratios and MTM Based on
a Minimum Variance Hedge

Hedge	$\hat{\beta}_1$	Obs.	Net MTM per $100	MTM Volatility	Average Basis	Basis Volatility
A: Analysis of Comparable Time Period						
20-yr BMA swap	0.3445	256	3.4304	0.2858	1.1007	0.0444
20-yr LIBOR swap	0.3182	256	2.0224	0.2728	0.8421	0.0596
Municipal futures	0.5508	256	0.1991	0.2726	0.9718	0.0272
U.S. T-bond futures	0.3144	256	2.1384	0.2611	0.9001	0.0307
10-yr swap futures	0.3975	256	1.6671	0.2702	1.0234	0.0623
B: Analysis of Entire Time Period						
20-yr BMA swap	0.2436	998	14.4406	0.2571	1.1442	0.0288
20-yr LIBOR swap	0.2628	1749	10.5611	0.2721	0.9444	0.0378
Municipal futures	0.5508	256	0.1991	0.2726	0.9718	0.0272
U.S. T-bond futures	0.2629	998	10.6716	0.2373	0.9047	0.0317
10-yr swap futures	0.3658	543	1.9786	0.2634	0.9758	0.0818

This hedging strategy has an inherent call on the direction of the market. The predominant gains in MTM for the hedges are due to the low hedge ratios dictated by the minimum variance methodology and the decrease in interest rates over the time period. Although this methodology produces the minimum variance in the daily MTMs, it does not provide for minimum values of the cumulative MTM.

In addition to hedge ratios and MTM, average yield basis and yield basis volatility are measured for 256 trading days for which all of the data are available. The basis volatility is the standard deviation of basis over the time period. The lowest standard deviation is 0.0272 for the municipal note futures contract. Based on net MTM and the standard deviation of basis, the municipal futures contract appears to be the most efficient hedge; however, the contract has traded for only about one year since it has been redefined. After many years of more dramatic basis shifts, a more accurate assessment can be made. Part B shows the same analysis over the maximum time period of available data starting on January 2, 1997. Although the data are not directlly comparable, the performance for hedge alternatives is shown.

STABILITY OF HEDGE RATIOS

Effective hedging requires the hedger to make an accurate estimate of the hedge ratio. In the municipal market, hedge ratios are unstable and require the hedger to adjust the size of the hedge position, especially for long-term hedges. Exhibit 12.13 shows empirical hedge ratios for NYCWFA bonds. The hedge ratios were estimated from a regression of spot market price changes on 20-year LIBOR swap price changes for a lagging 60-day period. The hedge ratios range from 0.012 to 0.614 and are volatile. Similar volatility is found if the analysis is performed with BMA swaps or U.S. Treasury bond futures as the hedges.

COST-OF-CARRY

A major concern for hedgers in the fixed-income market is the cost-of-carry (COC) on the hedge instruments. COC is a function of the relationship between short-term and long-term interest rates. The COC is a measure of hedging cost over time.

For interest rate swaps, we can estimate the COC by measuring the net interest accrual over the life of the swap. For an at-market swap, the

EXHIBIT 12.13

Hedge Ratios Estimated for 20-year LIBOR Swap
with a Lagging 60-day Regression

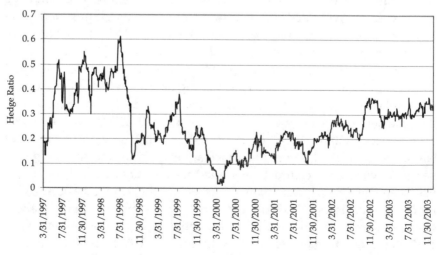

Date

expected net present value of the interest accrual is equal to zero at inception. As interest rates change, expectations change. One result of the change in expectations is a change in the price protection of the underlying position. A second result is a change in the COC of the hedge.

As an example of COC, consider the NYCWFA bond from above. An investor in this bond expects to receive the yield y on the bond over the life of the investment. Assuming the investor can finance the position at three-month LIBOR r, the expected annual payoff is equal to $y - r$. The $25 million bond can be hedged with a quarterly reset 20-year LIBOR swap, whereby the investor pays fixed and receives three-month LIBOR. The amount of the swap will be determined by the hedging strategy. In this example the investor is unaffected by movements in r because the funding costs are offset by the floating swap receipt. The net cost of the hedge is equal to the fixed rate swap rate minus r. Exhibit 12.14 shows the cash flows for this example.

Using the daily data described above, we estimate COC for each of the hedge instruments over different periods of time. We eliminate the

EXHIBIT 12.14

Cash Flows for a Municipal Bond Hedged
with a LIBOR Swap

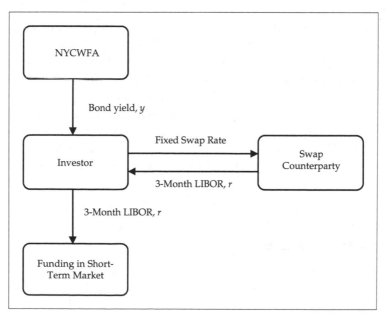

municipal futures contract from this analysis since it has not been trading for a meaningful period of time. We break the data into four subsets based on data availability. The first subset begins on January 2, 1997 and has 1749 observations. The only consistent data available over that time period were for the 20-year LIBOR swap. The second subset begins on January 3, 2000 and includes 20-year LIBOR swaps, 20-year BMA swaps, and U.S. Treasury bond futures and has 998 observations per variable. The third subset begins on October 26, 2001 to include the 10-year swap futures contract and has 543 observations per variable. The final subset begins on December 20, 2002 in order to include the municipal futures contract and has 256 observations per variable. All of the data end on December 31, 2003.

To measure COC for short LIBOR and BMA swaps, we deduct the actual quarterly LIBOR and BMA reset rates from the fixed swap rate. We assume that each swap begins on the first day of the time period and that the fixed rate is equal to the at-market swap rate. The daily swap accruals are cumulated, and an average daily COC is calculated. The notional par amount of the swap is set at $25 million.

Since interest rate futures contracts settle quarterly, the COC can be estimated from the price differential when contracts roll. For short interest rate futures, the COC is estimated from the cumulative change in contract value on the day the contract rolls net of market changes on that day. From this number, a daily COC is estimated, assuming a total position of $25 million.

Exhibit 12.15 summarizes the COC findings for each subset of data based on $25 million hedge positions. The hedging costs vary by time period and hedge instrument. For the 20-year LIBOR swap, for example, average daily COC is $2656.88 over the four-year period and decreases to $1784.19 over the seven-year period. Results must be adjusted by the appropriate hedge ratios to compare among hedges. For example, a $25 million bond hedged with LIBOR swaps at a ratio of 50% would have had one-half the COC. The appropriate hedge ratio with a BMA swap would be different for the same bond, and the COC would have to be adjusted accordingly.

CALLABLE BONDS

Most municipal bonds include call provisions consisting of a 10-year non-call period. The issuer possesses a combination of a European option to

E X H I B I T   12.15

Historic Daily Cost-of-Carry for a $25 Million Position

Hedge	Average Daily COC $n = 1749$	Average Daily COC $n = 998$	Average Daily COC $n = 543$	Average Daily COC $n = 256$
20-yr BMA swap	—	2,010.61	2,055.50	2,149.89
20-yr LIBOR swap	1,784.19	2,656.88	2,755.68	2,710.90
U.S. T-bond futures	—	2,239.45	3,179.41	3,282.58
10-yr swap futures	—	—	3,012.96	3,864.36
Municipal futures	—	—	—	3,128.99

the first call date and a Bermudan option from the first call date until the maturity of the bond. For example, for a 30-year callable bond with standard call provisions, the issuer has a 10-year European call option and a 20-year Bermudan call option. Exhibit 12.16 shows a time line of the call option on a typical 30-year municipal bond.

Callable bonds complicate the hedging issues in the municipal market. Callable bonds exhibit negative convexity when changes in yields cause the bonds to price to the call date rather than the maturity date. A bond priced to its call date has a much lower duration than the same bond

E X H I B I T   12.16

Time Line for a Typical Call Option on a 30-Year Municipal Bond

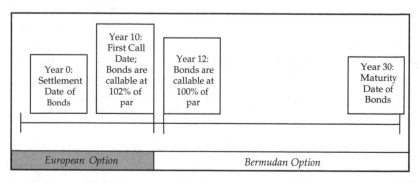

priced to its maturity date. For the small changes in yields near the coupon rate, the changes are minor. For example, a bond that sells for par will be valued at par, whether it is priced to the call date or maturity date. For the larger changes in yield, however, the price volatility can be considerable.

If callable bonds are hedged to maturity and interest rates fall below the coupon, the bonds are overhedged. If callable bonds are hedged to the first call date and rates rise above the coupon, the bonds are underhedged. In addition, for a long-term hedge, there is a risk that the bond or the hedge ultimately has a longer maturity. The amount of risk in a callable bond depends on the difference between the duration to call and the duration to maturity. For example, a 12-year bond with a 10-year call has less price volatility than a 30-year bond with a 10-year call. If the 12-year bond is priced alternatively to call or maturity, the difference in price is smaller than that of the 30-year bond. Exhibit 12.17 shows the price yield function of these two bonds, assuming both bonds have a 5.00% coupon. The bonds have the same price when priced to the call date. However, as interest rates rise and the bonds are priced to maturity, the 30-year bond exhibits much more price volatility than the 12-year bond.

Most municipal bonds are ultimately called. Since the call options are 10 years away, even if the bonds are issued in a period of relatively low interest rates, the bonds will have rolled down the curve substantially by the first call date. For example, a 25-year municipal bond callable in 10 years will be a 15-year bond on the first call date. Assuming an upward-sloping yield curve, the 15-year yield is typically much lower than the 25-year yield. If the bonds are not called on the first call date, the issuer has an additional 15 years to call the bonds. In addition, the issuer has the ability to advance refund the bonds by using one of several methods to lock in rates as the first call date approaches. This increases the window for the issuer to monetize its option.

Recall from our discussion of noncallable bonds that a duration-based approach for hedging interest rate risk is inappropriate for the municipal market because of basis changes. Although the duration relationship affects the hedge ratio, shifts in basis have a larger influence on the appropriate hedge ratio. A hedger must choose the maturity of the hedge, and adjustments may be necessary as the underlying bonds season.

Example: To analyze the volatility of a callable bond, we select a callable sewage disposal revenue bond issued by the City of Detroit, Michigan, and dated November 1, 1995. The bonds have a 5.25% coupon and mature on

EXHIBIT 12.17

Price/Yield Comparison for 12-Year and 30-Year Municipal
Bonds Callable in 10 Years

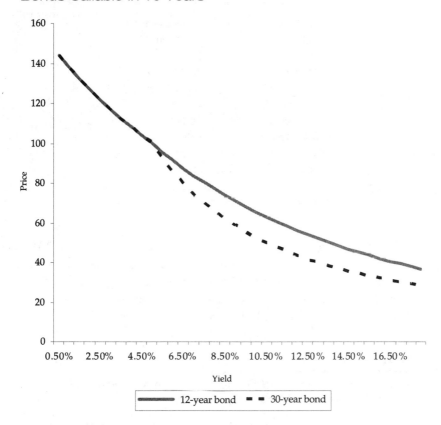

July 1, 2021. The first call date is July 1, 2005, at a premium of 101%, and the first par date is July 1, 2007. A description of the bonds is given in Exhibit 12.18.

We collected daily prices and yields from January 2, 1998 to December 31, 2003. Over this time period, the bonds are alternatively priced to call (928 days) and to maturity (627 days). Exhibit 12.19 shows the historic prices relative to par. Based on market convention, the prices that fall below the par line are priced to maturity and the prices above the line are priced to the call date.

The obvious problem with hedging a callable bond is the shift in basis that accompanies alternative pricing between call and maturity. A static hedge ratio will not be efficient if the bond is priced to both call and

EXHIBIT 12.18

Description of Detroit Sewage Bond

Dated Date	November 1, 1996
Maturity	July 1, 2021
Coupon	5.25%
Call Dates	7/1/2005 @ 101
	7/1/2007 @ 100
Ratings	AAA/Aaa
Credit Support	MBIA
Yield-to-Maturity*	5.262
Price	99.842
Duration	13.101

*Pricing statistics as of January 2, 1998.

maturity for an extended period of time. As shown in Exhibit 12.19, the basis falls significantly when the bond is priced to call for an extended period of time. This is evident in the time period beginning mid-year 2002. A decrease in basis is expected because the comparison becomes one of short-term municipal rates with the seasoned long-term LIBOR swap rates.

EXHIBIT 12.19

Historic Price and Yield Basis of Detroit Michigan Sewage Disposal Bonds

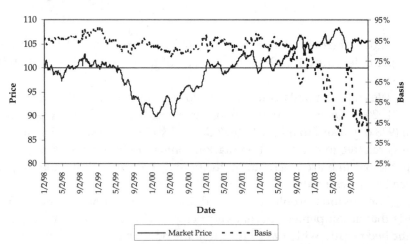

The duration differentials when the bonds and hedges are mismatched will compound the hedging inaccuracy.

A callable bond can be hedged with exchange-traded options, such as long call options on U.S. Treasury note futures.[7] The long call options offset the embedded short call options on the municipal bonds. Although this approach may work for short periods of time, it is not cost effective. Options on taxable bonds are generally more expensive than embedded municipal bond options. Therefore, the costs of directly hedging the call options will exceed the yield benefits from owning a callable bond.

ISSUER HEDGING STRATEGIES

In the previous sections we have discussed strategies used by municipal bond investors or portfolio managers to manage interest rate risk. Municipal bond issuers also need to manage interest rate risk at it applies to them. An issuer can use derivatives to hedge against rising interest rates, to lock in current interest rates, or to maximize the value of its call option. In this section we discuss hedging strategies as they apply to the municipal bond issuer.

VARIABLE-RATE EXPOSURE

Issuers of variable-rate debt are exposed to rising interest rates. One way for an issuer to protect against this risk is by buying an interest rate cap. Interest rate caps are similar to a portfolio of call options. Like interest rate swaps, they are based on a notional principal amount. A cap rate is established when the contract is traded. If interest rates exceed the cap rate over the calculation period, the cap owner receives a payment.

Interest rate caps can be expensive. To reduce the expense of an interest rate cap, an issuer can use an interest rate collar. Under a long collar, the issuer will simultaneously buy an interest rate cap and sell an interest rate floor. The proceeds of the interest rate floor are used to offset the cost of the interest rate cap. Using a collar, the issuer forfeits the benefits of interest

---

7. This can also be accomplished by buying a swaption. The cost, however, generally makes this strategy prohibitive.

rates below the floor rate in exchange for a less expensive cap. The issuer's net exposure is limited to interest rates between the floor and the cap rates.

Example: Consider an issuer of $50 million floating-rate bonds that reset weekly based on the BMA rate. The issuer can enter into an interest rate cap with a cap rate of 5.00% and a notional amount of $50 million. The issuer will make an up-front payment for the cap.[8] If BMA exceeds 5.00%, on average during the cap reset period, the issuer will receive a payment. The net effect is a maximum interest rate exposure of 5.00% plus the cap fee on the variable-rate bonds.

Another strategy for an issuer is the use of an interest rate swap to hedge interest rate exposure. A municipal issuer using a pay-fixed receive floating swap can effectively transform floating-rate bonds into fixed-rate bonds. A municipal issuer can use an interest rate swap to create a synthetic fixed-rate bond.

Example: A municipality has $100 million in tax-exempt floating-rate bonds. The bonds reset weekly based on the BMA rate and generally reset at BMA + 20 basis points. The maturity of the bonds is 30 years. The municipality would like to hedge the exposure to interest rate changes by creating a synthetic fixed-rate bond in the swap market. Exhibit 12.20 shows the structure of the BMA swap. Under the terms of the swap, the municipality agrees to pay the at-market swap rate of 4.50% and will receive the BMA rate plus + 20 bps. The cash inflows on the swap are sufficient to pay the interest payments on the bonds. The net result for the municipality is a fixed interest payment of 4.50% on its bonds.

HEDGING THE VALUE OF AN EMBEDDED CALL OPTION

Callable bonds give an issuer the ability to capture low interest rates if they prevail in the future. Because of the European nature of the call option, savings cannot be realized before the first call date. In many cases, however, one of several techniques designed to take advantage of low interest rates can be used to lock in current market interest rates.

---

8. Alternatively, the issuer can amortize the payment for the cap by making quarterly or semiannual payments.

EXHIBIT   12.20

Synthetic Fixed-Rate Bonds Using Municipal Swap

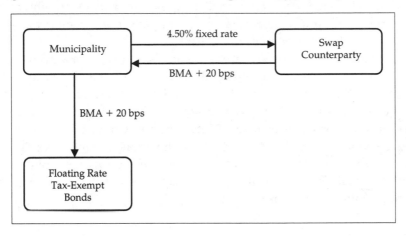

ADVANCE REFUNDING

One way for an issuer to hedge against higher interest rates is to lock in current rates by advance refunding its bonds. An advance refunding is accomplished by issuing bonds, called *refunding bonds*, for use in a current refunding on the first call date. A sufficient number of bonds are issued to pay the call price of the bonds, including call premium and underwriter's discount, cost of issuance, and debt service on the existing bonds until the call. The proceeds from the issuance of the bonds are placed in an escrow account and invested until the first call date.

FORWARD-DELIVERY BONDS

Certain issuers cannot advance refund their bonds because of regulatory restrictions.[9] In addition, some issuers are restricted from advance refunding bonds based on the use of proceeds of the original issue. The regulations

---

9. Bonds issued after March 14, 1986 can be refunded only one time prior to their call date. That is, a refunding issue that advance refunded post-1986 bonds cannot be advance refunded. Bonds issued prior to March 14, 1986 can be refunded two times. For example, if a bond was issued in 1980 and was advance refunded in 1988 with a callable bond with a 10-year noncallable period, the refunding issue could be refunded one additional time before its call date in 1998.

are designed to minimize the number of municipal bonds outstanding by eliminating coincident issues prior to a call date, which lowers the competition for U.S. Treasury securities. The regulations do not prohibit an issuer from issuing taxable bonds or entering into other arrangements to lock in a level of interest rates in the future.

An alternative to an advance refunding is the use of forward-delivery bonds. An issuer can issue bonds in the current market with a delayed delivery date that coincides with the first call date. The issuer will pay the current rates plus the forward premium, which will be determined by market conditions and the level of interest rates. Under this strategy, the issuer establishes fixed rates on the refunding bonds without waiting for the first call date. This strategy is inefficient if the forward premium is high. For example, if the call date is several years in the future, the forward premium will be prohibitive.

FORWARD-DELIVERY SWAP

Another alternative to advance refunding is a forward delivery swap. Swaps can be structured with a delayed start date on the interest accruals. An issuer can structure a forward-delivery swap such that the starting date coincides with the first call date on the existing bonds. On the first call date, the issuer will issue a sufficient amount of floating-rate bonds to pay all costs associated with calling the existing bonds. At the same time, the issuer begins its forward swap agreement, which requires it to pay a fixed rate and receive a floating rate. The issuer hedges interest rates by creating a synthetic fixed-rate bond in the future. The net cost to the issuer is the fixed payment on the swap, which is equal to the current swap rates plus a forward premium.

SELLING A SWAPTION

A variation of a forward delivery swap is the sale of a swaption. A swaption buyer has a European option on a swap. As a hedge against interest rates, a municipal issuer can sell a swaption with a notional amount equal to the principal on the underlying bonds. The exercise date of the swaption is the first call date. If the option is exercised, the municipality pays the predetermined fixed rate and receives a floating rate. At the same

EXHIBIT 12.21

Summary of Hedging Techniques for Municipal Issuers

	Current Market	**First Call Date**
Advance Refunding	• Refunding bonds issued • Outstanding bonds escrowed to first call date	• Old bonds called with proceeds of refunding issue
Forward-Delivery Bonds	• Outstanding bonds unaffected • Issuer enters into a forward agreement to issue bonds on first call date • Structure of bonds is set	• Current refunding bonds issued • Outstanding bonds are called with proceeds of variable-rate issue
Forward Delivery Swap	• Outstanding bonds unaffected • Issuer enters into a swap agreement to begin on first call date • Fixed swap rate is set	• Variable-rate bonds issued • Outstanding bonds are called with proceeds of variable-rate issue • Swap pays variable rate to issuer and issuer pays fixed rate
Swaption	• Outstanding bonds unaffected • Issuer sells the right to enter into a swap agreement to begin on first call date • Fixed swap rate is set	**(A) Swaption is exercised** • Variable-rate bonds issued • Outstanding bonds are called with proceeds of variable-rate issue • Swap pays variable rate to issuer and issuer pays fixed rate **(B) Option not exercised** • Outstanding bonds unaffected
Option	• Issuer sells option and receives option premium	**(A) Option exercised** • Current refunding bonds issued • Outstanding bonds called with proceeds of current refunding bonds **(B) Option not exercised** • Outstanding bonds unaffected

Based on Exhibit 4 in Cusatis (1996).

time, the municipality issues floating-rate bonds, the proceeds of which are used to refund the outstanding issue of bonds. The net result is a synthetic fixed rate for the issuer. If the swaption is not exercised, the issuer retains the ability to current refund the bonds. This hedging strategy provides the issuer with an upfront payment and transfers the option to a swap dealer.

SELLING AN OPTION

There is a variation to the swaption structure whereby the issuer sells an option to an investor. In the years prior to the first call date, when an issuer would otherwise advance refund its bonds, a portion of an issuer's European option exists. The issuer can sell the European option to an investor. The issuer sells an investor the right to purchase current refunding bonds on the first call date. In exchange for an option premium, the investor can take delivery of a prespecified amount of bonds with prespecified coupons and amortization, on the first call date.

If the option is exercised, the issuer must deliver the refunding bonds. The debt service on the current refunding bonds is structured to mirror the debt service on the outstanding bonds from the call date to the maturity of the outstanding bonds. The option premium represents the savings in debt service for the issuer. If the option is not exercised, the issuer retains the ability to current refund at a future date. The five hedging strategies described above are summarized in Exhibit 12.21.

COMPARISON OF HEDGING ALTERNATIVES

Hedge	Pros	Cons
BMA Swaps	Customized terms	High transaction costs, basis risk
LIBOR Swaps	Customized terms	High transaction costs, basis risk
Interest Rate Futures	Liquid, low transaction costs	Standard terms, tracking risk, daily mark-to-market, basis risk
Futures Options	Removes exposure to calls	Expensive
Swaptions	Preserves upside potential	Expensive

SUMMARY

In this chapter we described the task of hedging municipal bonds. The market consists of many different issuers, and, because of this, bonds correlate at different levels with market hedges. Most municipal hedges are cross-market and for many reasons do not always track the municipal market. Most municipal bonds are callable, and the resulting negative convexity adds to the difficulty of hedging.

The largest tracking error occurs when taxable yields and municipal yields move independently. A measure of the relationship between municipal bond yields and taxable yields is referred to as *basis*, and changes in this relationship are called *basis shifts*. We showed that hedge ratios are very sensitive to small changes in basis. We also showed that basis historically has increased when rates decreased. For this reason, an efficient cross-market hedge requires a lower hedge ratio than suggested by current basis.

In this chapter we showed that *ex post* hedge ratios based on current basis are inefficient. Hedge ratios based on minimum variance as estimated from regression analysis are much lower than those estimated based on current basis. An *ex ante* hedge ratio can be constructed if an estimate of expected basis exists.

There are many hedging strategies for the municipal issuer. Issuers can effectively protect against interest rate exposure from variable bonds with interest rates caps or collars. They can also create synthetic fixed-rate bonds with the use of an interest rate swap. There are many strategies for optimizing the value of a municipal call option.

REFERENCES

Cusatis, Patrick. "Monetizing the Value of a Municipal Call Option." *The Financier: ACMT* 3, no. 3 (August 1996), 24–31.

Cusatis, Patrick. "In Search of an Optimal Hedge Ratio for the Municipal Market." Working paper, Penn State University—Harrisburg, 2004.

Ederington, L. "The Hedging Performance of Low-grade Bond Funds." *Journal of Finance* 34, no. 1 (1979), 157–70.

Gray, Gary, and Patrick Cusatis. *Municipal Derivatives: Uses and Valuation.* New York: Irwin Professional Publishing, 1995.

CHAPTER 13

Corporate Bonds

The corporate bond market is the largest long-term debt market, accounting for more than 20% of all outstanding bonds in the United States. According to the Bond Market Association, corporate bond issuance increased by almost 14% to $743.6 billion in 2003. There was approximately $4.4 trillion in corporate bonds outstanding as of the end of 2003.

Like the municipal market, the corporate bond market consists of many unique issuers and generally requires a cross-market hedge. Unlike the municipal market, credit is a primary concern for corporate investors. Corporate bonds default at a much higher rate than municipal bonds. Changes in credit perception can adversely affect the value of a hedged corporate bond portfolio. It is important for a hedger to understand the trading characteristics of the underlying bond or portfolio relative to the value of a hedge.

In this chapter we examine hedging techniques for corporate bonds. We begin by discussing credit spreads. Since the corporate market requires cross-market hedging, spreads are very important. We develop hedge ratios and strategies for hedging corporate bonds. We examine several aspects of the corporate bond market. We examine market changes over a four-year period, using a corporate bond index as a measure of the market. We select an individual bond and examine *ex post* and *ex ante* hedge ratios. We also create a portfolio of corporate bonds and calculate *ex ante* hedge ratios over a four-year period. Finally, we discuss hedging and risk management techniques for the corporation.

CREDIT RISK

The most important characteristic of a corporate bond portfolio is its credit risk. Credit risk refers to the likelihood that a corporation will be unable to make a scheduled interest or principal payment or that the market's perception of this likelihood will change. Corporations can be analyzed based on credit ratings and are generally classified as investment grade or speculative grade. Investment grade includes all bonds rated Baa3/BBB− or above by Moody's Investors Service (Moody's) and Standard & Poor's Corporation (S&P), respectively. All bonds rated Ba1/BB+ or below by Moody's and S&P, respectively, are considered speculative grade.

Speculative-grade corporate bonds have a high incidence of default. Exhibit 13.1 displays cumulative corporate bond default rates from 1986 to 2000 compiled by S&P. Bonds are categorized by S&P Rating, investment grade, and speculative grade. Speculative grade bonds have a 24.58% cumulative default rate over the 15-year period. Bonds rated BBB, which are investment grade, have a 4.48% cumulative default rate. Overall, investment-grade corporate bonds have a relatively low incidence of default.

Credit risk has two implications for a portfolio of corporate bonds. First, a default on an interest or principal payment has valuation effects on the bonds. Portfolio managers will generally hedge default risk by holding a diversified portfolio of credits or by making credit default swaps. Second, credit risk can cause tracking problems for a portfolio, even if the portfolio has no incidence of default. Changes in credit perceptions can cause large price swings as the market revalues bonds to include credit risk. For example, in 2002 Ford Motor Corporation and TYCO Corporation both experienced credit difficulties that led to downgrades by the major credit agencies. The market increased the probability of default on these bonds and revalued them downward. Both corporations continued to make scheduled interest and principal payments, and the market eventually revalued the bonds upward. However, in the interim a cross-market hedged portfolio of these corporate bonds was inefficient.

The level of credit quality is used to determine the appropriate hedge in the corporate bond market. High-credit quality bonds correlate more closely with U.S. Treasury securities than lower credit quality bonds. Landes, Stoffels, and Seifert (1985) find that a hedge based on a U.S. Treasury index is less effective as credit quality declines. For low-credit quality bonds, the use of an equity index derivative (such as S&P 500 futures) may be appropriate. Grieves (1986) shows that a combination of equity index

EXHIBIT 13.1

Corporate Bond Average Cumulative Default Rates (%), 1986–2000

S&P Rating	1986	1987	1988	1989	1990	1991	1992	1993	1994	1995	1996	1997	1998	1999	2000
AAA	0.00	0.00	0.03	0.06	0.10	0.18	0.26	0.40	0.45	0.51	0.51	0.51	0.51	0.51	0.51
AA	0.01	0.04	0.09	0.16	0.25	0.37	0.53	0.63	0.70	0.79	0.85	0.92	0.96	1.01	1.07
A	0.04	0.11	0.19	0.32	0.49	0.65	0.83	1.01	1.21	1.41	1.56	1.65	1.70	1.73	1.83
BBB	0.22	0.50	0.79	1.30	1.80	2.29	2.73	3.10	3.39	3.68	3.91	4.05	4.22	4.37	4.48
BB	0.98	2.97	5.35	7.44	9.22	11.11	12.27	13.35	14.29	15.00	15.65	16.00	16.29	16.36	16.36
B	5.30	11.28	15.88	19.10	21.44	23.20	24.77	26.01	26.99	27.88	28.48	28.96	29.34	29.68	29.96
CCC	21.94	29.25	34.37	38.24	42.13	43.62	44.40	44.82	45.74	46.53	46.84	47.21	47.66	48.29	48.29
Investment grade	0.08	0.19	0.31	0.51	0.72	0.95	1.17	1.37	1.54	1.71	1.84	1.93	2.00	2.06	2.14
Speculative grade	4.14	8.34	11.93	14.67	16.84	18.64	19.98	21.09	22.05	22.85	23.46	23.88	24.22	24.45	24.58

Source: *Municipal Rating Transitions and Defaults*, Standard & Poor's (2001).

futures and U.S. Treasury bond futures is an effective way to hedge corporate bonds subject to default risk.[1] The intuition behind the use of equities to hedge corporate bonds is that as credit quality declines, bonds become increasingly like equity. Therefore, a corporate bond with a high likelihood of default will correlate highly with the value of the common stock of the corporation.

For the reasons outlined above, corporate bonds must be evaluated based on credit quality and performance relative to the other taxable markets such as U.S. Treasuries. As in the municipal market, the relative performance of corporate bonds is important to a hedger. In the next section we analyze the historic movement of corporate spreads.

CORPORATE SPREADS

The corporate bond market is a spread market. Yields are typically quoted relative to yields on a nearby maturity U.S. Treasury bond in basis points (bps). For example, if the yield on a 10-year U.S. Treasury note is 5.00%, a 10-year corporate bond with a yield of 6.50% will be quoted as "U.S. Treasuries + 150 bps." This is a method of benchmarking yields on corporate bonds. Changes in this spread over time affect the value of the bonds and can create tracking risk for a hedge.

The corporate bond spread historically has been volatile. To examine historical changes in the spread, we use the Lehman Brothers Credit Index, which includes investment-grade bonds issued by corporations and noncorporate entities. The index was first compiled in 1973 and includes over 3,000 publicly issued U.S. corporate and noncorporate debentures and secured notes. For inclusion in the index, a bond must meet certain credit and maturity guidelines, including an investment grade rating and a maturity date of at least one year.

We measured the difference between the index and the 10-year constant maturity U.S. Treasury (CMT) and 10-year LIBOR swaps from January 3, 1995 to December 31, 2003. Exhibit 13.2 shows the results.

The LIBOR spread averaged 0.491 and ranged from −0.303 to 1.257. The CMT spread averaged 1.049 and ranged from 0.062 to 2.164. The sum-

---

1. Many studies have examined the use of equities to hedge corporate bonds. See also
    Cornell and Green (1992), Ioannides and Skinner (1999), Marcus and Ors (1996),
    and Weinstein (1985).

E X H I B I T   13.2

Historic Corporate Bond Spreads

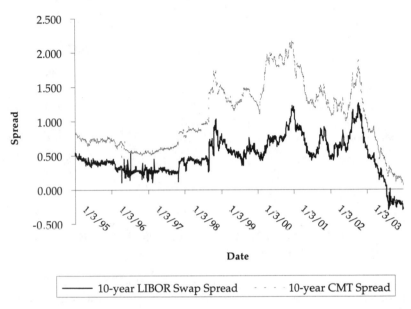

mary statistics for both spread measures are shown in Exhibit 13.3. LIBOR spreads are higher than CMT spreads because the absolute level of the CMT is lower than LIBOR.

OPTION-ADJUSTED SPREAD

A common method for measuring corporate bond spreads is to calculate an *option-adjusted spread* (OAS). A callable bond is worth less than an otherwise noncallable bond because the investor has sold a call option to the issuer in exchange for a higher yield. An option pricing model can be used to value the call option but does not adjust the value for liquidity and credit risk. For this reason, the observed market value (yield) of the bond will typically be lower (higher) than the value dictated by the option pricing model. The OAS is the difference in yield that equates the market price and the theoretical value of the bond. An OAS is valuable for comparing callable bonds to other fixed-income instruments. Since the value of the call is removed, OAS allows for a direct comparison among fixed-income securities.

E X H I B I T   13.3

Descriptive Statistics on Corporate Yield Spreads,
1995–2003

	LIBOR Spread	CMT Spread
Mean	0.491	1.049
Median	0.466	0.957
Standard Deviation	0.274	0.480
Minimum	−0.303	0.062
Maximum	1.257	2.164

HEDGING CORPORATE BOND MARKET RISK: STATIC CAPITAL MARKETS

Since corporate bonds generally require a cross-market hedge, the sensitivity of a portfolio to spreads is an important determinant of the effectiveness of a hedge. As a starting point, we consider the example of static capital markets. Under the assumptions of static capital markets, corporate bonds trade at a static spread to the taxable benchmark. Bond spreads under static capital markets are a constant function of the risk of the corporate bonds. Exhibit 13.4 outlines a static capital markets scenario under which a 10-year noncallable corporate bond is hedged with a 10-year LIBOR swap. Spreads are assumed to stay constant at 49.1 bps, the historic average spread, for a given change in swap yields. Annual fluctuations in 50-basis-point increments are assumed for a maximum fluctuation of 150 basis points in either direction. Swap prices are calculated under the assumption of a parallel shift in implied forward rates, which allows the swap to be priced as a bond with a coupon equal to the established fixed rate. For both the bond and the swap, modified duration is calculated for each time period. One can calculate the present value of a one-basis-point change, PV01, for the swap and the bond, by multiplying the appropriate modified duration by the price of the bond or swap. For example, for the swap, the present value of a one-basis-point change in yields is calculated as follows:

$$PV01(swap) = D_m(swap)P_t(swap)$$

An *ex ante* hedge ratio h^* is estimated as follows:

$$h^* = \frac{PV01(\text{bond})}{PV01(\text{swap})}$$

An *ex post* hedge ratio h is calculated based on the ratio of the actual change in the corporate bond price to the change in the swap price:

$$h = \frac{P_t(\text{bond}) - P_{t-1}(\text{bond})}{P_t(\text{swap}) - P_{t-1}(\text{swap})}$$

where $P_t(\text{swap})$ and $P_t(\text{bond})$ are the price of the swap and bond at time t, respectively. The resulting hedge ratios result in a zero net price change for a hedged portfolio.

The values of h^* and h are shown in Exhibit 13.4. Because of the static basis assumption, the hedge ratios are close in value. The breakeven

EXHIBIT 13.4

Static Capital Markets Hedge Ratios

n	0	1	2	3	4	5	6
Pricing Date	1/1/04	1/1/05	1/1/06	1/1/07	1/1/08	1/1/09	1/1/10
Spread	0.491%	0.491%	0.491%	0.491%	0.491%	0.491%	0.491%
Change in Rates		+0.50%	+0.50%	+0.50%	−0.50%	−0.50%	−0.50%
Corporate Bond							
Yield	5.49%	5.99%	6.49%	6.99%	4.99%	4.49%	3.99%
Price	100.000	96.560	93.836	91.807	102.565	104.434	105.495
Modified Duration	7.617	6.974	6.320	5.650	5.078	4.356	3.585
PV01(bond)	0.076	0.067	0.059	0.052	0.052	0.045	0.038
LIBOR Swap							
Yield	5.00%	5.50%	6.00%	6.50%	4.50%	4.00%	3.50%
Price	100.000	96.488	93.719	91.671	102.604	104.491	105.554
Modified Duration	7.795	7.125	6.445	5.750	5.153	4.411	3.622
PV01(swap)	0.078	0.069	0.060	0.053	0.053	0.046	0.038
Hedge Ratios							
h^*		0.977	0.980	0.982	0.984	0.985	0.987
h		0.979	0.984	0.990	0.984	0.990	0.999

hedge ratios range from 0.979 to 0.999. The slight differences in the *ex post* and *ex ante* hedge ratios are due to differences in convexity between the swap and the bond.

HEDGING CORPORATE BOND MARKET RISK: VOLATILE CAPITAL MARKETS

The assumption of constant corporate spreads is unrealistic. We showed that the spread between corporate bonds and LIBOR swaps ranged from −30.3 bps to 125.7 bps from January 2, 1995 to December 31, 2003. For this reason, *ex ante* hedge ratios based on duration can be inefficient in volatile markets.

Ex post hedge ratios are very different from *ex ante* hedge ratios if spreads change. For example, if the corporate bond spread started at −30.3 bps and increased to 125.7 bps, the historic low and high spreads, the *ex post* hedge ratios are more than 1.5 times as high as those required under a static spread market. Exhibit 13.5 summarizes the results of this example. Breakeven hedge ratios range from 1.405 to 1.567. In this example, corporate bond yields are increasing more quickly than LIBOR swap rates; therefore a higher hedge ratio is required. If the spreads had decreased over the time period, a much lower breakeven hedge ratio would have resulted.[2]

HISTORIC CHANGE IN SPREAD

Corporate spreads change based on the level of interest rates and market events that affect credit perception and liquidity of the corporate bonds. Changes in corporate bond spreads historically are inversely related to changes in interest rates. These movements, while they may have a business cycle component, are not entirely determined by the level of interest rates. The relationship between the 10-year LIBOR swap spread and 10-year LIBOR swap yields from January 3, 1995 to December 31, 2003 is

---

2. When arbitrary changes in spreads are introduced, it is possible for the *ex post* hedge ratio to be negative. This implies that the best hedge for a long corporate bond is a receive-fixed swap. This can occur, for example, when corporate bond values decrease and long swap values increase because of a change in spreads. In this scenario, a breakeven hedge ratio would require a long position in a swap to offset the gain of the long bond position.

EXHIBIT 13.5

Volatile Capital Markets Hedge Ratios

n	0	1	2	3	4	5	6
Pricing Date	1/1/04	1/1/05	1/1/06	1/1/07	1/1/08	1/1/09	1/1/10
Spread	−0.303%	−0.041%	0.219%	0.479%	0.738%	0.998%	1.257%
Change in Rates		+0.50%	+0.50%	+0.50%	+0.50%	+0.50%	+0.50%
Corporate Bond							
Yield	4.70%	5.46%	6.22%	6.98%	7.74%	8.50%	9.26%
Price	100.000	94.656	90.539	87.550	85.635	84.788	85.050
Modified Duration	7.906	7.193	6.481	5.764	5.033	4.281	3.499
PV01(bond)	0.079	0.068	0.059	0.050	0.043	0.036	0.030
LIBOR Swap							
Yield	5.00%	5.50%	6.00%	6.50%	7.00%	7.50%	8.00%
Price	100.000	96.488	93.719	91.671	90.337	89.734	89.901
Modified Duration	7.795	7.125	6.445	5.750	5.034	4.290	3.513
PV01(swap)	0.078	0.069	0.060	0.053	0.045	0.038	0.032
Hedge Ratios							
h^*		1.014	0.990	0.971	0.957	0.948	0.943
h		1.522	1.487	1.459	1.435	1.405	1.567

shown in Exhibit 13.6. Changes in the two data series have a correlation of −0.4371.

To further examine the relationship between spread and interest rates, we estimate the historic change in the corporate bonds/LIBOR swap spread for a change in the yield on 10-year LIBOR swaps. The regression equation takes the form

$$\Delta s = \beta_0 + \beta_1 \Delta y(\text{swap}) + \varepsilon$$

where

Δs	= change in spread
β_0	= intercept coefficient
β_1	= change in spread attributable to change in swap yield
$\Delta y(\text{swap})$	= change in swap yield
ε	= error term, $E(\varepsilon) = 0$

EXHIBIT 13.6

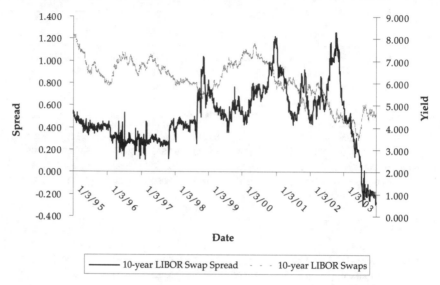

Relationship between LIBOR Spread and LIBOR Swap Yields

Date

———— 10-year LIBOR Swap Spread   - - - - 10-year LIBOR Swaps

The relationship is examined daily from January 3, 1995 to December 31, 2003. As a measure of the corporate market, we use the yield on the Lehman Brothers Credit Index. The regression statistics are summarized in Exhibit 13.7. The regression analysis results in an estimate of $\hat{\beta}_1$ equal to -0.002652, which is significant at the 0.01 level.[3] This suggests that, on average, a one-basis-point increase (decrease) in swap yields leads to a decrease (increase) in spreads of 0.002652, and a 50-basis-point increase (decrease) in swap yields corresponds to a decrease (increase) in spreads of 0.1326.

EX ANTE OPTIMAL HEDGE RATIO

Corporate bond spreads are an important concern for a hedger of corporate bonds. If not separately hedged, the hedger must make a decision either to trust historic basis levels or to form expectations on future spread levels. If spread changes were independent of movements in the market, hedge ratios based on average basis changes would provide a reliable hedge.

---

3. The regression has an adjusted R^2 of 0.19.

EXHIBIT 13.7

Historic Change in Spreads—Regression Statistics, January 3, 1995 to December 31, 2003 ($n = 2251$)

	Coefficients	Standard Error	t-statistic	p value
Intercept	−0.000008	0.000008	−1.0466	0.2954
Δy(swap)	−0.002652	0.000115	−23.0445	0.0000

We solve for an *ex ante* hedge ratio based on expected changes in spreads. A solution for the *ex ante* estimate of the hedge ratio h^* for a one-basis-point increase in swap yields given an expected shift in spreads Δs_t is as follows:

$$h^* = \frac{[(s_0 + \Delta s_t) + (y_0(\text{swap}) + 0.01) - y_0(\text{bond})](100)\text{PV01}(\text{bond})}{\text{PV01}(\text{swap})}$$

where

$\quad s_0 \qquad\qquad$ = spread at time 0
$\quad \Delta s_t \qquad\qquad$ = expected change in basis from time zero to time t
$\quad y_0(\text{swap})$ = swap yield at time 0
$\quad y_0(\text{bond})$ = bond yield at time 0

To estimate the hedge ratio for a larger change in swap yields, the +0.01 in the numerator is replaced with the actual percentage swap yield change and the denominator is multiplied by the swap yield change. Since the hedge ratio is duration-based, it is not accurate for large yield shifts.

Example: Consider the estimate of the hedge ratio for a one-basis-point increase in swap yields, given an increase in spreads of 0.001. Assume a corporate bond has a current yield of 5.491% and a PV01 of 0.076. A swap of the same maturity as the bond has a current yield of 5.00% and a PV01 of 0.078. The starting spread is the historic average LIBOR spread of 49.1 bps. The *ex ante* hedge ratio is estimated as follows:

$$h^* = \frac{[(0.491 + 0.001) + (5.01) - 5.491](100)(0.076)}{0.078} = 107.18\%$$

As in the municipal market, the difficult task in the corporate market for an *ex ante* approach is estimating expected spreads. Historically, spreads are a function of changes in the supply and demand of corporate bonds and changes in credit perception. Although spreads have been shown to have a business-cycle component, they are difficult to forecast. Changes in spread make it difficult to establish a consistent long-term hedging strategy.

HISTORIC CORPORATE BOND AND HEDGE DATA

We use the Lehman Brothers Credit Index as a measure of changes in the corporate market for a four-year period from January 3, 2000 to December 31, 2003. We construct a database of relevant hedging vehicles for the same time period. The beginning of this period corresponds with the respecification by the CBOT of the U.S. Treasury futures contracts.

In the swap market, we collect daily prices on LIBOR swaps with 10-, 20-, and 30-year tenors. The swap prices are based on quarterly reset interest rate swaps versus three-month LIBOR flat. In the futures market, we collect daily prices for the U.S. Treasury note, U.S. Treasury bond, and S&P 500 futures contracts. Exhibit 13.8 lists descriptive statistics based on the hedge data.

E X H I B I T 13.8

Summary of Historic Corporate Bond Market and Hedge Data

	Exchange	Mean	Median	Standard Deviation	Obs.
Lehman Brothers Credit Index	—	102.49	102.46	4.94	999
LIBOR Swaps					
10-year	OTC	113.33	112.64	8.83	999
20-year	OTC	116.69	116.06	10.46	999
30-year	OTC	119.33	118.32	12.18	999
Futures					
10-year U.S. T-note	CBOT	107.09	106.45	6.43	999
U.S. Treasury bond	CBOT	104.82	104.09	6.44	999
S&P 500 Futures	CBOT	1148.86	1123.50	208.69	999

The relationship between the hedge data and the market index can be examined by calculating minimum variance hedge ratios and adjusted R^2 measures with the use of regression analysis. We also compute sample correlation coefficients r between the hedge data and the market index. Whereas each corporate bond is unique and requires a specific hedge ratio based on its characteristics, the index provides us with information about the general relationship among hedges and the corporate bond market. We calculate minimum variance hedge ratios for selected hedge instruments based on the following equation:

$$\Delta P(\text{index}) = \beta_0 + \beta_1 \Delta P(\text{hedge}) + \varepsilon$$

where

$\Delta P(\text{index})$	= change in index price
β_0	− intercept coefficient
β_1	= minimum variance hedge ratio
$\Delta P(\text{hedge})$	= change in price of the hedge instrument
ε	= error term, $E(\varepsilon) = 0$

Sample hedge ratios $\hat{\beta}_1$, adjusted R^2 values, and correlation coefficients are presented in Exhibit 13.9. The hedge ratios for the fixed-income hedges range from 0.3021 for the for the 30-year LIBOR swap to 0.6531 for the U.S. Treasury note futures. The adjusted R^2 values range from 0.7417 for the 30-year LIBOR swap to 0.8610 for the U.S. Treasury note futures. Correlations between price changes for the fixed-income hedges range from 0.8614 for the 30-year LIBOR swap to 0.9280 for the U.S. Treasury note futures. Although the correlations and adjusted R^2 values are high for all of the fixed-income hedges, the hedge ratios are lower than would be expected based on relative durations. This is due to the fact that minimum variance hedge ratios are affected by changes in spreads over time. The *ex ante* hedge ratios h^* are shown in Exhibit 13.9. These hedge ratios are based on the ratio of PV01(index) to PV01(hedge).[4] The minimum variance hedge ratios are consistently lower than the *ex ante* hedge ratios.

The changes in the S&P 500 futures contract have a significant relationship with changes in corporate bond prices. Based on the regression, however, we see that S&P 500 futures explain a small portion of the total

---

4. The Lehman Brothers Credit Index has a modified duration of 5.649 and a price of 95.114 as of January 3, 2000. Therefore, PV01(index) is 0.0537.

EXHIBIT 13.9

Sample Corporate Bond Market Relationships

Hedge	h^*	$\hat{\beta}_1$	Adj. R^2	r	Obs.
10-year LIBOR swap	0.7662	0.5953*	0.7721	0.8788	998
20-year LIBOR swap	0.5190	0.3604*	0.7609	0.8724	998
30-year LIBOR swap	0.4500	0.3021*	0.7417	0.8614	998
U.S. T-note futures	0.6883	0.6531*	0.8610	0.9280	998
U.S. T-bond futures	0.5407	0.4341*	0.8425	0.9180	998
S&P 500 Index Futures	—	−0.0042*	0.0399	0.2022	998

*Significant at the .01 level.

variation of changes in corporate bond prices. This result is intuitive, since the relationship between the stock indices and corporate bonds increases as credit declines. The Lehman Brothers Credit Index consists of quality credit issues.

HEDGING EXAMPLE: ONE CORPORATE BOND

To describe and analyze the corporate bond hedging process, we begin by selecting a sample corporate bond issue. We select a noncallable Boeing Capital Corporation (McDonnell-Douglas) issue dated December 18, 1996 and due December 18, 2012. The bonds have a 7.375% coupon and were issued at par. The bonds are uninsured and are rated A/A3 by Standard & Poor's and Moody's, respectively. The total maturity size of the bonds is $20 million. The bonds are described in Exhibit 13.10.

We collect daily prices and yields on the Boeing Capital bonds from January 3, 2000 to December 31, 2003. We begin by examining the bond prices relative to a 13-year LIBOR swap over the time period. Exhibit 13.11 shows the relationship between the prices of the bond and a seasoned 20-year LIBOR swap over the time period. The prices track closely over time.

Using the historic Boeing bond prices, we calculate hedge ratios for a 13-year LIBOR swap and U.S. Treasury bond futures based on the following equation:

$$\Delta P(\text{bond}) = \beta_0 + \beta_1 \Delta P(\text{hedge}) + \varepsilon$$

EXHIBIT 13.10

Description of Boeing Capital
Corporation Bond

Dated Date	December 18, 1996
Maturity	December 18, 2012
Coupon	7.375%
Call Date	Non-callable
Ratings	A/A3
Yield-to-Maturity*	7.879
Price	95.947
Duration	8.113
PV01	0.0778

*Pricing statistics as of January 3, 2000.

where

$$\Delta P(\text{bond}) = \text{daily change in price of the Boeing bond}$$
$$\beta_0 = \text{intercept coefficient}$$
$$\beta_1 = \text{minimum variance hedge ratio } h$$
$$\Delta P(\text{hedge}) = \text{daily change in hedge price}$$
$$\varepsilon = \text{error term, } E(\varepsilon) = 0$$

Exhibit 13.12 summarizes the results of the regression analysis, mark-to-market (MTM), average spread, and volatility of spread. The minimum variance hedge ratio is −0.8871 for the 13-year swap. The hedge ratio is −0.6729 for the U.S. Treasury bond futures.

MTM values represent the cumulative MTM over the hedging time periods. For a perfect hedge, the expected MTM is zero. The net MTM value for the 13-year LIBOR swap is −0.1703 per $100. For a $20 million dollar bond position, this equates to a net loss over the time period of $34,060. The U.S. Treasury bond is less efficient, with a net MTM loss of 3.8672 per $100 or a net loss of $773,440.

Exhibit 13.12 also shows the average yield spread and the standard deviation of the yield spread. The volatility of the U.S. Treasury bond futures spread is 0.4853, which is more than 1.5 times the volatility of the 13-year LIBOR swap spreads. LIBOR swaps have the advantage of seasoning

EXHIBIT 13.11

EXHIBIT 13.11

Historic Boeing Bond Prices and 13-Year LIBOR Swap Prices

with the bonds. Therefore, as time passes the hedge matches more closely and spreads are less volatile than in the U.S. Treasury futures market. We expect the 13-year swap to more closely hedge the value of the bonds because the maturity, duration, and convexity closely match those of the bonds.

Overall, the 13-year LIBOR swap performs well. Exhibit 13.13 shows the relative performance of the unhedged bonds and the bonds hedged with a LIBOR swap. The line labeled "MV hedged value" represents the net value of the bonds with a LIBOR swap hedge based on the minimum

EXHIBIT 13.12

Historic Hedge Ratios and MTM Based
on Minimum Variance Hedge

Hedge	$\hat{\beta}_1$	Obs.	Net MTM per $100	MTM Volatility	Average Spread	Spread Volatility
13-yr LIBOR swap	−0.8871	998	−0.1703	0.4622	1.0057	0.3054
U.S. T-bond futures	−0.6729	998	−3.8672	0.4971	0.9575	0.4853

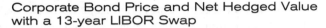

EXHIBIT 13.13

Corporate Bond Price and Net Hedged Value
with a 13-year LIBOR Swap

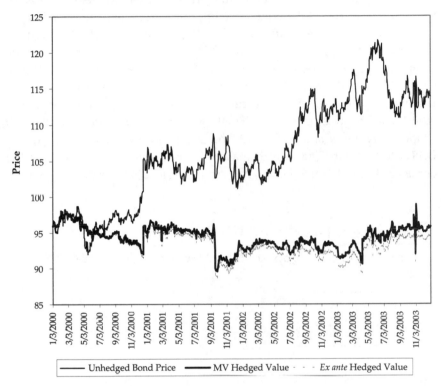

variance hedge ratio. The standard deviation of the unhedged bond prices is 7.003, and the standard deviation of the net hedged position is reduced to 1.592. This analysis assumes the use of a minimum variance hedge ratio, which is calculated *ex post* and reflects changes in spread over the time period.

In practice, it is not possible to apply as accurate a hedge ratio. Based on the relative PV01's of the bond and swap, the *ex ante* hedge ratio is 94.46%. In this example, hedging *ex ante* based on duration would lead to an overhedged portfolio. Exhibit 13.13 also shows the results of the bonds hedged with a LIBOR swap based on an *ex ante* hedge ratio of 94.46%. The *ex ante* hedge ratio is less efficient than the minimum variance hedge ratio and leads to higher volatility and MTM losses.

LIBOR SWAP STRUCTURE

Assume an investor purchased the Boeing bonds described above for settlement on January 3, 2000 at a dollar price of 95.947 to yield 7.879%. To hedge the price risk of the bonds, the investor can structure a plain vanilla LIBOR swap with a maturity date of 2012. The investor will pay the fixed swap rate and receive three-month LIBOR. Assuming the investor uses the *ex ante* hedge ratio, the notional principal amount of the swap is (0.9446) (20,000,000) = $18,892,000. The fixed swap rate for a 13-year swap as of January 3, 2000 was 7.352%. The cash flows on this swap are shown in Exhibit 13.14. The investor receives a yield of 7.879% (approximately, through coupon payments and accretion) and receives (0.9446)(three-month LIBOR) on the swap. The investor pays the short-term financing rate on the bonds and pays the fixed swap rate of (0.9446)(7.352%) = 6.945. The cash

E X H I B I T   13.14

Cash Flows on Corporate Bond Hedged with a LIBOR Swap

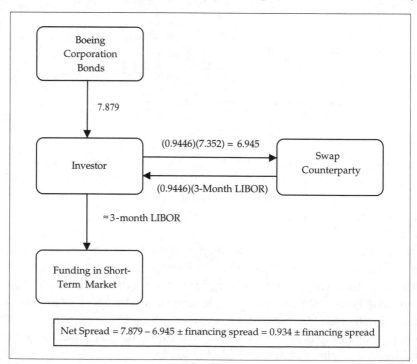

flow diagram represents the approximate annual cash flows. The bond cash flows are semiannual, and the swap cash flows are netted quarterly.

In this example, the net spread is 0.934% ± financing spread. If the investor finances the investment at 94.46% of three-month LIBOR, then the funding spread is zero; otherwise there is a funding adjustment. The investor retains the credit risk of the bonds but has transferred most of the interest rate risk with the interest rate swap.

BASIS SWAPS

Most of the interest rate risk of a corporate bond position can be hedged with an interest rate swap. However, since spreads can be volatile, and an investor must make an *ex ante* hedge ratio decision, the investor has basis risk. An investor who is concerned with basis risk can hedge shifts in spreads by entering into a *basis swap* in addition to an interest rate swap. Since the investor in the example is long a corporate bond and short a swap, the investor has exposure to widening credit spreads. Corporate credit spreads will widen under two different sets of market conditions. First, spreads will widen if corporate rates increase more than LIBOR swap rates. If this happens, corporate bonds decrease in value and the swap underperforms. Second, spreads will widen if LIBOR swap rates decrease by more than corporate rates. Under this scenario, the LIBOR swap decreases in value by more than the increase in bonds. Both cases lead to net loss on the hedged portfolio.[5]

In a basis swap two parties agree to exchange cash flows based on different yield curves, such as the corporate and the LIBOR curves. If an investor has exposure to wider spreads, as in the example, the investor will want to receive the corporate rate and pay the LIBOR rate. The swap can be structured as fixed-for-floating or floating-for-floating, based on the needs of the investor.[6]

Exhibit 13.15 shows the cash flows on a typical basis swap. The swap involves the exchange of the three-month commercial paper rate (a floating

---

5. This assumes that spreads are initially positive.
6. An alternative to a basis swap is a credit spread option. The investor can buy an option to sell the underlying corporate bond at a prespecified spread to LIBOR swap rates, for example. The value of the option will increase as credit spreads widen, thus offsetting the underperformance of the hedge. This alternative requires the payment of an upfront premium and is generally more expensive than a basis swap.

EXHIBIT 13.15

Typical Corporate Basis Swap

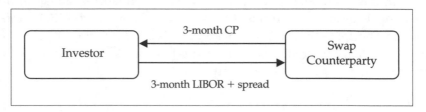

rate) for three-month LIBOR plus a spread established as of the pricing date (also a floating rate). Under the terms of the swap, the investor receives the commercial paper rate and pays three-month LIBOR. If credit spreads widen, the basis swap will increase in value and offset the underperformance of the LIBOR swap.

CREDIT DEFAULT SWAPS

Our discussions on credit spreads have been concentrated on changes in credit perceptions that adversely affect the relative valuation of a bond and a hedge. If an investor is concerned with the risk that an issuer will fail to pay a scheduled interest or principal payment, the investor can enter into a *credit default swap*. A credit default swap is an agreement under which a counterparty (the investor) agrees to make periodic payments and the other counterparty makes a payment only if a predefined credit event occurs. The periodic payments are determined by the expected default probabilities over the life of the swap. Credit events can include ratings downgrades, bankruptcy, or a missed interest or principal payment. The purpose of the swap is to make the investor whole if a credit event occurs. Exhibit 13.16 shows the cash flows on a typical credit default swap.

HEDGING EXAMPLE: CORPORATE BOND PORTFOLIO

In this section we create a three-bond portfolio of corporate bonds and outline the procedures for measuring and hedging portfolio risk. We begin by selecting a portfolio of investment-grade, noncallable bonds. The bonds consist of the Boeing Capital Corporation issue from the previous example,

EXHIBIT 13.16

Typical Credit Default Swap

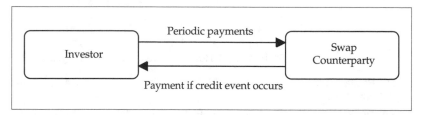

a Caterpillar, Inc. issue with a coupon of 9.375% maturing 3/15/2021, and a Lowe's Companies issue with a coupon of 8.190% maturing 9/12/2022. Descriptions of the three issues are shown in Exhibit 13.17.

Assume a portfolio manager is long a total of $100 million in various amounts of these three issues on January 3, 2000. The manager holds $20 million of the Boeing issue, $75 million of the Caterpillar issue, and $5 million of the Lowe's issue. The manager wants to hedge against interest rate risk in the portfolio. To calculate an *ex ante* hedge ratio, we begin by calculating the modified duration of the portfolio. The modified duration of a portfolio, D_p, is equal to the value-weighted average of the modified durations of individual bonds. Exhibit 13.18 shows the pricing statistics of the corporate bond portfolio as of January 3, 2000. The market value of the portfolio is $110,503,000. The value weights are based on the market values of each bond relative to the market value of the portfolio.

Using the value weights and the modified durations of the individual bonds, we calculate a modified duration of the portfolio of 9.406. Therefore

EXHIBIT 13.17

Corporate Bond Portfolio Description

Issue	Rating	Coupon	Maturity	Options
Boeing Capital Corp. (McDonnell-Douglas)	A3/A	7.375%	12/18/2012	None
Caterpillar Inc.	A2/A	9.375%	3/15/2021	None
Lowe's Companies Inc.	A2/A	8.190%	9/12/2022	None

EXHIBIT 13.18

Corporate Bond Portfolio Pricing Statistics

Issue	Par Amount ($million)	Price*	Yield	D_m	Value Weight	D_p
Boeing Capital Corp. (McDonnell-Douglas)	20	95.942	7.879	8.113	17.4%	1.409
Caterpillar Inc.	75	115.040	7.900	9.657	78.1%	7.540
Lowe's Companies Inc.	5	100.695	8.121	10.028	4.6%	0.457
Total	**100**	**110.503**			**100.0%**	**9.406**

*As of January 3, 2000.

the PV01 of the portfolio is equal to $(9.406)(110.503)/100 = 10.394$. The PV01 of a 20-year LIBOR swap was 10.353 as of January 3, 2000. Therefore, the *ex ante* hedge ratio h^* is

$$h^* = \frac{\text{PV01(portfolio)}}{\text{PV01(swap)}} = \frac{10.394}{10.353} = 1.004$$

This hedge ratio assumes that the portfolio weights and the relative durations of the portfolio and the swap will remain relatively constant. Applying this hedge ratio over a long period of time in a volatile market will not result in an efficient hedge. Changes in interest rates and credit spreads will change the appropriate *ex ante* hedge ratio. Exhibit 13.19 shows the relative performance of the bond portfolio on a hedged and un-hedged basis. The hedged portfolio performs well over the time period be-cause the durations of the portfolio and swap remained relatively stable.

HEDGING CALLABLE BONDS

In the previous examples we concentrated on noncallable bonds. A hedge for a callable bond is a combination of a hedge on a noncallable bond and a hedge of the call option. Several approaches can be taken to hedging callable bonds. The appropriate approach depends on the characteristics

EXHIBIT 13.19

Corporate Bond Portfolio Price and Net Hedged Value
with a 20-year LIBOR Swap

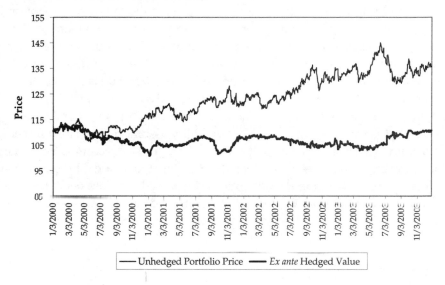

of the underlying bond, the likelihood of the option being exercised, and
the risk tolerance of the investor. Below we outline several hedging strategies and the risks associated with each.

Hedging to the call. An investor can assume that the bonds will be
called on the first call date. A hedge ratio can be constructed based on the
duration to the call date adjusted for basis. In periods of high interest rates
relative to the coupon on the bonds, a portfolio of callable bonds will be
underhedged with this approach. For bonds with 10 or 20 years beyond
the call date, this approach may not be appropriate.

Hedging to maturity. An investor can assume that the bonds will
not be called on the first call date. A hedge ratio can be constructed based
on the duration to the maturity date adjusted for basis. In periods of low
interest rates relative to the coupon on the bonds, a portfolio of callable
bonds will be overhedged with this approach. Since a decrease in interest
rates in the municipal market is typically accompanied by a shift in basis,
this approach can be costly in low-interest-rate markets.

Hedging to the midpoint. An investor can pick the midpoint between the call date and maturity date. A hedge ratio can be constructed

based on the duration to the midpoint adjusted for basis. This will lower the volatility relative to the other approaches when interest rates are high or low.

Hedging the call option. Another approach is to hedge the option by buying exchange-traded options. For example, a portfolio manager can hedge the negative convexity in a portfolio of callable corporate bonds by buying call options on U.S. Treasury note futures. The long call options offset the short call options on the corporate bonds. While this approach may work for short periods of time, it is not cost effective. As we have discussed, options are the most expensive hedge. When the corporate bond is purchased, it is priced based on current volatility assumptions in the market. Volatility will change as the bond seasons. An increase in volatility will lead to hedge costs that exceed the benefit from selling the option. Therefore, the costs of directly hedging the call options can exceed the yield benefits from owning a callable bond. Conversely, if volatility decreases, an investor can buy a cheaper option in the market to lock in an option spread.

PUTTABLE BONDS

Some corporate bonds contain a put to the issuer if the price falls below a prespecified strike price. For example, if a corporate bond is puttable at 100, an investor can sell the bonds to the issuer at a price of 100 on or after the exercise date. An investor will exercise this put option if the price falls below 100. The put is a hedge for the investor and removes the price risk of the bonds at or below the put price. An investor in puttable bonds has purchased a hedge in exchange for a lower yield on the bonds.

A concern for an investor in puttable bonds is the solvency of the issuer. If there is substantial credit risk, the put has limited value. The need for the put option can correlate with adverse credit events for the issuer. In addition, there may be a period of several years when the put cannot be exercised. Over this time period the issuer's credit can deteriorate. An investor in puttable bonds must evaluate the credit condition of the issuer when determining the value of the put option as a hedge.

COST-OF-CARRY

Cost-of-carry (COC) refers to the cost of carrying a hedge if the market does not change. In the fixed-income market, cost-of-carry is a function of the slope of the yield curve, is generally positive for a short position, and varies over time. A hedge that costs more to carry may be worth the extra cost if it has a high correlation with the underlying asset.

We estimate the COC for a 20-year LIBOR swap and the U.S. Treasury bond futures contract from January 3, 2000 to December 31, 2003. To measure COC for 20-year pay-fixed LIBOR swaps, we deduct the quarterly LIBOR reset rates from the fixed swap rate. We assume that the swap settles on the first day of the time period and the fixed rate is set at the at-market swap rate. The daily swap accruals are cumulated and an average daily COC is calculated. The notional par amount of the swap is set at $25 million. For interest rate futures, the COC is estimated by cumulating the change in contract value on the day the contract rolls net of market changes on that day. From this number, a daily COC is estimated, assuming a total position of $25 million.

Exhibit 13.20 summarizes the daily COC findings for the two hedges based on $25 million hedge positions. For the 20-year LIBOR swap, average daily COC is $2,656.88 over the four-year period. For the U.S. Treasury bond futures, average daily COC is $2,239.45 over the four-year period. For comparability, the results must be adjusted by the appropriate hedge ratios.

ISSUER STRATEGIES

Corporations can use derivative products to protect against changes in interest rates. A corporation with a proposed bond issue is subject to interest rate risk. An increase in interest rates will increase the cost associated

EXHIBIT 13.20

Historic Daily Cost-of-Carry
for a $25 Million Position

Hedge	Average Daily COC $n = 998$
20-yr LIBOR swap	2,656.88
U.S. T-bond futures	2,239.45

with the pending bond issue. Prior to the first call date, an issuer of callable bonds may want to lock in rates that allow for the efficient call of the underlying bonds. In this section we outline hedging strategies that accomplish these goals.

FORWARD-DELIVERY BONDS

Forward-delivery bonds allow a corporation to lock in rates for a future bond issuance. A corporation can issue bonds in the current market with a delayed delivery date that coincides with a forward date when proceeds are needed, such as the first call date. The corporation will pay the current rates plus a forward premium. Under this strategy, the issuer establishes fixed rates on a future bond issue without waiting for the forward date to price the issue. This strategy is inefficient if the forward premium is high. If the bond issuance is several years in the future, the forward premium will be prohibitive.

FORWARD-DELIVERY SWAP

Swaps can be structured with a delayed start date. A corporation can structure a *forward-delivery swap* such that the starting date coincides with the need for bond proceeds. If the firm needs proceeds to call bonds, on the first call date the corporation will issue a sufficient amount of floating-rate bonds to pay all costs associated with calling the existing bonds. At the same time, the corporation begins its forward swap agreement as the fixed-rate payer. The issuer has hedged interest rates by creating a synthetic fixed-rate bond in the future. The net cost to the issuer is the fixed payment on the swap, which is equal to the current swap rates plus a forward premium.

SELLING A SWAPTION

A variation of a forward delivery swap is the sale of a swaption. A swaption buyer has a European option on a swap. As a hedge against interest rates, a corporation can sell a swaption with a notional amount equal to the expected bond issue. The exercise date of the swaption corresponds to the forward date when proceeds are needed. If the option is exercised, a swap dealer pays a variable rate and the corporation pays the predetermined fixed rate. At the same time, the corporation issues variable-rate bonds. The net result is a synthetic fixed rate. If the swaption is not exercised, interest rates are lower and the hedge is not needed. The three hedging strategies described above are summarized in Exhibit 13.21.

EXHIBIT 13.21

Summary of Hedging Techniques for Corporations

	Current Market	First Call Date
Forward Delivery Bonds	• Outstanding bonds unaffected • Corporation enters into a forward agreement to issue bonds on first call date • Structure of bonds is determined	• Bonds are issued • Outstanding bonds can be called with proceeds of variable-rate issue
Forward Delivery Swap	• Outstanding bonds unaffected • Corporation enters into a swap agreement to begin on future date • Fixed swap rate is set	• Variable-rate bonds issued • Outstanding bonds can be called with proceeds of variable-rate issue • Swap pays variable rate to corporation and corporation pays fixed rate
Swaption	• Outstanding bonds unaffected • Corporation sells the right to enter into a swap agreement to begin on first call date • Fixed swap rate is set	**(A) Swaption is exercised** • Variable-rate bonds issued • Outstanding bonds can be called with proceeds of variable-rate issue • Swap pays variable rate to corporation and corporation pays fixed rate **(B) Option not exercised** • Outstanding bonds unaffected • Corporation issues current delivery bonds

COMPARISON OF HEDGING ALTERNATIVES

Hedge	Pros	Cons
Interest Rate Futures	Liquid, low transaction costs	Standard terms, tracking risk, daily mark-to-market, spread risk
LIBOR Swaps	Customized terms, no tracking risk	High transaction costs, spread risk
Futures Options	Removes exposure to calls	Expensive
Basis Swaps	Customized terms	Removes upside potential
Credit Default Swaps	Removes all credit risk	Can be expensive, counter-party risk can be substantial

S U M M A R Y

In this chapter we outlined techniques for hedging corporate bonds. An important consideration for corporate bond investors is credit risk. Credit risk has the obvious implications of a payment default. More important is the volatility in bond prices caused by changes in perception of credit risk, even if bonds do not default. Corporate bond spreads have been volatile over time and introduce inefficiency into a hedged portfolio.

We developed *ex post* and *ex ante* hedge ratios and examined their performance historically. *Ex post* and *ex ante* hedge ratios vary because *ex post* ratios are adjusted for changes in spreads over time, whereas *ex ante* hedge ratios are not. To the extent basis is relatively static, *ex ante* hedge ratios perform efficiently.

Callable bonds are difficult to hedge because the use of exchange-traded options over a long period of time is generally cost prohibitive. There are several techniques that an investor can use to reduce the risk of a call option without directly hedging the call option. An investor can hedge to either the call date or maturity date, or a midpoint between these dates. The appropriateness of such a strategy will be determined by the characteristics of the underlying bonds or portfolio.

A corporation may need new money in the future or may want to call bonds that are not currently callable. There are several hedging strategies for corporations that need to issue bonds in the future. Forward-delivery bonds, forward-delivery swaps, and swaptions are an effective way for an issuer to establish fixed-rate financing in the current market.

REFERENCES

Bookstaber, R., and D. Jacob. "The Composite Hedge: Controlling the Credit Risk of High-Yield Bonds." *Financial Analysts Journal* 42, no. 2 (1986), 25–36.

Cornell, B., and Kevin Green. "The Investment Performance of Low-Grade Bond Funds." *Journal of Finance* 46 (March 1991), 29–48.

Cusatis, Patrick, and Martin Thomas. "The Effects on Changes in Spread on Corporate Bonds." Working paper, Penn State University–Harrisburg, 2004.

Grieves, R. "Hedging Corporate Bond Portfolios." *Journal of Portfolio Management* (Summer 1986), 23–25.

Ioannides, Michalis, and Frank S. Skinner. "Hedging Corporate Bonds." *Journal of Business Finance and Accounting* 26, nos. 7 and 8 (Sept/Oct 1999), 919–44.

Landes, L., J. Stoffels, and J. Seifert. "Duration-Based Hedge: The Case of Corporate Bonds." *Journal of Futures Markets* 5, no. 2 (1985), 173–82.

Marcus, Alan J., and Evren Ors. "Hedging Corporate Bond Portfolios Across the Business Cycle." *Journal of Fixed Income* (March 1996), 56–60.

Weinstein, M. "The Equity Component of Corporate Bonds." *Journal of Portfolio Management* (Spring 1985), 37–41.

Woodell, Collen, Leo Brand, and William Montrone. "Municipal Rating Transitions and Defaults." *Standard & Poors Ratings Direct*, June 13, 2001.

CHAPTER 14

Mortgages

A mortgage is a loan secured by real estate. The real estate serves as collateral for the loan and the lender has the right to foreclose against the property in the event of default by the borrower. Mortgages fall into two general categories. *Residential mortgage loans* are those secured by residential properties. *Nonresidential mortgage loans* are those secured by commercial and farm properties. While there are many different types of mortgages available to borrowers, the most common are fixed-rate mortgages, which require the mortgage to be repaid with a series of equal monthly payments. As of the first quarter of 2004, there was more than $9.6 trillion in total mortgages outstanding in the United States. More than three-fourths of these mortgages were secured by single-family residences.

Mortgages and mortgage-backed securities (MBSs) have unique risk characteristics that must be managed by mortgage lenders and MBS investors. In this chapter, we examine hedging techniques for companies facing exposure to the risks of fixed-rate mortgage lending. We discuss alternative methods of hedging with futures contracts and options. Although the methods are applicable to lenders and investors, our focus is on risks to lenders.

THE MORTGAGE MARKET

Every sector of the mortgage market has grown in recent years. Exhibit 14.1 shows summary data on the dollar amounts of mortgages outstanding

EXHIBIT 14.1

Mortgages Outstanding, 1997–2004 (billions of dollars)

Year	Home	Multifamily Residential	Commercial	Farm	Total
1997	3,939.5	300.1	833.1	90.0	5,162.7
1998	4,306.1	331.3	921.0	96.6	5,655.0
1999	4,727.5	368.7	1,057.2	102.3	6,255.7
2000	5,142.5	400.8	1,168.9	108.9	6,821.1
2001	5,664.6	445.9	1,282.0	116.3	7,508.8
2002	6,353.2	489.0	1,387.8	124.8	8,354.8
2003	7,171.2	544.2	1,518.6	132.2	9,366.2
Q1 2004	7,375.9	550.8	1,556.7	134.1	9,617.5

Source: Federal Reserve statistical release, *Flow of Funds Accounts of the United States*, Federal Reserve Board of Governors, June 10, 2004.

from 1997 to 2004. As of the first quarter of 2004, there was a total of $9.617 trillion in mortgages outstanding in the United States. Home mortgages comprised 76.7% of all mortgages in 2004. Home and commercial mortgages are the fastest-growing sector, increasing by 87% over the time period.

Most mortgages are funded through a process known as *securitization*. In a securitization, mortgages are pooled and used as collateral for the issuance of MBSs, which are then sold to investors. The largest issuers of MBSs are the Government National Mortgage Association (Ginnie Mae), the Federal National Mortgage Association (Fannie Mae), and the Federal Home Loan Mortgage Corporation (Freddie Mac). Fannie Mae and Freddie Mac are government-sponsored entities (GSEs) that buy mortgages from the original lenders and securitize them. Only *conforming mortgages*, those that conform to a standard set of underwriting guidelines, are purchased by these agencies. Loans not conforming to these guidelines are known as *nonconforming mortgages*. Many large lenders fund their loans through private securitizations, which may include conforming and nonconforming mortgages.

Exhibit 14.2 presents data on agency and private mortgage securitizations. Agency and GSE-backed pools comprised more than 75% of securitized mortgage receivables in the first quarter of 2004, and more than 96% of these were home mortgages. Private securitizations have grown from 17% of total mortgage pools in 1997 to more than 24% in 2004.

EXHIBIT 14.2

Mortgage Pools Outstanding, 1997–2004 (billions of dollars)

	Home	Multifamily Residential	Commercial	Total
		Agency and GSE-Backed Mortgage Pools		
1997	1,788.1	37.8	0.0	1,825.8
1998	1,970.2	48.3	0.0	2,018.4
1999	2,234.7	57.5	0.0	2,292.2
2000	2,425.6	66.0	0.0	2,491.6
2001	2,748.5	81.6	0.0	2,830.1
2002	3,063.7	94.5	0.0	3,158.2
2003	3,373.4	114.7	0.0	3,488.0
Q1 2004	3,397.8	111.4	0.0	3,509.2
		Privately Issued Mortgage Pools		
1997	280.4	20.9	74.9	376.3
1998	360.6	33.9	123.4	517.9
1999	399.4	42.0	157.3	598.7
2000	432.8	47.5	187.1	667.4
2001	505.0	53.5	225.7	784.3
2002	563.2	59.0	252.1	874.4
2003	696.1	67.1	295.7	1,058.9
Q1 2004	754.7	68.8	303.8	1,127.2

Source: Federal Reserve statistical release, *Flow of Funds Accounts of the United States,* Federal Reserve Board of Governors, June 10, 2004.

Investors may purchase mortgages directly or invest in MBSs. Most securitized mortgages are *mortgage passthrough securities,* which represent a claim against a pool of mortgages. Investors in passthrough securities receive a *pro rata* share of the cash flows from the underlying pool of mortgages, less servicing fees. Most mortgage passthrough securities are agency securities, issued by Ginnie Mae, Fannie Mae, or Freddie Mac. Agency passthroughs include various levels of guarantees in interest and principal provided by the issuing entity.

Mortgages are typically priced at a spread over the 10-year U.S. Treasury note rate. Exhibit 14.3 shows the average rate on new mortgages for the period 1971–2004. Mortgage rates reached a high of 18.63% in October 1981 and have fallen steadily since that time. Mortgage rates fell from 8.54% in June 2000 to 5.24% in June 2003. In June of 2004, the average mortgage rate was 6.30%.

PREPAYMENT RISK

Most borrowers have the right to prepay their mortgages before the stated maturity of the loan. Some prepayments occur because borrowers move or simply decide to shorten the term of the mortgage through early repayment of principal. The primary determinant of mortgage prepayments is the level of mortgage rates relative to the current mortgage rate. Borrowers have a strong incentive to prepay if rates have fallen, because they can pay off the original loan with a new loan at a lower rate.

EXHIBIT 14.3

Average Contract Rate on Commitments for Fixed-Rate First Mortgages, 1971–2004

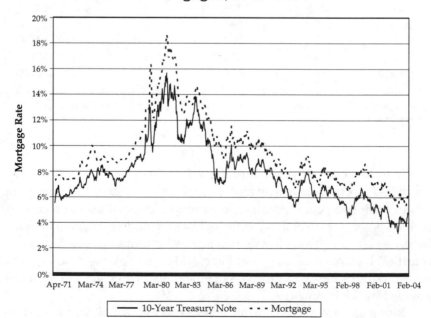

The prepayment option granted to homeowners becomes more valuable as mortgage rates decline. Borrowers can refinance their mortgages at lower rates of interest, thereby returning principal to the lender. The reduction in the expected life of a mortgage when interest rates fall and prepayments rise is known as *contraction risk.* Contraction risk has two implications for investors. The first is that the value of mortgages or MBSs will increase at a decreasing rate as mortgage rates decline, a characteristic known as *negative convexity.* Negative convexity limits the upside price potential of mortgages associated with declining interest rates, similar to a callable bond. The second implication for investors is that they must reinvest the principal at a lower rate of interest. This is known as *reinvestment risk.*

Bonds typically decline in value as interest rates rise because the cash flows are discounted at a higher rate. This decline in value is compounded with mortgages because with rising interest rates, borrowers have less incentive to refinance and prepayment rates fall. The extension of time until expected cash flows are received is known as *extension risk.*

Contraction and extension risk imply that the duration of a mortgage portfolio or MBS will decrease as interest rates fall and rise as interest rates rise. Hence, the effective term of a mortgage may be significantly different from the stated term, depending on the level of interest rates. Exhibit 14.4 shows the price-yield relationship between mortgage values and interest rates for a pool of 8.00% mortgages. The graph shows negative convexity at lower interest rates. As interest rates fall, the value of the portfolio increases because the cash flows are discounted at lower rates of interest. As rates continue to fall below 8.00%, some borrowers refinance and return principal to the lender, and the value of the portfolio increases, but at a decreasing rate. As rates rise above 8.00%, the value of the portfolio falls because the cash flows are discounted at a higher rate of interest and borrowers have less incentive to refinance.

COLLATERALIZED MORTGAGE OBLIGATIONS

Collateralized mortgage obligations (CMOs) are securities backed by a pool of passthrough securities or mortgages. The underlying cash flows in a CMO are reallocated to different bond classes called *tranches.* Payments from the underlying mortgages flow to the tranches in such a way that different classes of bonds have different maturities. Short-term tranches

EXHIBIT 14.4

Mortgage Portfolio Value and Interest Rates

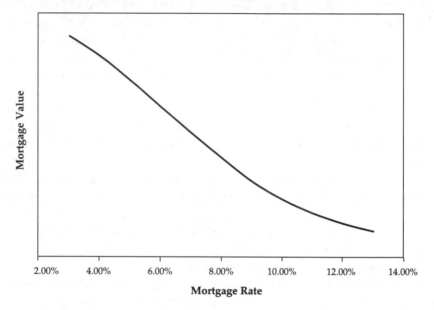

provide relatively more protection against extension risk, and long-term tranches provide more protection against contraction risk.

There are a number of different CMO structures, but all have the characteristic that the cash flows are restructured among the tranches. The benefit of CMOs lies in their multiclass structure. While the underlying prepayment risk of the pool still exists, the contraction and extension risk is redistributed to the different tranches. Hence, these risks can be assumed by investors most able to bear them.

HISTORIC MORTGAGE DATA

For the examples presented in this chapter, we use weekly data on GNMA 6.00% passthrough securities for the period June 2000–December 2004. Our hedges were constructed with the CBOT 10-year U.S. Treasury note futures contract and options on the 10-year U.S. Treasury note futures. The mortgage rate data we use is the average contract rate on commitments for 30-year conventional fixed-rate first mortgages. We use the 10-year constant maturity rate on U.S. Treasury notes for our U.S. Treasury note data.

RISKS OF INVESTING IN MORTGAGES

Investors in mortgages and mortgage passthroughs face the same fundamental risks as faced by a bondholder. Increases in interest rates will decrease the value of the investment, and decreases in rates will increase the value of the investment. The impact on value is affected by the negative convexity associated with prepayments on the underlying loans.

Exhibit 14.5 shows the relationship between mortgage rates, GNMA passthrough prices, and 10-year U.S. Treasury note futures prices. As interest rates fall, the GNMA prices begin to level off, demonstrating the negative convexity of the price/yield relationship for mortgages. The U.S. Treasury prices show convexity throughout the range of mortgage rates.

The relationship between mortgage and U.S. Treasury futures prices depends on several factors. The convexity of the price/yield relationship

EXHIBIT 14.5

Price/Yield Relationship for 6.00% GNMA Mortgages and 10-Year U.S. Treasury Note Futures Contracts, June 2000 to December 2004

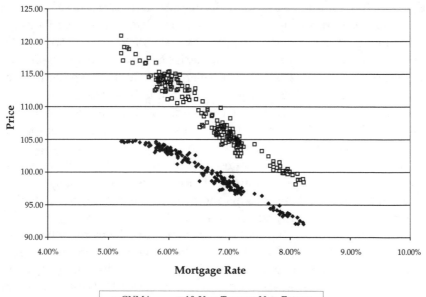

for mortgages is affected by the weighted average coupon (WAC), which is the average mortgage rate of the portfolio. Prepayments on the mortgage portfolio increase when borrowers can refinance at lower rates. Hence the negative convexity is more pronounced when rates fall to or below the WAC. The spread between mortgage rates and U.S. Treasury note rates will also affect the relationship. If spreads widen, mortgage prices fall relative to U.S. Treasury prices. In general, the price/yield relationship for U.S. Treasury notes will be more convex than that for mortgages.

MORTGAGE PIPELINE RISK

Mortgage lenders take positions in mortgages and in mortgage-related securities at various stages of the mortgage origination process. The risk to each lender depends on the time period for which the positions are held and the characteristics of the portfolio. As a consequence, mortgage lenders face several types of risk.

In addition to the fee income earned from origination, lenders who sell loans profit by selling loans above cost. The origination process requires mortgage lenders to commit to a mortgage interest rate while the loan is in process, typically for a period of 30–60 days. If rates rise before the loan goes to closing, the value of the loans will decline and the lender will sell the loans at a lower price. Borrowers benefit from this arrangement because they have locked in the lower mortgage rate. The risk that mortgages in process (in the pipeline) will fall in value prior to their sale is known as *mortgage pipeline risk.* Lenders often hedge this exposure by selling forward their expected closing volume or by shorting U.S. Treasury notes or futures contracts.

Mortgage pipeline risk is affected by *fallout.* Fallout refers to the percentage of loan commitments that do not go to closing. As interest rates fall, fallout rises because borrowers who have locked in a mortgage rate are more likely to find better rates with another lender. Conversely, as rates rise the percentage of loans that close increases. Mortgage lenders use sophisticated tracking systems and models to estimate fallout. Fallout rates are typically in the range of 20–40%.

Fallout affects the required size of the hedging instrument because it affects the size of the pipeline position to be hedged. At lower rates, fewer loans will close and there will be a smaller required position in the hedging instrument. Mortgage lenders often use a dynamic hedging strategy to manage pipeline risk, which adjusts the size of the position in the hedging instrument based on revised estimates of fallout. Lenders also use put options on U.S. Treasury note futures to hedge against the risk of fallout.

RETAINED INTERESTS IN MORTGAGES

In a stripped mortgage-backed security, payments are allocated to different classes of investors. Interest-only securities (IOs) are stripped mortgage-backed securities that only receive interest on the outstanding principal in the pool. Principal payments are allocated to principal-only securities (POs). Mortgage lenders often retain interests in IOs.[1]

IO cash flows are sensitive to prepayment rates. Since the IO receives interest on the outstanding principal balance, prepayments reduce the cash flows received by investors. As interest rates increase, both the IO cash flows and the discount rate on cash flows increase. At lower mortgage rates, the increase in cash flows has a stronger effect than the increase in discount rates. For mortgage rates less than the WAC and for a range of mortgage rates above the WAC, IO values tend to increase as rates rise. Conversely, as mortgage rates decline and prepayments rise, IOs tend to decline in value. Mortgage lenders hedge the risk associated with declining mortgage rates by using instruments that increase in value as rates decline.

Companies faced with exposure to the risks of mortgages can choose from several hedging methods. The appropriate method is determined by the cash flows associated with each method, the size of the position to be hedged, the expiration of the hedge, and the goals of the hedger. In the examples that follow, we discuss the hedging of mortgages with U.S. Treasury futures and options on U.S. Treasury futures.

HEDGING MORTGAGE PRICE RISK
WITH U.S. TREASURY NOTE FUTURES

U.S. Treasury note futures can be used to hedge mortgage price exposure by providing the hedger with a cash flow stream that offsets losses in their spot position. The resulting net cash flows from the combined positions in the mortgage and the futures contract effectively establish a fixed price received

---

1. Mortgage servicing rights (MSRs) are similar to retained interest. The primary source of cash flow on an MSR is the revenue related to the servicing of mortgages, which is similar to that of an IO.

for the mortgage. If the mortgage price is highly sensitive to changes in the futures price, a larger number of futures contracts will be required to generate sufficient cash flows to establish an effective hedge. The number of contracts required for a minimum variance hedge is calculated as

$$N^* = \frac{V_M}{V_H} h^*$$

where

N^* = units (contracts) of the futures contract
h^* = *ex ante* hedge ratio
V_M = market value of the mortgage position
V_H = market value per contract of the hedging instrument

The hedge ratio h^* can be estimated by observation of the price changes between the mortgage and hedging instrument or as a ratio of durations. The *ex ante* hedge ratio from the duration estimate is equal to

$$h^* = \frac{D_M}{D_H}$$

where D_M is the modified duration of the mortgage portfolio and D_H is the modified duration of the hedging instrument. The duration of the mortgage portfolio will depend on estimates of prepayments and the characteristics of the portfolio.

Example: A company owns mortgage-backed securities with a face value of $10,000,000 and is concerned that increases in interest rates will reduce the value of the portfolio. The company has estimated the duration of the mortgage portfolio to be 2.37 at the current level of interest rates. The company decides to hedge with a short position in the December 2001 10-year U.S. Treasury note futures contract. The duration of the U.S. Treasury note futures is estimated to be 6.01. On October 12, 2001, mortgage rates are 6.58%, and the price of the GNMA securities is 99.797. U.S. Treasury note futures prices are 108.563, and each futures contract has a face value of $100,000. The company closes its position on December 7, 2001, when mortgage rates have risen to 6.84%, GNMA prices have fallen to 97.266, and futures prices have fallen to 105.281.

The hedge ratio is estimated as the ratio of the durations on the mortgage and futures contract:

$$h^* = \frac{D_M}{D_H} = \frac{3.46}{6.01} = 0.5757$$

The number of contracts needed to hedge the mortgage portfolio is equal to

$$N^* = \frac{V_M}{V_H} h^* = \frac{9,979,700}{108,563}(0.5757) \approx 53$$

Exhibit 14.6 summarizes the transactions and the company's gains and losses on each position.

The gain on the short futures position is an offset to the reduced price of the mortgage-backed securities. The unhedged value of mortgages has decreased by \$253,100 (\$9,979,700 − \$9,726,600), and the futures position increased by \$173,946. Exhibit 14.7 shows the daily net value of the hedged and unhedged positions during the period.

In the above example, the durations of the mortgage portfolio and of the hedging instrument change as interest rates rise. The effect on the duration of the mortgage portfolio is likely to be more pronounced if there is a large change in prepayments. The size of this effect will depend on the composition of mortgage rates in the portfolio. To maintain an effective hedge, the hedger should recalculate duration at the new level of interest rates and adjust the hedge ratios accordingly.

EXHIBIT 14.6

Cumulative Payoff to Short Futures Hedge on Mortgages

Date	Position	Futures Price	Cumulative Payoff
10/12/01	Sell 53 Futures Contracts	\$108.563	$108.563 - S_n$
12/7/01	Buy 53 Futures Contracts	\$105.281	$S_n - 105.281$
Cumulative Payoff at Maturity		53,000 (\$108.563 − \$105.281) = \$173,946	

EXHIBIT 14.7

Dollar Value of Hedged and Unhedged Position
in Mortgage-Backed Securities, October 12, 2001 to
December 7, 2001

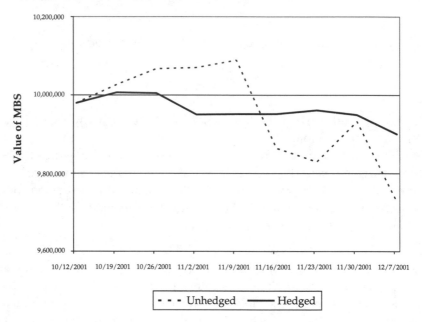

HEDGING MORTGAGE PIPELINE RISK WITH OPTIONS

Mortgage lenders face the risk that loans in the pipeline will be sold at a
loss in the future because of fluctuating interest rates. This situation is
complicated by the fact that the size of the position will also fluctuate
with interest rates. As rates rise, the position to be hedged remains large
because a larger percentage of loans in the pipeline will go to closing. As
rates fall, the position to be hedged decreases in size as loans fall out of the
pipeline.

Effective hedging of a mortgage pipeline requires that the hedge
adjust for both the fluctuations in mortgage value and the size of the position. Mortgage lenders can adjust for both effects through the use of U.S.
Treasury note futures options. A long position in a futures put option
gives the holder the right to assume a short position in a futures contract
at a prespecified delivery price, the strike price. For U.S. Treasury note
futures put options, the option will be exercised in a rising rate environ-

ment if U.S. Treasury prices fall below the strike price. If prices remain above the strike price, the option will expire unexercised. Hence, a larger short position in futures will be associated with rising rates, and a smaller position will be associated with falling rates.

Example: A mortgage lender has $10,000,000 of mortgage loans in the pipeline on July 15, 2003. The loans are expected to close on August 15, 2003. The lender believes that if rates remain at or above their current level of 5.52%, they will close 90% of the pipeline. However, if rates fall, the lender believes that they will close 50% of the loans.

September put options on 10-year U.S. Treasury note futures with a strike price of 115 are currently trading at a premium of $1.109. Each futures contract is for the delivery of a $100,000 face-value U.S. Treasury note, and the futures price is currently $115.016. Hence, the premium on a put option is $1,109 per contract.

If rates remain at or above current levels, the lender will need to hedge a $9,000,000 position in mortgages. If rates fall, the lender will need to hedge a $5,000,000 position. The lender estimates that the hedge ratio, which measures the change in mortgage price per change in U.S. Treasury note price, is equal to 0.40.

Two transactions are made to establish the hedge. The lender takes a short position in U.S. Treasury note futures to hedge the $5,000,000 position and purchases futures options to hedge the $4,000,000 position. The number of futures contracts required to hedge the $5,000,000 position is calculated as

$$N^* = \frac{V_M}{V_H} h^* = \frac{5,000,000}{115,016}(0.40) \approx 17$$

The number of futures options required to hedge the additional $4,000,000 position is calculated as

$$N^* = \frac{V_M}{V_H} h^* = \frac{4,000,000}{115,016}(0.40) \approx 14$$

If rates rise and U.S. Treasury note prices fall below 115, the lender exercises the options. The combined short positions of 31 futures contracts are sufficient to hedge the $9,000,000 position in mortgages. If rates fall below current levels, the options expire out of the money and the lender has a short position in 17 contracts, which is sufficient to hedge the $5,000,000 of loans remaining in the pipeline.

The above hedge is effective in both rising and falling interest rate markets. However, the hedge is expensive because the net value of the hedged positions is reduced by the premium paid for the options. The cost of the put options is equal to $15,526 ($1,109 times 14 contracts). In practice, this type of hedge would be established with put options with different exercise prices to account for the fallout associated with different levels of interest rate changes.

COMPARISON OF HEDGING ALTERNATIVES

Hedge	Pros	Cons
U.S. Treasury futures	Liquid, low transaction costs	Standard terms
		Daily mark-to-market
		May require rolling hedge
		Basis risk
		No benefit from favorable interest rate movements
Options on U.S. Treasury futures	Benefit from favorable interest rate fluctuations	Expensive

S U M M A R Y

Mortgages have unique risk characteristics that must be managed by mortgage lenders and investors. In this chapter, we examined hedging techniques for companies facing exposure to the risks of fixed-rate mortgage lending. We discussed alternative methods of hedging with futures contracts and options.

Mortgages are funded through a process known as securitization. In a securitization, mortgages are pooled and used as collateral for the issuance of mortgage-backed securities, which are then sold to investors. Most securitized mortgages are mortgage passthrough securities, which represent a claim against a pool of mortgages. Mortgage passthrough securities are often restructured and sold as collateralized mortgage obligations (CMOs). CMOs redistribute the risk of mortgages to different classes of bondholders.

Mortgages have an embedded put option, which gives borrowers the right to prepay their mortgages before the stated maturity of the loan. As a result, the price/yield curve for mortgages exhibits negative convexity. We discussed the implications of negative convexity for investors in mortgages and for mortgage lenders. Negative convexity implies that mortgage investors may have limited price appreciation associated with a decrease in rates.

We discussed the risks and hedging needs of investors and lenders in the mortgage market. As rates change investors may need to adjust hedge ratios because of the negative convexity of mortgages. We discussed mortgage pipeline risk and the effect of negative convexity and fallout on hedging strategies. Finally, we provided examples of hedging strategies for investors and lenders that use U.S. Treasury note futures and futures option contracts.

REFERENCES

Burghardt, Galen. *The Eurodollar Futures and Options Handbook*. New York: McGraw-Hill, 2003.

Countrywide Financial Corporation. *2003 Annual Report*. Calabasas, CA.

Fabozzi, Frank J., Ed. *The Handbook of Fixed Income Securities*, 6th Ed. New York: McGraw-Hill, 2001.

Federal Reserve Board of Governors. Federal Reserve statistical release, *Flow of Funds Accounts of the United States*. Washington, D.C.: Federal Reserve Board of Governors, June 10, 2004.

Taglia, Pete. "Risk Management Case Study: How Mortgage Lenders Use Futures to Hedge Pipeline Risk." *Futures Industry Magazine*, September/October 2003.

SUMMARY OF NOTATION

TIME VALUE OF MONEY

PV	present value
FV_n	future value in year n
$PVIFA_{n,r}$	present value interest factor of an annuity for n years at $r\%$
$FVIFA_{n,r}$	future value interest factor of an annuity for n years at $r\%$
EAR	effective annual rate
PMT	annual loan payment
C	annual cash flow
n	number of years
t	time
m	number of compounding periods or intervals per year
q	partial compounding period
e	base of natural logarithm, equal to 2.7182818

STATISTICS

$f(x)$	probability density function of x
$F(x)$	cumulative density function of x
$N(x)$	cumulative normal probability density for x
μ_X	population mean of X
$\overline{X}$	sample mean of X
σ_X^2	population variance of X
$\sigma_{\overline{X}}$	standard error of sampling distribution
σ_X	population standard deviation of X
s_x	sample standard deviation of X
$COV(X,Y)$	population covariance

C_{XY}	sample covariance
ρ_{XY}	population Pearson correlation coefficient
r_{XY}	sample correlation coefficient
SSE	sum of squared errors
SSR	sum of squares from regression
SST	total sum of squares
R^2	coefficient of determination
β_0	regression intercept coefficient
β_1	regression slope coefficient
$\hat{\beta}_0$	estimated regression intercept coefficient
$\hat{\beta}_1$	estimated regression slope coefficient
$\hat{Y}_i$	predicted value of Y
α	level of significance
ε	error term

FIXED INCOME MATH

F	face value or principal of a bond
c	annual coupon rate on a bond
C	interest cash flow or coupon payment in dollars equal to cF
y	market discount rate or yield to maturity on a bond
y_c	yield-to-call
Δy	change in market yields
AI	accrued interest
P	bond price
ΔP	change in price
ΔP_D	change in bond price due to duration
ΔP_K	change in bond price due to convexity
P_c	clean price of a bond
P_d	dirty price of a bond, $P_c + \text{AI}$
D	Macaulay's duration
D_m	modified duration
D_p	price duration of a portfolio
K	convexity
w_t	value weight

FUTURES

F_0	initial futures price
F_t	futures price at time t
S_0	initial spot asset price
S_t	spot asset price at time t
S_n	spot asset price at maturity
G	carrying cost
g	carrying costs as a percentage of spot price
r_d	annual domestic interest rate
r_f	annual foreign interest rate
CTD	cheapest-to-deliver
CF	conversion factor
DO	deliverability option
$D_{futures}$	modified duration of futures contract
D_{CTD}	modified duration of CTD
DIV_0	current dividend
d	continuous dividend yield

SWAPS

c	fixed swap rate
PV_{fixed}	value of fixed rate leg of the swap
$PV_{floating}$	value of the floating leg of the swap
I_t	floating coupon at time t
V_{fixed}	value of a swap for a fixed rate payer
$V_{floating}$	value of a swap for a floating rate payer
D_m^{fixed}	modified duration of fixed leg
$D_m^{floating}$	modified duration of floating leg
D_{fixed}^{swap}	modified duration of a swap for a fixed rate payer
er	exchange rate
$r_t(1)$	discount rate in time t in terms of currency 1
$r_t(2)$	discount rate in time t in terms of currency 2
TROR	total rate of return
b	percentage of LIBOR, basis

OPTIONS

X_c	exercise price of a call option, interest rate cap rate
X_p	exercise price of a put option
X_f	interest rate floor rate
$V_0(c)$	initial value of call option
$V_0(p)$	initial value of put option
u	proportionate increase in asset price
d	proportionate decrease in asset price
Δ	delta of an option
$\Gamma(c)$	gamma of a call option
$\Gamma(p)$	gamma of a put option
a	speed of adjustment to the mean
$V_0(\text{cap})$	value of an interest rate cap
$V_0(\text{floor})$	value of an interest rate floor
τ	individual cap period

TERM STRUCTURE

r_t	discount rate at time t
$_{t-1}f_t$	forward rate from $t-1$ to t
r_n	annualized zero-coupon yield
Q	quoted price for a Eurodollar futures contract
$B(t_1,t_2)$	time t_1 price of a zero-coupon bond that matures at time t_2
T_t	number of days until the end of time period t

GENERAL HEDGING

h^*	ex-ante hedge ratio
h	ex-post hedge ratio
N^*	ex-ante number of futures contracts
$\hat{\beta}_1$	minimum variance hedge ratio
COC	cost-of-carry
V_s	market value of spot position
V_h	market value of hedging position

COMMODITES/CURRENCIES

ΔS_t	change in the spot exchange rate or price at time t
ΔF_t	change in futures or forward exchange or price at time t

EQUITIES

β	beta, systematic risk of an asset
r_s	return on a stock
r_m	return on the market
r_p	return of the portfolio
β_p	beta of a portfolio
σ_p	standard deviation of a portfolio

MUNICIPAL BONDS/CORPORATE BONDS

PV01(swap)	present value of a 1 basis point change for swap
PV01(bond)	present value of a 1 basis point change for bond
$P_t(\text{swap})$	price of a swap at time t
$P_t(\text{bond})$	price of a bond at time t
$\Delta P(\text{bond})$	change in bond price
$\Delta P(\text{index})$	change in index price
$\Delta P(\text{hedge})$	change in hedge price
$y_0(\text{swap})$	swap yield at time 0
$y_0(\text{bond})$	bond yield at time 0
$\Delta y(\text{hedge})$	change in yield on the hedge instrument
$\Delta y(\text{swap})$	change in swap yield
b_0	basis at time 0
Δb_t	expected change in basis from time zero to time t
s_0	corporate bond spread at time 0
Δs_t	change in corporate bond spread

MORTGAGES

D_M	modified duration of a mortgage
D_H	modified duration of hedge
V_M	value of mortgage position
V_H	value of hedge

INDEX